PRAISE FOR *RESETTING MANAGEMENT*

Resetting Management is a compelling treaty on modern leadership, where leaders have to distribute power across and beyond their organizations, and where a real competitive advantage lies in learning to learn, by exercising a combination of strategic and organizational agility together with intellectual humility. In a world of platitudes, this is a book that actually makes a difference by resetting the way we look at the world.
Alexis Nasard, CEO, Kantar

In *Resetting Management*, Stéphane Girod and Martin Králik methodically review how one needs to lead in modern society. Behind polite and constructive build-up and analysis, the recipe is unrolling. But make no mistake, the title sets the tone, and it's brutal: 'Reset the way you and I lead, or... get out of the way.'
Antoine Ernst, Chief Transformation Officer, Japan Tobacco International

The beauty of *Resetting Management* is that it doesn't profess that there is only one way to obtain business agility. The book is filled with inspirational examples of companies following different paths towards agility as well as practical models that help us analyse our own company to select the best path forward.
Cecilie Heuch, Chief People and Sustainability Officer, Telenor Group

Resetting Management clarifies the different facets of agility and presents very practical tools and frameworks that will help businesses shed their rigid corporate planning, seize the opportunities of the digital era and continuously renew their competitive advantage.
John J Zhang, former Director, Strategy and Corporate Development, Midea Group

Agility is one of the hottest concepts in the world of business today, but what does it really mean? This book provides the answer – it's the most comprehensive guide to business agility available, full of deep insights into the challenges and tensions involved, and with practical takeaways for leaders and managers everywhere.
Julian Birkinshaw, Professor of Strategy and Entrepreneurship, London Business School

Girod and Králik have cracked the code on how to prosper in an increasingly unpredictable future. The true Management 4.0 playbook for competitive advantage in the Fourth Industrial Revolution. Learn how to achieve the needed strategic adaptability – via extreme customer centricity, innovative agility and flexibility, constant balancing of trade-offs and much more.

Mikael Ronnblad, Group Executive Board Member, Fortum Corporation (Europe), and Board Member, Valo Ventures (USA)

In reading *Resetting Management*, I found the words, concepts and real-life case studies addressing the exact sort of issues that I, as a CEO, am dealing with these days. It's an excellent book combining academic rigor with accessible and applicable examples that help provide a roadmap for anyone leading a company through today's ever-changing, technology-driven business and social environment.

Mike Federle, CEO, *Forbes*

We live in a world of accelerating change, where the future is less and less an extrapolation of the past. To thrive in this environment, we need organizations with an 'evolutionary advantage' – a capacity to change as fast as change itself. *Resetting Management* is a must-read for anyone who's serious about making resilience and agility a core competence.

Michele Zanini, Managing Director, Management Lab, and co-author of *Humanocracy*

Thought-provoking, incisive and holistic, *Resetting Management* is the most comprehensive book I have read on business transformations. The value of this book lies in the integration of strategic, organizational and leadership agility, which are usually treated in a siloed way. I have found it particularly relevant for my work in strategy, M&A and post-merger integration.

Moncef Tanfour, Group Vice President Strategic Development and Integration, Grundfos

Resetting Management unpacks thoroughly the 'Why' and the 'What' of how organizations can leverage agility to thrive in the realities of the new world. Rather than a one-shoe-fits-all approach, the authors provide practical insights with lots of corporate examples which allows anyone to calibrate and personalize the transformation of their business.

Parag M Parekh, VP Global Digital Sales, Adidas

Resetting Management is really about playing to win! It is insightful and even disturbing to realize how conservative we can still be in our management approaches. It's time for a reset. This book gives the keys to reshape our future thanks to the entrepreneurial energy that strategic, organizational and leadership agility create.

Patrick Rasquinet, CEO, La Prairie

Resetting Management

Thrive with agility in the age
of uncertainty

Stéphane J G Girod
and Martin Králik

Publisher's note

Every possible effort has been made to ensure that the information contained in this book is accurate at the time of going to press, and the publishers and authors cannot accept responsibility for any errors or omissions, however caused. No responsibility for loss or damage occasioned to any person acting, or refraining from action, as a result of the material in this publication can be accepted by the editor, the publisher or the author.

First published in Great Britain and the United States in 2021 by Kogan Page Limited

2nd Floor, 45 Gee Street	122 W 27th St, 10th Floor	4737/23 Ansari Road
London	New York, NY 10001	Daryaganj
EC1V 3RS	USA	New Delhi 110002
United Kingdom		India

www.koganpage.com

Kogan Page books are printed on paper from sustainable forests.

ISBNs

Hardback	978 1 78966 719 6
Paperback	978 1 78966 717 2
Ebook	978 1 78966 718 9

British Library Cataloguing-in-Publication Data

A CIP record for this book is available from the British Library.

Library of Congress Cataloging-in-Publication Data

Names: Girod, Stéphane J. G., author. | Králik, Martin, author.
Title: Resetting management: thrive with agility in the age of uncertainty / Stéphane J.G. Girod and Martin Králik.
Description: London ; New York, NY: Kogan Page, 2021. | Includes bibliographical references and index.
Identifiers: LCCN 2021010016 (print) | LCCN 2021010017 (ebook) | ISBN 9781789667172 (paperback) | ISBN 9781789667196 (hardback) | ISBN 9781789667189 (ebook)
Subjects: LCSH: Industrial management. | Adaptability (Psychology)
Classification: LCC HD31.2 .G57 2021 (print) | LCC HD31.2 (ebook) | DDC 658–dc23
LC record available at https://lccn.loc.gov/2021010016
LC ebook record available at https://lccn.loc.gov/2021010017

Typeset by Integra Software Services Pondicherry
Print production managed by Jellyfish
Printed and bound by CPI Group (UK) Ltd, Croydon CR0 4YY

To Adriaan and my parents,
thank you for everything – Stéphane

In memory of Z A – Martin

CONTENTS

LIST OF FIGURES

LIST OF TABLES

ACKNOWLEDGEMENTS

We are extremely grateful to all the people, too numerous to mention, who have contributed to this book and whose ideas have inspired us. They include participants in executives programmes and the people who helped us develop case studies.

We would like to particularly thank: All the editorial and production team of Kogan Page, Erik Meijer, Britta Meijer-Nehring, Prof Jean-François Manzoni, Prof Anand Narasimhan, Cédric Vaucher, Thomas Andresen, Séverine Jourdain, Tomas Björkholm, Michael Göthe, Henrik Kniberg, Joakim Sundén, Cecilie Heuch, Maarten van Beek, Vincent van den Boogert, Tanja Tierie, Herman Tange, Mandy Brouwer, Karim Cherif, Lisa Duke, Moncef Tanfour, Sara Svedjedal, Eduarda Philadelpho Fernandes de Pina, Tammy Lowry, Marc Vollenweider, Vincent du Sordet, Delia Fischer, Vincenzo Palatella, Alice Tozer, Sally Peck, Christel Gachet, Daniele Chicca, Alexander Ross, Anna Dunand, Feikje Dunnewijk, Michael Wade, Lindsay McTeague, Dorien van Leeuwen, Maurice Jetten, Michael Leckie, Ibrahim Gokcen, John Wisdom, Prof Bernard Jaworski, Christian Laurent, Prof Øystein Fjeldstad, Prof Michael Watkins, Claus-Bernhard Pakleppa, Jean-Louis Barsoux, Corina Windischmann, Fiona Dekker, Rolf Birkhofer and Mateja Panjan.

PREFACE

Management has never rhymed with plain sailing. In every era, it faces a new set of challenges. Although only time will tell regarding the extent to which the 2020 COVID-19 crisis changed the rules of the game, you have probably already drawn two lessons: First, the 2020 crisis crystallized the reality of our complex world. Because the world economies are interdependent, an incident in Wuhan, China escalated into a global pandemic that shut down societies worldwide. It vividly illustrated that complexity breeds uncertainty. Is today's degree of uncertainty higher than in the past? The jury is out on that. What 2020 taught us was that ignoring uncertainty is not an option for businesses that seek to remain relevant and to expand.

Second, two months into the crisis some companies were successfully adapting by innovating and transforming. Others remained dazed and subdued. Why? The answer has to do with their varying degrees of business agility. Faced with acute forms of uncertainty, many firms were seized with paralysis. And yet, some were able to deal with it, embrace it rather than fear it, move ahead and prepare to resume growth.

This book is a journey into the principles and practices of business agility that is broadly defined as adaptability and flexibility. The COVID-19 crisis amplified and accelerated major shifts in the way businesses function. But before the crisis, a profound shift was already underway in management practice, brought on by the realization that uncertainty and complexity required better responses. Since then, developing the capabilities for flexibility and adaptation has become even more important.

From the early 2000s, the limits of the dominant approach to management began to come into full view. Rooted in hierarchy and bureaucracy, the approach had changed very little in the previous hundred years. The post-2000 business world of complexity, disruption and blurring boundaries has little use for it. Contrary to predictions, this doesn't mean that hierarchy and bureaucracy will disappear altogether.

About the Research

We conducted original empirical research using semi-structured interviews with 60 executives at 10 non-digital native incumbents (billion-dollar and multi-billion-dollar companies) in both business-to-business (B2B) and business-to-customer (B2C) industries before and during the crisis. In May 2020, we surveyed 550 executives across industries about their perception of agility. We also engaged in discussions with 200 senior executive participants during agility-focused workshops at the Institute of Management Development (IMD). In addition, we conducted a large review of secondary data and public sources to triangulate our interview data.

Because agility is still an emergent phenomenon, we used an inductive research design based on comparative case studies to build new theories and frameworks that will guide management practice. Our industry and sample selections were intertwined and guided by theoretical considerations.

Through empirical research, a literature review and interactions with executives, we have discovered that, across industry sectors, many businesses are resetting their approach to strategizing, organizing and leading.

It is more likely that as businesses embrace agility, they will be greatly simplified and reinvented into systems that facilitate, not stifle.

The book leverages both new and existing research (see box above). Across industry sectors, organizations are reorienting their approach to strategizing, organizing and leading. Specifically, they are resetting management towards business agility in three ways:

1 Embracing the new business context. They understand that business agility goes far beyond rolling out agile processes like scrum. Whereas agile processes are methodologies, agility is a set of capabilities for releasing a new level of company-wide energy, innovation and entrepreneurship. It is about responding to disruption while still delivering on strategy with rigour and efficiency.

2 Mastering the principles of business agility at three levels. In their quest for agility, executives are seeking to develop flexibility at three levels: in the way they strategize, design their organization, and lead themselves and others. Beyond agile, their focus is on business agility as a more holistic reality. They are redefining hierarchy, mindsets, ego and the meaning of success. This is set to be agility's greatest battleground.

3 Adapting the way their business transforms. In the past, companies stuck to strict delineations: 'traditional' precluded 'experimental'. 'In-house expertise' discouraged open innovation. Growing one's business agility means minimizing these trade-offs and managing competing demands much more effectively. At the same time, as they develop agility and explore one or many futures, businesses are bound to encounter new, unexpected trade-offs and challenges. This will require that leaders and indeed the entire workforce test and improvise new solutions.

These are the three ways of resetting management that form the structure of this book. If you master them, your business will not just survive, it will thrive.

Who Should Read This Book

This book should be of interest to you if you are, or are aiming to be, a:

- Senior executive of a large, established company and you wish to work out how you and your teams can adapt and compete in a world of start-ups, ecosystems and tech giants. You are seeking not only to understand but also to thrive in the resulting context of high uncertainty.

- Scholar of strategy, organizational design and leadership. You should be able to make meaningful discoveries in this book as well.

The book aims to combine a highly practical perspective with academic rigour, challenging the clichés and simplifications that continue to surround agility. It acknowledges that some readers are doubtful and sceptical about the concept of agility. It also reflects the reality of 2020s executives who are anxious and hopeful to usher in the next, more flexible and versatile paradigm of management – the one this book terms 'business agility'.

To give this paradigm clearer contours, the book presents you with new tools, frameworks and case studies, sensitively placed in context. It shows you how to distinguish the old from the new in the current interest in agility, thus helping you separate the hype from ongoing deep-seated change.

You may also wonder about the link between agility and digital. The company examples throughout the book will show you that digital is both a driver and a solution, an enabler of agility. In fact, digital and agility transformation can go hand in hand. This is why agility is a natural evolution of concepts that appeared in the last 25 years and which, thanks to digital, are finding traction in large businesses. This is also what makes agility stand apart from its predecessors such as ambidexterity and even some of the older meanings attached to the category of strategic agility.

How To Use This Book

Many examples that researchers present as 'best practice' today (eg Nokia, Kodak, Intel) become a disappointment tomorrow. Therefore, inventing your new or next practices is more important than following rapidly outmoded best practices. In addition, every company has to find its form and degree of agility by following the principles detailed in this book. How they choose to implement them will depend on their creativity and originality. The examples that are presented here will give you inspiration and perspectives on how companies respond to similar problems through their own emergent practices. The examples are also meant to help you ask the right questions. The COVID-19 crisis revealed how vulnerable many companies were to uncertainty and how rigid their response was. This book is a guide to future-proofing and crisis-proofing your business.

You will find the book's chapters grouped into three sections: Part One (Chapters 1 and 2) is a call for action, setting up the Why of business agility. Part Two (Chapters 3–7) will walk you through company stories of building agility and the resulting new landscapes in business strategy, organizing and leadership; in other words, the What. Part Three (Chapters 8–10) is the How of agility transformation; it will guide you onto a path of successful transition and help you resolve the challenges you are bound to encounter along the way.

By using the book's diagnosis tools, you may find that what you really need is to improve on one particular dimension of business agility. Perhaps for your business, strategic or organizational agility should be the priority. Feel free to prioritize them in your reading. Also, don't hesitate to use the tools with your teams. Remember that the spirit of agility is to try, test, learn and adapt. Experiments are about starting small and, if successful, growing. Of course, a big part of the success of a business depends on how well it aligns strategy with the environment, and organization with strategy. Thus, you may well discover that working on one level of business agility will inspire you to work on the other two levels as well. The book gives you all the necessary tools to do that.

PART ONE

A Call to Action (Why)

01

Why Agility?

FIVE LESSONS FROM THIS CHAPTER

1 Agility is on everybody's lips and yet its understanding remains largely intuitive.
2 Among executives, the lack of clarity has produced a range of conflicting perceptions and emotions.
3 Hidden in this fog of confusion is the reality that the business environment in the 2020s requires a radically new management paradigm.
4 Current management models, rooted in bureaucracy and hierarchy, are fast becoming – or have become – constraining and out of touch.
5 Agility is a mission-critical quest.

Business Agility – That Elusive Concept

We live in a world where business agility is recognized by its absence rather than its presence. It is the hidden piece of the puzzle. Like most executives, you can tell when 'something' has been missing from your company's strategy and performance. In fact, you might be constantly told to 'embrace agility or be left behind'. But beyond this fear factor, there has been little clarity on how to go about developing agility and what flavour of agility is right for you and your business.

Great expectations coupled with sketchy understanding have conspired to give the concept of agility an air of something mythical and nearly miraculous. In many minds, agility conjures up a secret ingredient, a magic spell or a panacea: 'If only we could figure *it* out and plug *it* into our company… Surely that would turbocharge our growth and competitive strengths once and for all.' As with most fuzzy and overblown aspirations, some executives are inclined to dismiss agility altogether: It sounds like another fad, here today and gone tomorrow. In a survey of 550 executives across industries that IMD conducted in May 2020, 36 per cent of respondents were unclear on the meaning of agility; some believed it was just a buzzword.

The range of emotions among these executives is summarized in Table 1.1. As you start reading this book, where do you stand?

Table 1.1 How executives view agility

View of agility	Description / justification
Enthusiastic	Agility will bring our company to the next level. I cannot wait to sink my teeth into this challenge and help reinvent how we do things around here.
Hopeful	We're optimistic about the potential, particularly of agile methods. But we need to understand it better and in a more holistic way.
Confused	Agility seems to mean 'whatever we want it to mean'. Does it relate to software only or to management in general?
Conservative	If it ain't broke, don't fix it!
Sceptical	Sounds like a buzzword. Everyone's jumping on the bandwagon. Will it provide clear accountability and oversight?
Ambivalent	Looking at the risks involved, do we invest resources into what may be a passing trend?
Fearful	Enough with the 'A' word! For all I know, our hard-won efficiency and discipline will go out the window. Worse, I will lose power and influence in the organization.
Apprehensive	We know we have to do something to survive, but we have misgivings.
Narrow, piecemeal	We'll set up scrums and squads; that should be enough.
Jaded	Seen it all before. It's just another efficiency exercise – like lean, once upon a time.

(*continued*)

Table 1.1 (Continued)

Split	Some love it, some loathe it (often top management vs middle management).
Wait and see	With COVID-19, we're trying to salvage cash, suppliers, brands. Is this really the time for large-scale experiments?
Resistant	Sounds like more hassle than it's worth. This could easily snowball into massive change. Do we even have the muscle to embark on something like that?

Often, agility is reduced to 'agile', which is shorthand for agile methods and processes derived from software development. This is because many leaders don't understand that agile methods will not work in a vacuum, without important changes in the other dimensions of the organization (Chapter 9). In a 2020 IMD seminar with a multinational insurance company, 47 per cent of the participants were not clear on the difference between business agility and agile methods (which was their default understanding of what agility is about).

Meanwhile, for most executives, their grasp of agility remains largely intuitive. They hear business gurus and eminent scholars describe agility as *constantly* rethinking, reinventing, reconfiguring, and generally 'keeping your strategy *moving* as fast as your business'.[1] It makes a lot of sense – but sounds frantic and exhausting, like telling someone to put in double hours every day. At the same time, the exhortations are hardly new: 40 years ago, company bosses were already complaining about hyper-competition. GE's Jack Welch called the 1980s a 'white-knuckle decade' and predicted that the 1990s would be worse.[2] A study on US manufacturing between 1950 and 2002 showed sharp upticks in volatility and 'increased heterogeneity of returns'.[3] For most businesses, safe bets were few and far between long before the rise of China, digital and social media.

Those who thought of agility as a fad may have expected the 2020 COVID-19 crisis to stamp out all talk of such initiatives. It didn't. In fact, agility is now touted as *the* way of tackling the new and next normal. Instead of emulating and learning from best practices, businesses have to invent a set of next practices. What becomes important is sense-making, testing and learning to adapt on the go. All of these define 'agility' (Chapter 2). Among managers at the aforementioned insurance firm, 65.5 per cent believed their company should press on with agility transformation, despite the challenges brought on by the crisis.

From Complexity to Pervasive Uncertainty

Why is that? The key word here is uncertainty. Business agility, and the flexibility it provides, is the way of embracing this uncertainty, rather than fearing it or, worse, ignoring it.

Even if your ideas about agility are vague, you will not be oblivious to the changes that have taken place in the business environment. By now, you may have seen your company's competitive advantage come under pressure. How to make sense of and find patterns in the change that surrounds you?

To come to grips with a new reality, managers need tools – in this case, cognitive handles. VUCA – a word defined by volatility, uncertainty, complexity and ambiguity – once promised to be such a handle when it arrived on the scene in 1987. However, as time went by, the realization sank in that perhaps VUCA wasn't a single, four-legged beast to be tamed, but rather four different species of a beast, each provoking a distinct response.[4]

More recently, scientists exploring VUCA have borrowed concepts and theories from natural systems (weather patterns, biological populations) and applied them to organizational systems. They have suggested that much of what today's businesses are trying to determine has to do with the challenge of operating as complex adaptive organisms. Within such entities, the lines between incremental and discontinuous change are far from clear-cut. Regardless of intentions, it doesn't take much to stumble and tip over from one into the other.[5] Similarly, small changes in one part of the system may produce disproportionate effects in other parts (see the Miele vignette below).[6] In these terms, enterprises of today are living at 'the edge of chaos'.[7] What they are grappling with on a daily basis is an ongoing process of adapting, all the while sensing that one misstep may send them hurtling into radical change.[8]

A Good Problem to Have? Depends On Your Level of Agility

Miele, the well-known German global leader in high-end home appliances, was wrong-footed by the 2020 pandemic. At the outset of the crisis, it was hit by component factory shutdowns in Asia. Furthermore, expecting the crisis to dent household income and consumption, the company revised its production plan downwards. What happened in reality was the opposite: Confined to their homes, people started giving them a vigorous spring-cleaning. In doing so, they realized that many of their appliances were in need of an upgrade. As a result, Miele saw a jump in orders that it was unprepared to cope with.

Much of this complexity – and the resulting uncertainty – has been brought on by the higher degree of interconnections in the global economy, particularly the dramatic expansion in trade and investment flows. Since 1990, the total volume of imports and exports relative to global GDP has grown threefold. With such upward momentum, any correction such as the 2008 financial crisis and the COVID crisis will produce great shocks in the system.[9]

In essence, what is it that businesses are adapting to? Frameworks like STEEP help us group the drivers of change, in this case into social, technological, economic, environmental and political. Each comes with its own set of moving targets, dynamics of acceleration and shifts in power. The cumulative effect of digital alone on legacy companies has been likened to a vortex (Figure 1.1) – a force that pulls everything in and compels business offerings and value chains to shed their non-digital aspects, then reshuffles the resulting digital value into disruptive business models.[10] Digital entails a pervasiveness of software – and the software release process is inherently continuous and ambiguous, exerting pressure on non-digital components to adapt.[11] Additionally, digital provides but also demands immediacy through platforms such as social media. All of this takes place in a digital universe whose size, ie the volume of data that is created and

Figure 1.1   The digital vortex

How significant will the impact of digital disruption be on your organization?

SOURCE IMD Global Center for Digital Business Transformation, 2019

copied – more than doubles every two years. Thus from 2010 to 2020, this universe is estimated to have grown about 50-fold.[12]

Digital has flooded every business segment with new entrants. They are reinventing the rules of competition by bringing customer-centricity to a new level. To gain even more edge, they employ teams of data scientists and have established themselves as attractive employers for data talents in general. As a result, Tesla's connected car project, for instance, has shown consumers that a vehicle could be as advanced, personalized and intuitive to operate as a smartphone, and just as integrated with the user's digital lifestyle – whether that involves controlling features via apps or bringing their Netflix settings and preferences inside the car with them. Tesla thinks about cars differently than most carmakers: 'It's not just some sort of transport utility device with no soul and no character.'[13]

The COVID-19 crisis shattered the last illusions some legacy businesses may have harboured that they could escape the pull of the digital vortex. Digital platforms have blurred and dissolved the boundaries between industries and, increasingly, companies, and replaced them with ecosystems. In addition, where platforms once mainly supported suppliers and third-party innovators, today they bring together a widely distributed workforce, challenging how companies think of work outputs and productivity. In aggregate, today's complexity creates levels and manifestations of uncertainty that those who coined the term VUCA could not have anticipated.

Concurrently, confusion persists as to whether managers should act upon one, some or all VUCA dimensions. What is emerging is that complexity is the main driving force, leading to the consequences of volatility and, crucially, high uncertainty.[14]

This is why doing nothing is not an option – unless you accept decline. It is why you keep hearing, 'Be more agile.' Here is the good news: If you do create the conditions of agility, you will no longer fear the uncertainty. Instead, you will use it to your advantage in growing your business. How to create those conditions; where to start; and what pitfalls to avoid – that's what this book was written to show you.

Why It's a Management Reset

History shows us that when systems, structures or ruling classes outlive their usefulness, they are cast away – often ruthlessly and violently. In 2018, when a front-page story in the *Harvard Business Review* declared 'The end of bureaucracy', it was a daring yet timely statement: Bureaucracy and hierarchy have reached the end of an era. Despite their adaptations over the decades, with their many layers of command they were simply built to support a model of predictable, linear business and competition that doesn't exist anymore. This is not to say the business landscape of the future will be devoid of hierarchy, but that hierarchy is likely to be radically different from what it has been until now.

Crucially, bureaucracies have a knack for preventing managers from doing what they were hired to do by clogging their time with information requests, paperwork and other distractions. (These take precedence over everything – especially customers and products – because whoever initiated that request is now 'waiting'.) This on top of endless meetings of little more than ritual value: A 2014 study by Bain & Co. revealed that in a single large company, supporting and running the weekly executive committee meeting devoured 300,000 working hours a year.[15]

Traditionally, bureaucracies adjusted to external changes through restructuring. Freeze–change–refreeze; academics called the cycle 'punctuated equilibrium'.[16] Whatever the nature of the restructuring, the end point was one where 'order has been restored'. Similarly, the old world of best practices was built on cause-and-effect relationships that could be anticipated. Risk was managed because the risks were known and could be quantified.

In a turbulent environment, those expectations don't hold water anymore. In today's management, practices are emergent; they escape replication. Cause and effect are often only discernible in retrospect. Risk management gives way to uncertainty management.[17] Although scholars have acknowledged this reality for the past 15–20 years, the 'how' has remained stubbornly difficult – something this book aims to help you overcome by guiding you onto a path of implementation.

The top-down, authoritarian mould of management is a particularly tough sell to the millennial workforce. A cohort that grew up with always-on connectivity, random access and instant validation expects the work environment to morph into its own image. The old bureaucratic order thrived on impersonality; some go as far as talking about its dehumanizing effects. This was the corporate 'deal', and the previous generation – saddled with mortgages, car loans and consumer debt – endorsed it. But it is hardly a good match with young workers who are passionate about values and community;[18] who prefer experiences over material possessions; and who value sharing or renting over ownership. As the corporate world absorbs millennial perspectives, it adopts an inclusive, stakeholder view.[19] Increasingly, it regards short-termism as a trap, diverting the bulk of managers' time to issues of compliance and reporting while limiting the space for open-ended thinking that is indispensable for competitiveness and growth.

In the bureaucracy, silos may have existed for good reasons. In the next management paradigm, collaboration needs to replace them. Case in point: A Chinese smart homes company IMD worked with. By now, China's highly digital customers are accustomed to being presented with an integrated view of different product options and offerings. To fashion these new 'phygital' retail experiences, data must be collected across families of products. It takes sophisticated data analytics to identify viable consumer segments in this market. Internally, however, the company continues to be siloed by divisional P&Ls. Marketing, consumer journeys, customer data are fragmented by business line. Divisional heads are rewarded on how much they grow their own business, not the company-wide business.

In another example, carmaker Lamborghini realized that great products are not enough for today's consumers. What they demand are new experiences and ongoing interactions with the brands they like. Its exclusive, invitation-only mobile app named Lamborghini Unica does just that by connecting the buyer's physical and digital touchpoints into a coherent, engaging customer journey where daily upgrades can take place. Of course, to make this happen the company had to integrate its own inner workings, aggressively breaking down walls to make sense of Big Data and help every employee connect to the firm's purpose.

Lamborghini's initiative shows that great customer experience and data-driven cross-selling and upselling won't happen without internal collaboration.[20] These stronger internal linkages militate against the processes that support traditional risk management bureaucracies. Key performance indicators (KPIs), enterprise resource planning (ERP) and others were designed to provide maximum visibility at the top. Effectively crowding out new businesses, they entrench the tyranny of the core business (Chapter 3). This curtails the potential for new skills to integrate with the core business and regenerate it.

The New Environment Requires New Managerial Capabilities

Entering the 2020s, the discipline of management has come full circle. Leaders and managers have been tasked with building a new world of management, one that reflects the realities of pervasive uncertainty. Particularly as digital transforms strategy and competition, there has been greater impetus for discovering what agility really is and developing the muscle to implement it at multiple levels. This is the promise, but also the challenge, of business agility (Figure 1.2):

- Building the capacity that is necessary to assess the new environment.
- Acting on that environment at the levels of strategy, organization and leadership.

Decades of academic research established that higher performance depends on external and internal alignment. External alignment comes from strategy, which functions as the eyes of the company, navigating threats and seizing opportunities. Attention to execution is just as important, mobilizing scarce resources and leading the organization in a way that infuses life into the selected strategy through internal alignment.[21] In an uncertain environment, businesses that seek higher performance need to embed flexibility, experimentation,

Figure 1.2   An uncertain environment requires that companies adapt how they strategize, organize and lead

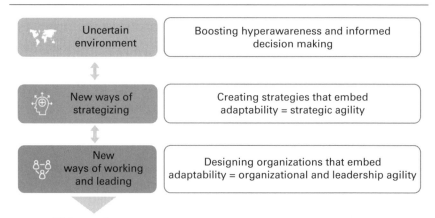

adaptability and resilience in the way they strategize, organize and lead. Alignment doesn't go out of the window, but agility gives it new dynamics. If handled well, business agility can generate the benefits described in Table 1.2.

Table 1.2   Building business agility: What are the benefits?

Release the creative and entrepreneurial potential of the firm to grow and remain relevant

Improve adaptability and resilience to unexpected changes

Strengthen employee engagement through direct measurement of their impact and more say in decision making

Place customers centre stage

Speed up the pace of innovation in response to digital disruption

Continue reducing costs

Make digital transformation stick

Remove 'busyness' and allow leaders to concentrate on the firm's vision and direction

It has become clear that companies will not survive if their senior executives fail to embrace the opportunity that the rise of agility presents. The following chapters will provide you with the keys to unlocking this opportunity. They will:

- Outline the types of capabilities and behaviours your firm will need to develop in order to strengthen its strategic, organizational and leadership agility, thus achieving continued growth in uncertain contexts.

- Help you understand how to make agility transformation your own – reflecting your company's context, purpose and capabilities. The message has been drowned out for too long that not all companies need the same shape, degree or flavour of agility.

- Explain how you can calibrate and sequence agility transformation in a way that matches the realities of your business.

- Inspire you to develop new strategic, organizational and leadership routines along the dimensions of experiment–learn–respond.

- Demonstrate that agility doesn't mean chaos, loss of power and total absence of hierarchy.

- Show that the capacity to absorb and respond to change has to be embedded in the organization's design, leadership styles and strategizing processes. With the days of 'freeze–tweak–refreeze' corporate reorganizations and restructurings behind us, agility cannot be about making changes to the organization at regular intervals anymore. Instead, flexibility and adaptability become the norm, while steering clear of chaos.

Business agility goes far beyond what managers have come to know as 'agile' (ie agile methods and processes – scrum, squads, tribes). It is a way of responding to uncertainty in a holistic and informed way. It is about how leaders lead and companies organize themselves, their operations, strategies and their employees' work to succeed and grow, not just survive, in this age of uncertainty and disruption. More than a methodology, agility is a philosophy and a mindset of embracing uncertainty as an opportunity. It is not just about performance but also about organization-wide empowerment and learning. This is the 'why' of agility and the reason it has become a critical quality in to-day's business.

Endnotes

1 McGrath, R G (2013) *The End of Competitive Advantage: How to keep your strategy moving as fast as your business*, Harvard Business Review Press

2 D'aveni, R A (2010) *Hypercompetition*, Simon and Schuster

3 Thomas, L G and D'Aveni, R (2009) The changing nature of competition in the US manufacturing sector, 1950—2002, *Strategic Organization*, 7 (4), pp 387–431

4 Bennett, N and Lemoine, J (2014) What VUCA really means for you, *Harvard Business Review*, **92** (1–2)

5 Girod, S J G and Whittington, R (2015) Change escalation processes and complex adaptive systems: From incremental reconfigurations to discontinuous restructuring, *Organization Science*, **26** (5), pp 1520–35

6 Miller, J H and Page, S E (2009) *Complex Adaptive Systems: An introduction to computational models of social life*, Princeton University Press

7 Brown, S L and Eisenhardt, K M (1998) *Competing on the Edge: Strategy as structured chaos*, Harvard Business Press

8 Girod, S J G and Karim, S (2017) Restructure or reconfigure? Designing the reorg that works for you, *Harvard Business Review*, **95** (2), pp 128–32

9 Girod, S J G (2020) The Emperor's new clothes, COVID-19 and leadership, www.imd.org/research-knowledge/videos/The-Emperors-New-Clothes-COVID-19-and-leadership-Episode-1 (archived at https://perma.cc/87SR-3HCY)

10 Bradley, J, Loucks, J, Macaulay, J, Noronha, A and Wade, M (2015) *Digital Vortex: How digital disruption is redefining industries*, Global Center for Digital Business Transformation: An IMD and Cisco initiative, pp 6–16

11 Gothelf, J (2014) Bring agile to the whole organization, *Harvard Business Review*, **92** (11)

12 Gantz, J and Reinsel, D (2011) Extracting value from chaos, *IDC iView*, 1142, pp 1–12

13 Butler, C (2019) Tesla's plan to leave the auto industry behind on in-car infotainment, CNBC, 23 November, www.cnbc.com/2019/11/23/teslas-plan-to-leave-auto-industry-behind-on-in-car-entertainment.html (archived at https://perma.cc/2UER-NLBF)

14 Subramaniam, M and Piskorski, M J (2020) How legacy businesses can compete in the sharing economy, *MIT Sloan Management Review*, **61** (4), pp 31–37

15 Mankins, M (2014) This weekly meeting took up 300,000 hours a year, *Harvard Business Review*, **92** (4), p 29

16 Romanelli, E and Tushman, M L (1994) Organizational transformation as punctuated equilibrium: An empirical test, *Academy of Management Journal*, **37** (5), pp 1141–66

17 Snowden, D J and Boone, M E (2007) A leader's framework for decision making, *Harvard Business Review*, **85** (11), p 68

18 Weber, J (2017) Discovering the millennials' personal values orientation: A comparison to two managerial populations, *Journal of Business Ethics*, **143** (3), pp 517–29

19 Cossin, D and Hwee, O B (2016) *Inspiring Stewardship*, Wiley

20 Bergmann, J (2020) Luxury brands learn customer engagement from Lamborghini, The 360 Blog, 25 February, www.salesforce.com/blog/2020/02/360-perspectives-luxury-brands-learn-from-lamborghini.html (archived at https://perma.cc/B4JB-Y4JU)

21 Miller, D (1987) Strategy making and structure: Analysis and implications for performance, *Academy of Management Journal*, **30** (1), pp 7–32

02

The What of Business Agility

Reshaping How Organizations Make Choices

FIVE LESSONS FROM THIS CHAPTER

1 The quest for being adaptive – which is broadly defined as agility – isn't new. Despite incremental adaptations, many firms saw little incentive in the last 30 years for expanding their focus to accommodate not just the core business but also next businesses. Thus they could get away with working within highly complex bureaucratic organizations, geared to making the core business even more efficient.

2 In the current management reset, business leaders need to embrace greater simplicity in what they do and how they do it but without becoming simplistic. Business agility results in reconciling the need to accelerate innovation pace (nimble) without descending into chaos (stable). Reconciling nimble and stable is about being prepared for unexpected changes that come with today's type and degree of business uncertainty. Reconciling simple and complex is about being sophisticated in the way a business responds to this uncertainty.

3 Contrary to popular belief, speed is only one aspect of business agility. Business agility is essentially about reducing the tensions between conflicting demands in order to achieve more flexibility.

4 As a way of minimizing 'either/or' trade-offs and embracing 'both/and' solutions, business agility works at three distinct levels: Strategic, organizational and leadership.

5 There's one quest but multiple paths. Every company needs to find its own flavour of agility that is best suited to its business circumstances.

The Old Fight Against Rigidity is Taking a New Turn

When the modern corporation was born in the 1920s, it thrived on military-style regimentation and predictability. These were the qualities that guided Henry Ford (1863–1947) to set up assembly-line factories and churn out the automobile, a sophisticated and costly-to-build product, at both an unprecedented large scale and low cost. Frederick Taylor (1856–1915) took the pursuit of efficiency even further, connecting highly specialized tasks into a linear chain that made each worker interdependent on each other and separated doers from thinkers. Mass manufacturing, mass media and mass culture became the order of the day. As Spanish philosopher José Ortega y Gasset (1883–1955) observed, the mass became 'everybody', with no room for outliers.[1] This was the birth, and celebration, of management as a science, and science at this time implied 'life as a machine'. The more mechanical a process – and workers themselves – could become, the higher volumes of output it could churn out, the better. Humans, once 'the measure of all things' for ancient Greeks, were now taken out of the equation, except as cogs in an industrial wheel. Even art took it upon itself to remove human elements from artistic works: Charlie Chaplin's 1936 film *Modern Times* is a timeless parody of this assembly-line culture and its crushing effects.

Bureaucracy and Hierarchy Have Been Capable of Adapting…

Modern enterprise gave rise to modern bureaucracy. Max Weber (1864–1920) saw the ascendance of bureaucracy as an expression of modern society's growing rationality and controllability.[2] Who better to control mass production than an army of bureaucrats, supported by large pools of typists and stenographers, all housed in modern cities' first steel-frame office towers?

The system was not entirely closed to modifications – so long as they improved efficiency. Guided by management innovations of his time, Alfred Sloan at General Motors (1875–1966) created the M-form or multidivisional form of hierarchy, which after the Second World War became the dominant enterprise structure and is still alive today.[3] In the M-form, the centre exerts control by setting targets for a number of semi-autonomous units such as business and country divisions. Armed with its own profit-and-loss account, each unit focuses on competitive strategy and operations, whereas top management concentrates on corporate strategy and budget allocation.[4] The M-form came with a degree of flexibility: Unlike in Henry Ford's paradigm, now it was possible to merge, transfer, separate, close and open divisions at will, a change process that is known today as 'reconfiguration'.[5]

When business internationalized in the 1970s and 1980s, hierarchy and bureaucracy evolved into a matrix organizational structure, which allowed for greater coordination among businesses and countries.[6] Thus hierarchy stuck around (Table 2.1). For all its shortcomings, it served corporations well by delivering practical results, ie getting things done, as well as the psychological value produced by a sense of order and security.[7]

… But Rigidity Never Ceased To Be a Constraint

The matrix was an improvement, but it was found to dilute accountability and slow down decision making. Meanwhile, despite clinging to the assembly line as both the backbone and a metaphor for their organizations, automobile manufacturers, in particular, started realizing

Table 2.1 How 20th-century organizations evolved in a predominantly linear environment

Strategy	Structure	Processes and IT	Leadership and people	Incentives and motivation
FORDIST ORGANIZATION (early 20th century until today) • Push one product to customers • Large inventories to respond to predictable demand • Vertical integration to support one core business	MULTIDIVISIONAL ORGANIZATION (early 20th century until today) • Businesses siloed by P&L and cost centres • Only top management has oversight	TAYLORISM (early 20th century until 1970s) • Split between doers and thinkers • High predictability of planning process • Speed thanks to routinized, predictable tasks • Efficiency	Experience trumps values	Salary and fixed contract
Focus on core business and core competences (1980s–2000s) Lasting competitive advantage	Delayering of hierarchies (since 1980s) Matrix organizations Project management structures (since 1980s)	Lean manufacturing • Quality circles • Six Sigma • Kanban (since 1970s)	Command-and-control leadership Communities of practice	Individual bonuses Team bonuses Vertical promotions

that centralized quality control was a contradiction in terms. It was workers on the factory floor, not the top management, who were closest to the problem and were in the best position to find a solution. This new approach to managing quality sparked process re-engineering and Lean Six Sigma, a new wave of empowerment pioneered by Japanese firms in the 1970s.[8]

Despite these evolutions, executives battled a growing sense of misalignment with new, highly complex and uncertain environments. Typical corporations of the late 20th and early 21st centuries often suffered from complacency due to previous success – the tyranny of their core business. (After all, what could be more reassuring than billing oneself as 'market leader'?) They viewed corporate functions as cost centres rather than value-creating units. They feared or were in denial of uncertainty and struggled to prepare for the next revenue streams, despite the surrounding threats and opportunities.[9] At the same time, layers of bureaucracy and internal complexity would turn employees inwards, away from customers, and delay decision making while blocking strategy execution. In the M-form, it was all-out competition for attention and funding.

Over time, executives came to accept that their organizations weren't built to deal with this uncertainty, velocity and volume of change. They also realized that the traditional organizational forms, which optimized for risk management in a predictable world, were unlikely to yield the necessary solutions.[10] This realization led them to search for adaptability. Only, at this juncture, adaptability could no longer be an end goal; it had to be an embedded capability.[11] Concurrently, the pressure to be more flexible became overwhelming. In a 2017 McKinsey survey, 50 per cent of CEOs rated their firms' performance in achieving dynamism and responsiveness as low.[12]

Previous Takes On Agility

This enduring challenge to be adaptive inspired organizational scholars to call for new forms of strategizing, organizing and leading. In particular, the interest in strategic agility among business scholars has grown significantly in the past 20 years or so. The 1990s focused on ambidexterity – the management dilemma of exploiting the core business while simultaneously exploring the next business.[13] This was presented as a pendulum, swinging between states of exploitation and exploration. Although a solid starting point and a worthy precursor of agility, ambidexterity took only a limited view of the many tensions and dilemmas today's managers have been tasked with resolving.

Around the turn of the century, the rise of what was seen as the New Economy prompted some observers to comment that having agility without a strategy was no better than having a strategy without agility.[14] Based on an in-depth analysis of Nokia, a 2008 study by Doz and Kosonen coined the term 'strategic agility'.[15] It entailed staying nimble and flexible, open to new evidence, always ready to reassess past choices and change direction in light of new developments, and the willingness and ability to turn on a dime. The authors showed strategic agility to be a combination of organizational, strategic and leadership factors – a perspective this book fully supports. Nonetheless, their study does not capture the multiple layers of hard choices and tensions senior executives grapple with as they attempt to infuse their companies with strategic agility. It also largely predates the digital era, which, as this book shows, has changed the What and the How as well as the Who of strategy.

More recent studies have discussed strategic agility in terms of changing course without losing momentum,[16] efficiently redirecting resources to value-creating and value-protecting (and capturing) higher-yield activities,[17] or transforming – quickly, creatively and intelligently – as fast as, or faster than, the environment changes.[18]

Meanwhile, the search for the right flavour of organizational adaptability has been afoot for many decades, giving birth to an array of concepts such as modular organization,[19] adhocracy,[20] latent organization,[21] project-based enterprise,[22] heterarchy[23] and others. Each uncovered a few additional if mostly theoretical contours of organizational designs that could help companies to embrace rather than fear complexity, unpredictability and rapid change.

In the 1990s, the search for ambidexterity inspired many to explore how to set up an organization to be ambidextrous.[24] Proponents of structural ambidexterity suggested that companies should place any and all experimentation with next businesses in separate entities. The contextual view of ambidexterity maintained that rank-and-file employees were the ones best suited to keep an eye out for next-business ideas as part of their day-to-day work.[25] But for all these bold concepts, tangible change remained confined to theory or to mid-sized firms.

Beyond strategy and organizing, in the past few years the quest for agility has also started to encompass leadership. In particular, the prevalence of digital and its emphasis on complexity and speed have brought about a management landscape where leadership is becoming decoupled from formal positions and instead distributed across organizations. Digital does not diminish the importance of leadership. If anything, authentic leadership today is as prized as ever.

The spotlight has been on how newer generations lead. Leaders like Microsoft's Satya Nadella are champions at sense-making, driven by acute curiosity about customers and technologies that allows them to read the industry ahead of others.[26] In fact, the CEOs of digital giants have all at some point been truly hands-on in the creation of new products or algorithms.[27] This is the paradigm that Simon Hayward describes in his 2018 book *The Agile Leader: How to create an agile business in the digital age*.[28] It presents agile leaders as those who enable and disrupt at the same time. While enabling through empathy, trust and clarity of direction, their digital literacy allows them to act as disruptors who remain close to the customer, question the status quo and create new ways of thinking.

Some among today's generation of new business leaders have been equally good at managing for efficiency, inspiring others and also proving their mettle as knowledge experts who contribute to leading scientific journals. (Elon Musk has published a number of patents, acting as a lead inventor in all of them.) It is not unreasonable to expect that in the digital age, where top leaders need to demonstrate their digital fluency, this trend of the CEO as a Renaissance person, voracious in their appetite for knowledge and learning, will become the norm even among non-tech companies.

To date, debates on leadership agility have often hinged on compiling lists of leadership attributes and competences, detached from their strategic and organizational contexts. Some practical roadmaps have emerged, pointing to the new spaces leaders need to occupy. But little attention has been paid to the tensions whose handling constitutes the core in this latest evolution of leadership: How to empower others rather than drive results directly, and yet retain a degree of control and overall visibility, especially over a consistent delivery of strategy.[29]

Agility or 'Agile'?

Over the past decade, non-digital-natives like General Electric (GE) and Airbus have embraced agile methods and processes as they sought to reinvent themselves from equipment manufacturers to service providers and leaders in new, 21st-century ecosystems. Almost instantly, agile methods have become the hot ticket for management consultants, trainers, coaches and other specialists around the world. The boom that ensued has obscured as much as explained what agility is about. It has fed the perception of agility as essentially a skillset, something that individual employees can be trained to 'pick up'. Coaches, trainers and change experts have added agile training to their existing list of products which include Kanban, extreme programming, project management, process audits, leadership, enterprise coaching, etc. It has also conflated agility with 'agile', ie agile methods such as scrum. An integrated view of agility at strategic, organizational and leadership levels remains a scarce commodity throughout the field.

Managerial literature on the subject has likewise focused on the mechanics of building agile teams and recruiting agile leaders, alongside promoting such novelties as daily stand-ups and stewarding rather than owning software code. For example, Steve Denning's 2018 book *The Age of Agile* suggests that with agile – where networks of small, cross-functional teams tackle tasks in short cycles, continually adjusting for customer feedback – even global giants can learn to act entrepreneurially. According to the book, as long as a sufficient number of teams have gone agile, they will organically give rise to agile units. By then, the efficiency gains and quality improvements that have been secured will result in operational (or firm) agility. With time, and once the innovation has spilled over into the external market, firm agility will produce strategic agility.[30] In reality, however, this is not automatically the case, unless you pay attention to the guidelines presented in our book.

Legacy Companies' Comfort Zone Perpetuates Rigidity

Despite efforts to become more adaptive, large legacy businesses often remain intrinsically rigid. Many have struggled to leave their comfort zone and continue to choose, almost at any cost, stability and a simplistic way of strategizing, on top of a highly complex way of organizing and leading. Inevitably, this leads them to a state of inertia.[31] Legacy companies are hardwired to expect stability and to anchor their planning around the core business. Fear of self-cannibalization is a primary driver of decisions. They typically operate in a present or a very short-term horizon and neglect signals of change. Over-confident in forecasting, they default on simplistic medium-risk scenarios. As a result, they are well aware of the surrounding uncertainty but it never quite factors into their decision making.

The consequence is that strategic planning becomes simplistic. It is usually so ordered and drawn-out that it galvanizes an inward-looking view, coupled with a relative inability to respond to unexpected changes fast enough. As executives pile data into spreadsheets, they become so confident that they no longer challenge their assumptions. Far from having a single goal that everyone can focus on, executives are negotiating next year's budget, competing for resources, maintaining and escalating prior commitments, fighting for their turf, impressing the board and thinking about succession.[32] The mindset is one of dominance and a zero-sum game. Most companies end up approving roll-on budgets and incremental steps that entrench the core business further. The result of trying to satisfy everyone is that resources are distributed too thinly to aim for meaningful, let alone game-changing outcomes. More often than not, flexibility and entrepreneurship have been shut out.

Organizationally, companies that are run as bureaucracies are overly complex; that is another source of rigidity. Keeping the bureaucracy running saps the organization of energy, attention and creativity. Multiple reporting, endless numbers of meetings, a multitude of policies and procedures to follow, gatekeepers up and down steep hierarchies aiming to keep busy even if they add little value to the customer – all of these are symptoms of overblown complexity.

Can You Outrun the Start-Ups? And Should You?

Disruptive start-ups, on the other hand, improvise and pivot as often as they need. Due to their small size and digital proficiency, they are simpler and leaner, hence organizationally more efficient. For some established players, this creates the temptation to speed up the clock to the level of new entrants. This is understandable: Digital feeds the perception that agility predominantly has to do with speed, ie with organizations responding instantly to any and all external developments. In a May 2020 survey by IMD, 66 per cent of 550 executives across industries defined agility as fast adaptation to uncertainty. 'We are too slow! Agile is what will get us there faster,' is a sentiment often heard from managers.

It is true that to get out of their old reactive mode, legacy companies need to act, respond and experiment faster. Yet this book argues that speed is only one dimension of organizational agility. (During the 2020 global pandemic, even such epitomes of speed as Uber and Airbnb ran into trouble.) The next few chapters will attempt to dispel this notion – and the broader theme of 'managing in an age of urgency' – as well as the impression that small-sized companies, especially SMEs and family businesses, have it made when it comes to building agility.

Agility is the Flexibility Businesses Gain by Reconciling Two Tensions

Business agility has to do with resolving two core tensions. The research that underpins this book has identified agility as the flexibility that large companies achieve in response to high uncertainty when they are as nimble as necessary but without becoming chaotic (nimble/stable); and, at the same time, as simple as necessary in their inner workings but without being simplistic (simple/complex). Addressing these two tensions at strategic, organizational and leadership levels makes a business more flexible and entrepreneurial in the face of 2020s uncertainty.

Stable and *Nimble*

Whether they are highly successful or already disrupted by new entrants such as digital natives and start-ups, legacy companies must shape the opportunities that result from unexpected change. There is no escaping the fact that they are hugely invested in their core business, and therefore they are rarely in a position to abandon it altogether. In fact, more often than not, they must find ways to improve and defend this core business. But they also need to become more experimental and faster. Flexibility and growth will depend on their ability to move the cursor (Figure 2.1) from 'stable' towards managing more effectively the tension between stable and nimble. When it can do that, the business is more prepared for unanticipated changes.

Clarins Group, the French-based global leader in the cosmetics industry, faced considerable pressures to shed rigidity during the COVID crisis (Figure 2.2). As the health crisis unfolded, Clarins had to test new hypotheses fast and use them to adapt on the go. But as a

Figure 2.1   Agility is the flexibility a business achieves when it can address two tensions

global leader in its segment, it also had to continue delivering on its existing strategy – with discipline and accountability – without sacrificing the internal stability that served the firm well for many years. It had to move faster on some topics, but it also had to be cautious in order to protect its established distribution network, brand and cash flow. Being nimble without grounding will result in chaos: Start-ups might get away with it but not large companies with strategic priorities, key customers and employees with established skillsets.

Complex and *Simple*

As you saw in the previous section, most large incumbent businesses are rigid because they are overly simplistic in the way they strategize. Their path to greater strategic agility consists of introducing a healthier dose of complexity in what they choose to do and how they strategize, but without becoming overly complex.

Their path towards greater organizational agility follows an opposite direction. Typically, their focus was on risk containment through heavy bureaucratic and waterfall innovation processes combined with hefty layers of management. Today, enterprises need to evolve past this tradition of bureaucracy and to simplify how they operate. However, large and diverse companies cannot afford to oversimplify; they have to leverage rather than jettison their scale that sets them apart from start-ups, as well as their significant resources, departments, roles, processes and IT systems. Their executives have to learn which parts of their organization need more simplicity; and where, on the other hand, a healthy level of complexity is required, even desirable. If it can achieve that, a business will become more sophisticated about how it deals with the surrounding uncertainty.

Consider Clarins again. It felt the need to forge cross-market commonalities that would push through its global digital initiatives to mitigate lockdowns. But it also wanted to remain relevant to customer needs in local markets. In times of crisis, the company wanted to reduce waste through efficiency but had to accept the right level of redundancies that necessarily resulted from attention to local relevance.

For large, established firms dealing with the turbulence of globalization, digital transformation, climate and social change, the journey

Figure 2.2   How the tensions of stable/nimble and complex/simple played out at Clarins Group

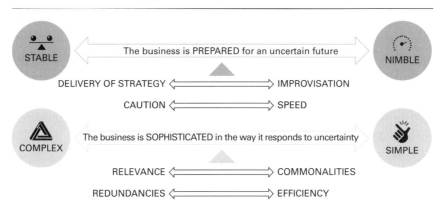

towards agility means emulating some of the start-ups' nimbleness and simplicity while leveraging the power of their scale.[33] As Nick Jue, the former CEO of ING Netherlands who initiated the bank's agility transformation said, 'I want to remain an elephant because I want to keep the power of the elephant. But I also want to be fast and flexible [like fintechs].'[34]

Conclusions

Facing Uncertainty Head-On By Pursuing 'Both/And' Solutions

A CEO's remit is to oversee growth and adaptability on the one hand and risk management, delivery of strategy and accountability on the other hand. Currently, this remit has expanded to embrace, rather than fear, uncertainty. If well applied, the attributes of nimbleness and simplicity enable innovation for top-line growth as well as adaptability to unpredictable changes and efficiency. Concurrently, the principles of complexity and stability enable strategy execution through resource slack, accountability and learning. Just as consistency can become rigidity, agility can become a lack of focus when it isn't tempered by consistency.[35]

Business agility is about paradox reconciliation, not simply about speed:[36] In today's management reset, you need to ensure control while at the same time relinquishing it, maintain uniformity while nurturing diversity, empower teams while avoiding chaos.[37] In the age of uncertainty, you, your team, and your organization need to learn to manage tensions, reconcile competing demands and introduce both/and solutions. Bridging organizations' inherent contradictions – those between rigidity and freedom, stability and nimbleness, routine and novelty – is at the heart of agility.[38]

Business agility is both a manifestation of and the driving force behind the ongoing management reset. Each of the following chapters in this book will reveal a different facet of that reset as well as agility's role in shaping the new, emerging paradigm of management.

There is No 'One Way' to Build Agility

This book suggests that there is no 'one way' of injecting agility into an organization. Agility comes in different colours, shapes and degrees, and every business needs to choose its own path. In charting this path, you will be able to identify the right fit between your organization and its environment, as well as address built-in organizational tensions. To minimize these tensions, instead of randomly trying on trendy tools and methodologies you will need to identify your organization's optimal position on the stable-vs-nimble and complex-vs-simple continuums.

As the next few chapters will show, much depends on industry conditions, B2B vs B2C, returns and profitability, degree of uncertainty, good vs declining performance, and national culture. We show that there is no one-size-fits-all, one-correct-way approach to building agility. Every organization needs to identify a form of agility that will suit its context, history, objectives and operating environment.

Endnotes

1 Ortega y Gasset, J (1993) *The Revolt of the Masses*, WW Norton & Company

2 Weber, M (2002) *The Protestant Ethic and the 'Spirit' of Capitalism and Other Writings*, Penguin

3 Chandler, A D (1990) *Strategy and Structure: Chapters in the history of the industrial enterprise*, vol 120, MIT Press

4 Williamson, O E (1975) *Markets and Hierarchies*, Free Press

5 Galunic, D C and Eisenhardt, K M (2001) Architectural innovation and modular corporate forms, *Academy of Management Journal*, **44** (6), pp 1229–49; Karim, S (2006) Modularity in organizational structure: The reconfiguration of internally developed and acquired business units, *Strategic Management Journal*, **27** (9), pp 799–823; Girod, S J G and Whittington, R (2015) Change escalation processes and complex adaptive systems: From incremental reconfigurations to discontinuous restructuring, *Organization Science*, **26** (5), pp 1520–35

6 Galbraith, J R (1971) Matrix organization designs: How to combine functional and project forms, *Business Horizons*, **14** (1), pp 29–40

7 Leavitt, H J (2003) Why hierarchies thrive, *Harvard Business Review*, **81** (3), pp 96–112

8 Hammer, M and Champy, J (2009) *Reengineering the Corporation: A manifesto for business revolution*, HarperCollins; Hammer, M and Hershman, L (2010) *Faster, Cheaper, Better: The 9 levers for transforming how work gets done*, Currency; Slater, R (2003) *Jack Welch and the GE Way*, Tata McGraw-Hill Education

9 Nunes, P F and Breene, T (2011) *Jumping the S-Curve: How to beat the growth cycle, get on top, and stay there*, Harvard Business Press

10 Teece, D, Peteraf, M and Leih, S (2016) Dynamic capabilities and organizational agility: Risk, uncertainty, and strategy in the innovation economy, *California Management Review*, **58** (4), pp 13–35

11 Girod, S J G and Whittington, R (2017) Reconfiguration, restructuring and firm performance: Dynamic capabilities and environmental dynamism, *Strategic Management Journal*, **38** (5), pp 1121–33

12 Ahlbäck, K, Fahrbach, C, Murarka, M and Salo, O (2017) How to create an agile organization, *McKinsey Quarterly*, 2 October, www.mckinsey.com/business-functions/organization/our-insights/how-to-create-an-agile-organization (archived at https://perma.cc/S3HZ-PD9A)

13 March, J G (1991) Exploration and exploitation in organizational learning, *Organization Science*, **2** (1), pp 71–87

14 Long, C (2000) Measuring your strategic agility, *Consulting to Management*, **11** (3), p 25

15 Doz, Y and Kosonen, M (2008) The dynamics of strategic agility: Nokia's rollercoaster experience, *California Management Review*, **50** (3), pp 95–118

16 Weber, Y and Tarba, S Y (2014) Strategic agility: A state of the art introduction to the special section on strategic agility, *California Management Review*, **56** (3), pp 5–12

17 Teece, D, Peteraf, M and Leih, S (2016) Dynamic capabilities and organizational agility: Risk, uncertainty, and strategy in the innovation economy, *California Management Review*, **58** (4), pp 13–35

18 Yeung, A and Ulrich, D (2019) *Reinventing the Organization: How companies can deliver radically greater value in fast-changing markets*, Harvard Business Press

19 Galunic, D C and Eisenhardt, K M (2001) Architectural innovation and modular corporate forms, *Academy of Management Journal*, **44** (6), pp 1229–49; Hoetker, G (2006) Do modular products lead to modular organizations? *Strategic Management Journal*, **27** (6), pp 501–18; Karim, S (2006) Modularity in organizational structure: The reconfiguration of internally developed and acquired business units, *Strategic Management Journal*, **27** (9), pp 799–823; Sanchez, R and Mahoney, J T (1996) Modularity, flexibility, and knowledge management in product and organization design, *Strategic Management Journal*, **17** (S2), pp 63–76; Schilling, M A and Steensma, H K (2001) The use of modular organizational forms: An industry-level analysis, *Academy of Management Journal*, **44** (6), pp 1149–68

20 Mintzberg, H and McHugh, A (1985) Strategy formation in an adhocracy, *Administrative Science Quarterly*, pp 160–97

21 Starkey, K, Barnatt, C and Tempest, S (2000) Beyond networks and hierarchies: Latent organizations in the UK television industry, *Organization Science*, **11** (3), pp 299–305

22 DeFillippi, R J and Arthur, M B (1998) Paradox in project-based enterprise: The case of film making, *California Management Review*, **40** (2), pp 125–39

23 Hedlund, G (1986) The hypermodern MNC-A heterarchy? *Human Resource Management (1986–98)*, **25** (1), p 9

24 Tushman, M L and O'Reilly III, C A (1996) Ambidextrous organizations: Managing evolutionary and revolutionary change, *California Management Review*, **38** (4), pp 8–29; Birkinshaw, J and Gibson, C B (2004) Building an ambidextrous organisation, Advanced Institute of Management Research Paper 003

25 O'Reilly III, C A and Tushman, M L (2013) Organizational ambidexterity: Past, present, and future, *Academy of Management Perspectives*, **27** (4), pp 324–38

26 Ancona, D (2019) Five rules for leading in a digital world, *MIT Sloan Management Review*, **61** (1), pp 1–4

27 Groysberg, B and Gregg, T (2020) How tech CEOs are redefining the top job, *MIT Sloan Management Review*, **61** (2), pp 21–24

28 Hayward, S (2018) *The Agile Leader: How to create an agile business in the digital age*, Kogan Page

29 Kinley, N and Ben-Hur, S (2020) *Leadership OS*, Springer International Publishing

30 Denning, S (2018) *The Age of Agile: How smart companies are transforming the way work gets done*, Amacom

31 Snowden, D J and Boone, M E (2007) A leader's framework for decision making, *Harvard Business Review*, **85** (11), p 68

32 Bradley, C, Hirt, M and Smit, S (2018) *Strategy Beyond the Hockey Stick: People, probabilities, and big moves to beat the odds*, John Wiley & Sons

33 Prange, C and Heracleous, L (eds) (2018) *Agility. X: How organizations thrive in unpredictable times*, Cambridge University Press

34 Calnan, M and Rozen, A (2019) ING's agile transformation – teaching an elephant to race, *Journal of Creating Value*, **5** (2), pp 190–209

35 Coleman, J (2017) The best strategic leaders balance agility and consistency, *Harvard Business Review*, **95** (1), pp 1–5

36 Smith, W K and Lewis, M W (2011) Toward a theory of paradox: A dynamic equilibrium model of organizing, *Academy of Management Review*, **36** (2), pp 381–403

37 Zhang, Y, Waldman, D A, Han, Y L and Li, X B (2015) Paradoxical leader behaviors in people management: Antecedents and consequences, *Academy of Management Journal*, **58** (2), pp 538–66

38 Lewis, M W, Andriopoulos, C and Smith, W K (2014) Paradoxical leadership to enable strategic agility, *California Management Review*, **56** (3), pp 58–77

PART TWO

A New Agility
Landscape (What)

03

Strategic Agility

A tech giant with a history that spans more than 100 years sounds like a contradiction. Yet IBM's longevity has come from an instinct for ruthlessly reinventing its business every 10 years or so – from hardware to software and services and, most recently, cloud and artificial intelligence – or what the company calls cognitive solutions. Through the years, IBM has thrived on changing its core – often by performing what some have described as 'a heart transplant on itself', scaling that change and making it stick.[1] The company never shied away from abandoning its established business model when the time came, such as by selling its PC division to China's Lenovo in 2005 to focus on IT services. Since 2014, it has again overhauled its business from mainframes and servers to software as a service. By 2017, close to half of its revenue came from the newly defined 'strategic imperatives' of analytics, cloud, security, social and mobile divisions.[2] At present, it seeks to re-emerge as the technological icon it used to be, this time as a leader in quantum computing, AI and blockchain. IBM has consistently used its scale to incubate trends, invest in new capabilities and restructure its offerings. In tandem with selling off older businesses to focus on bigger opportunities, it has, year after year, pursued aggressive acquisitions of specialized IT players. The $34 billion it paid in 2019 to buy open-source software provider Red Hat is considered the largest software acquisition, and one of the biggest tech deals, in history.[3] With equal consistency, the company has brought in new talent and diffused cultural change across the organization. These fights against gravity and natural rigidity have become a big part of what defines IBM.

Effective strategizing has always been about preparing for the long term in the short term, as IBM reminds us.[4] In an era where competitive advantage remains transient, Chapter 2 explained why maintaining a stubborn focus on the existing core business at the expense of speedy experimentation with next businesses leaves legacy companies unprepared for unexpected change. You also learned why cognitive biases and politics-as-usual prevent incumbents from approaching uncertainty and fast change with the right level of strategic sophistication.

Strategic agility is the critical flexibility that established companies achieve when they learn to navigate the tensions that occur in pursuing two high-level goals: 1) aiming to be nimbler without becoming reckless, and 2) strategizing with greater sophistication but without becoming overly complex. Strategy is still about choices, but the frontier for making those choices has shifted away from either/or and towards both/and decisions.

Moreover, managing the tensions of stable vs nimble and complex vs simple doesn't mean the same thing for all firms and all sectors. Every company must find the level of strategic agility that suits its circumstances. To calibrate what your company's needs are and where there are rigidities you need to address, you can use our Strategic Agility Assessment Test (Table 3.1).

Table 3.1   Introducing the Strategic Agility Assessment Test

Diagnosis: How *nimble* is our strategizing?	Very Poor 1	Poor 2	Avrg 3	Good 4	Very Good 5
We continuously experiment with next business models and opportunities					
We detect and act early on the looming threats to our competitive advantage					
We energetically fight the tyranny of the core business by self-disrupting					
We have a strategy process that enables us to detect and respond to important but unexpected changes rapidly					
We know how to test new opportunities small, then learn and scale if successful					
We only focus on big bets; we are not interested in scaling small businesses					
We reallocate resources and budgets to new opportunities as often as we should (eg by selling older businesses regularly)					
We behave as if our competitive advantage was only temporary					

Table 3.1   (Continued)

Diagnosis: How *nimble* is our strategizing?	Very Poor 1	Poor 2	Avrg 3	Good 4	Very Good 5
Our strategy process is sufficiently close to the frontline and future customers					
Our strategy process looks well beyond our industry boundaries					

Diagnosis: How *stable* is our strategizing?	Very Poor 1	Poor 2	Avrg 3	Good 4	Very Good 5
We innovate and protect our core business as much as we should					
We take the necessary time to assess whether external changes are mere blips or real pivot points					
We use dashboards and analytics that allow us to know how sound our core business is at any time					
We have a long-term and clear strategic vision					
We master a strategic planning process that allows us to protect our core business					
We do not pursue every single opportunity erratically					
Our financial and budget processes ensure that we finance our core business(es) as thoroughly as we should					
We strive to be the industry leader in our customers' eyes					

(continued)

Table 3.1   (Continued)

We are never overwhelmed by the number of strategic initiatives we pursue
Our portfolio of businesses, products, countries and/or customers is small enough to ensure good governance and sufficient resources and managerial attention
Our senior leadership team are united behind the execution of new strategic initiatives and businesses, even if they disrupt their own business
Our senior executives' incentives are aligned to share the gain of new business initiatives with those who lead these new initiatives
We know when to acquire companies and which targets to choose
We know how to integrate our acquired companies to leverage fully their expertise
We know which profiles and skills should be kept in house to protect our competitive advantage or develop the next one
We know which partnerships we should avoid; we have defined 'no-fly zones'

(continued)

Table 3.1   (Continued)

Diagnosis: How *simple* is our strategizing?	Very Poor 1	Poor 2	Avrg 3	Good 4	Very Good 5
Divisions that are ahead in digital transformation help those that are lagging behind					
Our leaders are united by one common understanding and language of digital transformation					

Diagnosis: How *complex* is our strategizing?	Very Poor 1	Poor 2	Avrg 3	Good 4	Very Good 5
Our portfolio of businesses, products, countries and/or customers is broad enough to mitigate environmental uncertainty					
We use powerful analytics that allow us to get fine-grained insights and make informed decisions about how large our portfolio should be					
We use powerful analytics that help us detect new and unexpected opportunities in our portfolio (of countries, products, and/or customers)					
In strategic brainstorming, senior executives do not hesitate to get out of their business turf and ideate for the company in general					
We have a culture of constructive confrontation to challenge our biases when we examine next business opportunities					

(continued)

Table 3.1   (Continued)

Our strategy process is diverse enough and gathers ideas well beyond the realm of management layers
If we need a board of millennials, we have one
We have a leading ecosystem of external partners
We know how to choose our partners and create differentiating value with them
We are seen as the partner of choice in our industry by start-ups

SOURCE Prof Stéphane JG Girod, IMD. Not to be used without permission

Strategic Agility is About Minimizing Trade-offs

Strategic agility is about minimizing trade-offs in order to remain flexible and grow in the face of uncertainty. The research behind this book discovered five important trade-offs, each marked by inherent tension (Figure 3.1).

Two of the trade-offs in Figure 3.1 have to do with the stable–nimble tension. The other three deal with the simple–complex tension. Two trade-offs refer to the What of strategy – eg strategizing for both the core business and the next business; managing a simple but diverse-enough portfolio. However, in and of itself, having a number of initiatives in place will not yield sufficient strategic agility. Firms also need to pay attention to the strategy processes they use for evaluating individual initiatives and reallocating resources. In other words, alongside the What of strategy, it is also How they strategize that matters.

Figure 3.1   Strategic agility is about minimizing five key trade-offs

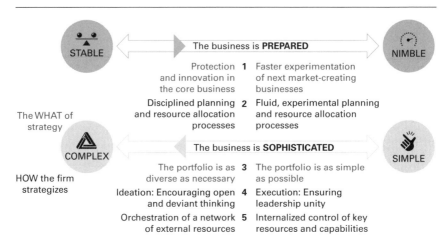

A firm that has learned how to minimize these trade-offs will emerge both prepared for change and sophisticated in its approach to change. Prepared because it will maintain a vibrant portfolio of options. Increasingly comfortable with a more fluid allocation of resources, it will be adroit at aggressively entering new markets and rapidly scaling up new businesses.[5] The company will also become more sophisticated: That means paying attention to weak signals; integrating insights on a continuous basis and making bold choices based on those insights; nurturing good quality (not just quantity) in its portfolio of future strategic directions; and achieving a new level of entrepreneurship through greater engagement of its stakeholders.

The journey towards strategic agility entails two steps. The first one is to be clear about which trade-offs need to be reconciled. That is the purpose of this chapter. We also acknowledge that reducing the tensions that occur when you want to pursue competing strategic demands is challenging. Chapter 8 will provide you with inspiration on how to tackle those challenges.

Finally, what Figure 3.1 reveals is that for most legacy companies, the journey towards strategic agility entails pushing the cursor towards more nimbleness. Whereas on the second tension, the journey usually begins by discarding the simplistic approach to strategy that doesn't sufficiently take into account uncertainty. Sophisticated strategizing means firms need to learn how to deal with the complexity of their external and internal environments, while at the same time keeping what they can simple.

Growing Both the Core Business and the Next Businesses

General Electric (GE) has a rich history of redefining its business successfully and repeatedly.[6] As early as the 1950s it set up its own corporate university in order to effect cultural and leadership change across the conglomerate. In the 1990s, at the height of the Jack Welch era, GE embraced the Six Sigma methodology to cut costs through the reduction of errors and defects.

Despite this track record, digital transformation with its new context and new levels of complexity presented GE with a tough challenge. The company's vision was to reposition itself from equipment maker to a leader in the Industrial Internet of Things (IIoT) space – a provider of smart machines and data analytics. In 2015 it set up a new division called GE Digital, a California-based software business that was tasked with developing GE's IIoT platform called Predix and the associated analytics and apps that Predix supported. However, GE's sturdy and structured industrial verticals business had been successful and stable for decades. Designing, developing and building machines, GE with industrials at its core spawned its own culture and its own set of incentives and rewards. The idea of blurring the lines, of co-creating with customers and co-envisioning industrial/digital solutions went against the grain of how things had been done for generations.

Similarly, wary of becoming displaced one day by cloud and digital giants, GE's direct competitor Siemens launched digital transformation in all of its businesses, assigning each its own level of priority and a similar amount of managerial attention. From the outset, the company actively involved all business units in the creation of its analytics platform, giving them a stake in the ground-breaking initiative's success.[7] It made sure it could deploy digital solutions to any current business opportunities. This included selling digital twins and virtual factory solutions to help customers speed up and cut the costs of complex project prototyping. In addition, Siemens also worked on the launch of its Industrial Data Analytics platform for IIoT, a new offering where the company uses predictive analytics to improve customers' asset reliability and performance. Going even further, Siemens started working on Mindsphere, a cloud-based platform-as-a-service (PaaS), where customers collect, analyse, visualize and store their own data and develop their own apps – without automatically sharing data with Siemens or necessarily owning Siemens-produced assets. Highly self- and industry-disruptive, this approach dramatically reshaped Siemens' customer relationships and profit formula.

Protecting the core business requires a great deal of innovation. But it is fast experimentation with next businesses that stretches a firm's strategic muscle. This is akin to rehearsing for unexpected disruptions. Yet this fast exploration need not take place in a separate universe: The old principle of resource relatedness when launching new revenue streams (as established products mature and new ones are launched) continues to apply.[8] Siemens succeeded because it engaged in digital transformation by relating it to the core business better and faster than GE did. Otherwise the core may fail to see the new initiative's relevance and value. Worse, it is likely to act as an antibody against next businesses.

In the consumer goods industry, cosmetics and beauty company Sephora, owned by LVMH since 1997, spent many years reinventing its core business around the digital consumer journey.[9] Confronted by the rise of global e-commerce giants like Amazon as well as new digital players in the beauty care segment, the company concentrated much of its innovation effort in protecting its core business. It brought its web development in house and paid as much attention to it as to physical products.[10] In 2016, Sephora launched its own app, incorporating augmented reality features. It also gained the upper hand in the next-market battle of omnichannel: Enhancing its brick-and-mortar network with in-store technologies, the company was successful in driving online traffic offline.[11] Venturing into a next business, it went as far as launching a monthly subscription service for the US market in 2015.

Cautiously defending its core business while experimenting with next businesses – largely through digital vehicles – instilled the right degree of strategic agility in Sephora. Despite the ongoing 'retail apocalypse', it experienced strong growth and continued to gain market share, especially in Asia and the Middle East.[12] In 2020, Sephora was LVMH's second-largest brand by sales. According to estimates, it accounted for about 60 per cent of sales at LVMH's selective retailing division and maintained double-digit profit margins.[13]

Three Horizons For Optimizing For Core Business and Next Business

Optimizing for both stable and nimble will typically play out across three different horizons (Table 3.2). Each horizon necessitates a different type of response to fast-moving digital disruptors.

The 'Disrupt' response is a reflection of the classic adage of 'the best defence is a good offence' – or the dictum, attributed to both President Lincoln and Peter Drucker, 'the best way to predict the

Table 3.2 Three horizons

Horizon	Action	Type of response	Description
1	Harvest	Defensive	• Invest in continuous innovation of the core business • Block disruptive threats from digital natives by optimizing businesses under attack
2	Occupy	Offensive	• Win the competition for new market by outcompeting digital rivals
3	Disrupt	Offensive	• Develop new business models to disrupt existing business • Create new markets before others do

SOURCE Adapted from A Jankovich and T Voskes (2018) *Make Disruption Work: A CEO handbook for digital transformation*, Vior Webmedia; and J Bradley, J Loucks, J Macaulay, A Noronha and M Wade (2015) *Digital Vortex: How digital disruption is redefining industries*, Global Center for Digital Business Transformation: An IMD and Cisco Initiative, pp 6–16 future is to create it'. It is fine to anticipate consumer, technology and industry trends. It is even better to be in a position of shaping and co-creating those trends.

Of course, each business needs to assess how far into the future it wants or needs to venture. Unlike GE or Siemens, Sephora didn't venture into horizon-3. Its subscription service is a horizon-2 initiative. On stable vs nimble, Sephora placed the cursor towards stable because the signals of what a horizon-3 strategy would require weren't clear yet. Rightly or wrongly, it did not perceive the same level of radical disruption as GE and Siemens did.

Protecting the core vs exploring the next businesses is a dynamic journey: Ideally, by the time the core becomes a sunset segment, the company has experimented with sufficient future options so that at least one next business is robust enough to take its place (see the previous IBM example above and upcoming Netflix discussion). By the same logic, once the next business becomes the new core, it will itself be susceptible to disruptive trends.

A Bit of Unconventional Planning…

Amidst COVID-19, Uber and Airbnb both announced downsizing as well as a retreat from future businesses. Learning new capabilities was useful and will without a doubt stand them in good stead in the future. But now is the time for caution and it is the core business that can deliver that. Circumstances called for liquidating assets in order to reinvest in and protect the core. In addition, a well-executed diversification will aim for producing counter-cyclical effects.

Similarly, since 2014 Swiss fluids engineering specialist Sulzer was affected by declining investments in oil and gas. To offset this trend, it made acquisitions in the mixpac systems segment and set up a new applicator division, on top of expanding its services business. The result is a diversified, low-cyclicality portfolio of core and next-business B2B end-market segments that is in a good shape to withstand crises like COVID-19. Sulzer's traditional oil market may have suffered but the company avoided facing adversity on all its horizons at one time.

Engaging in Both Disciplined and Experimental Planning

Sephora's parent, luxury goods conglomerate LVMH, is a good example of balancing discipline and rigour with experimentation in its approach to planning and resource allocation. When considering additions to its established portfolio of 75 Houses, LVMH used conventional financial planning and due diligence. Thus in 2019 when it completed its $3.2 billion acquisition of luxury hotels and travel firm Belmond, it was an extension of its position in hospitality where earlier it bought brands such as Cheval Blanc and Bulgari Hotels & Resorts. Around the same time, the group's $15.8 billion deal with Tiffany & Co helped it leapfrog Richemont in the fast-growing jewellery segment and in the US market.[14] These transactions were big financially but conservative in terms of strategy. They represented a win–win consolidation with other successful brands.

Concurrently, LVMH was aware of opportunities that its conventional planning process might miss. Around 2016–17, the company realized it was under-responding to the trend of social media influencers as well as to the rising market of ethnic and inclusive beauty. It invited singer Rihanna to create a new line of cosmetics named Fenty Beauty, followed by a lingerie line, Savage X Fenty. (Fenty's ready-to-wear fashion line was put on hold in early 2021.)

To address other strategic blind spots through fluid planning, LVMH launched the DARE programme (Disrupt, Act, Risk to be an Entrepreneur). DARE invited executives and employees alike to submit radical business ideas that related to themes such as green initiatives and the customer experience of tomorrow. The ideas were fine-tuned and pitched in fun-filled, rapid three-day cycles that emulated the lean start-up agile method (see Chapter 5) and culminated in a handful of initiatives getting selected for execution. DARE is designed to foster speedy innovation but also to challenge the siloed culture of individual Houses.

Top-Down and *Bottom-Up Strategizing*

Ever since Henry Mintzberg, there has been a debate about whether strategy should be top-down or bottom-up.[15] In a retreat from this either/or thinking, strategic agility allows firms to master both processes in parallel. Alongside top-down strategizing, LVMH's DARE is an example of a bottom-up process. It didn't just mirror conventional top-down strategizing, however. Rather, its value was in closing areas of vulnerability, improving innovation accuracy and spreading the impetus through applied learning – the way only an empowered frontline can, by observing disruptive behaviours among luxury consumers.

Disciplined planning remains useful in monitoring and deciding on the financing that will help the core business evolve. In addition, it helps avoid losing track of medium-term direction. To ensure discipline, it develops strong dashboards that regularly measure progress on priorities.[16] Where faster, or what is called issue-based, planning comes into play is in supporting new businesses' speedier experimentation as circumstances change and require quicker adaptation.[17] This may take the form, for example, of assigning an initiative to every substantial risk the organization has identified. Flagging a neglected business trend and matching it with an issue-based initiative allows a company to learn and to close gaps in its strategic capabilities and market positions.[18]

LVMH is not the only one. Increasingly, large companies pursue issue-driven strategy development.[19] Fortune 500 companies like Textron and Cardinal Health allow real-time issues to supersede annual calendar planning. They set up small teams, dedicated to fast project testing, which may operate outside the main decision hierarchy. If the long-term goals are too abstract and the short-term moves are largely tactical, they focus on the medium term as a fruitful territory.[20]

Nimbleness is Not Solely About 'Fast Strategy'

In some managers' minds, change has become synonymous with speed.[21] 'Fast strategy' is the stuff of many management books.[22] But despite the perception of an 'age of urgency',[23] faster doesn't necessarily mean better. What we found is that firms that are successful in achieving agility know when to stick to disciplined planning and when to opt for more fluid, experimental planning.

As defined in this book, nimbleness is not just about speed. It is also about experimenting and improvising to prepare for multiple futures.

A Bit of Unconventional Planning: Go Slow to Go Fast

In times of crisis, the clock often needs to be slowed down, not sped up, giving companies the time and space to think about the next big shifts. One needs to go slow in order to go faster. During COVID-19, the reality of sustainability has trumped speed for many businesses. Armani executives went on record saying the crisis was an opportunity for top-of-the-range lines to stop imitating fast fashion and to return to their original identity. The company has made a conscious effort to 'do less and do better' by stepping away from the industry trend of accelerating the production cycles and launching multiple collections every year.[24]

Maintaining Both a Simple and a Diverse-Enough Portfolio

In the 2000s, the consumer goods industry saw an avalanche of new products. Between 2002 and 2011, US consumer-goods companies raised the number of new products introduced annually by nearly 60 per cent.[25] Many product ranges became 'all things to all people', overlooking the fact that consumers often prefer fewer choices to more.[26] During Steve Jobs's tenure, the Apple product line-up contained only a handful of items, anchoring an entire digital media universe first in an iPod and later on an iPhone. It was precisely this simplicity that proved appealing to consumers.[27]

Today, the biggest brands are rationalizing their portfolios, hoping to free up resources and managerial attention. In 2019, Kellogg's sold its biscuit businesses including Keebler and Famous Amos to Ferrero for $1.3 billion, in order to focus on snacks and cereals. Danone similarly refocused its product range. However, this doesn't mean ignoring new growth opportunities: Kellogg's penetrated the protein bars segment, while Danone acquired a baby food company.[28] Meanwhile, in the age of new retail, Ikea is taking the opposite journey. Realizing the limitations of its gigantic out-of-town format, it is experimenting with four novel formats in 300 new stores. Ikea understands that in the context of its industry segment, attracting customers requires adding rather than diluting complexity in the store portfolio.

The dilemma at the heart of these moves is as follows: Too few offerings, countries, business lines may translate into leaving growth opportunities on the table; too many, and the budget is spread too thinly, communications costs rise, top management attention is stretched, and governance becomes too complex.

The 24/7 fresh-food supermarket 7Fresh is a bricks-and-mortar subsidiary of its digital-native parent JD.com, one of China's largest B2C online retailers. It represents the cutting edge of tech-enhanced shopping, providing facial-recognition-based self-checkout and smart shopping carts that connect with personal shopping lists, display products' nutritional value and help shoppers navigate the isles. Started in January 2018, 7Fresh was quick to launch 20 stores across China, each with an area of several thousand square metres.

Compared with JD.com's product range of hundreds of thousands, the 7Fresh selection is drastically streamlined. It is not just the product portfolio that 7Fresh is keeping as simple as possible in order to deliver efficiency and economies of scale: It is also its portfolio of customers. Whereas online, JD.com's appeal is very broad, 7Fresh focuses only on two segments: The urban young, and affluent urban families. This simplicity, however, doesn't mean limited choice and boredom. Using data analytics to study what customers actually buy, 7Fresh knows what to keep in stock and what to phase out. It also identifies patterns in online purchases, then brings in new products to test how they will perform in physical outlets.[29]

The 7Fresh approach is a good illustration of how embedded agility transforms decision making. The frontier where companies are

Figure 3.2   Pushing back on the frontier of making strategic trade-offs

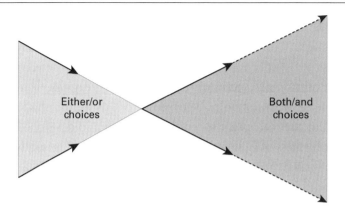

having to accept trade-offs is pushed further away, creating space for new, revolutionized strategizing (Figure 3.2). In consequence, companies like 7Fresh can keep their product portfolios both simple/efficient and complex enough to be sharply relevant to customers' evolving preferences.

A Bit of Unconventional Planning

The 2020 pandemic didn't dent digital-native retailers' intention to expand into bricks and mortar. The battle for convenience takes place in the omnichannel and in data integration between physical and digital channels. For example, to reduce human contact during the health crisis, 7Fresh installed smart vending machines in China's major cities.

Pursuing Both Diverse Ideation and Focused Execution

Accor is Europe's largest hospitality group. In a spate of acquisitions, it bought Mövenpick Hotels for $582 million and made a foray into home-sharing through Onefinestay. Seeking to attract younger, experience-led consumers[30] and facing growing pressure from Airbnb, Accor also set about searching for a new business model. Top management entrusted marketing with developing a millennial-friendly brand – but after two years of research, the results were underwhelming. Finally, Arantxa Balson, chief talent and culture officer, decided to turn the project over to a shadow board of millennial employees including six men and six women. In 2018, the Jo&Joe brand was born. Considered 'an urban shelter for millennials', the brand communicates creativity, flexibility and a strong sense of community. According to Balson, the shadow board succeeded in part because it focused on a vision and developed its point of view 'regardless of all internal and cost constraints'. The shadow board then gave birth to another innovation, a hotel subscription that provides people under 25 with a place to stay in any of the Accor hotels while hunting for a permanent abode.[31]

To strengthen the diversity of opinions and the richness of strategic ideation, Accor's CEO Sébastien Bazin instituted rotating 'devil's advocate' roles, challenging all executives to examine initiatives from outside their own area of responsibility. In particular, he tasked his team to stop looking only at Accor's traditional competitors and to consider the new entrants, including the mavericks.

Poor Execution Focus Will Undermine the Greatest of Innovations

In crafting successful strategies that respond to a company's areas of vulnerability as well as opportunity, it is important to make a distinction between the idea generation phase and the execution phase. Idea generation requires a non-threatening space that stimulates and accommodates a wide diversity of views. For business leaders, this diversity may be unsettling: Coming up with ground-breaking ideas is often an unorthodox process. Moreover, consulting the views of more people takes time and additional investment in communications. The process may well turn out to be too costly and complex to handle.

In the execution phase, politicking habitually kills the effective implementation of new strategic initiatives. Very often, once approval has been granted, the CEO's focus will have shifted elsewhere. Those whose main motivation was to please the boss will have moved on as well. To give a chance to next businesses, all leaders need to commit to the chosen direction with discipline. This is where simplicity of leadership unity should come from.

Many companies are single-mindedly committed to product and technological innovation. Where they fail is in applying equal discipline to anticipating, managing and building upon the outcomes of that innovation. The resulting disconnect between idea generation and execution will weigh down on a company's effort to build strategic agility. Kodak is a good example of the dangers of not mastering the two capabilities as a pair. There was no shortage of open thinking among the company's engineers, who invented the digital camera.[32] What brought about Kodak's downfall had less to do with the actual digital camera technology than with the company's leadership and its failure, in the execution phase, to commit to digital as the way of the future.[33]

Stepping Outside Familiar Patterns

Accor's success had a lot to do with the CEO's awareness that launching new ventures or even innovating in the core business cannot depend on one or just a handful of individuals. In the face of uncertainty, a single executive is unlikely to produce all the ideas or answers. In addition, decision-makers are often biased when evaluating options. Their first instinct is to reject novelty, looking for reasons why unfamiliar concepts might fail. When managers vet novel ideas, they are in an evaluative mindset. To protect themselves against the risk of a bad bet, they compare the new idea on the table to templates of ideas that have succeeded in the past. In other words, they are 'trapped in prototypes'.[34]

In the management reset, it is important to step outside familiar patterns and frame the pool of possibilities differently. Shifting the focus from 'What is the right answer?' to a simple 'Are we asking the right questions?' often provides a solid start. To avoid a leap in the dark, managers will do well to engage in thoughtful experimentation, consciously shifting or removing some of the core assumptions they would otherwise apply in a business-as-usual setting.[35] Another way to reinvigorate a company's decision making is by stimulating cognitive diversity, ie the breadth and depth of perspectives. The more diverse a team's backgrounds, the greater the pool of experiences that will inform its decisions.

Drawing On Both Internal and External Capabilities and Resources

A strong telco incumbent, Deutsche Telekom (DT) was highly motivated to protect its core business. At the same time, it had to respond to digital change, entering new segments to fight off start-ups and other tech companies who were eating away at its traditional business and disintermediating it.

In the 2000s, DT's big bet was on outsourcing. In 2007, the company transferred 55,000 IT services jobs to a newly formed subsidiary called T-Systems, with operations in Germany and India.[36] Over the next decade, DT adapted the outsourcing model and positioned itself as a partner in digitizing its clients' business with the use of standardized IT platforms.[37]

Internally, DT protected its core business of entertainment and communications through diversification in aviation connectivity, superior customer service and the 'un-carrier' strategy, providing maximum flexibility for the customer by eliminating traditional service contracts. It also identified its next B2C businesses in smart homes, smart speakers and security, bundling them into packages. In B2B, the company zoomed in on productivity services such as Big Data, cloud and cybersecurity.

Throughout, DT participated in worldwide innovation in the form of clusters and other group partnering. It set up an initiative called hub:raum, aimed at continuous scouting, incubation programmes, strategic investment and other forms of absorbing innovation from start-ups. It also attracted and created a meaningful dialogue with potential app developers and, through its network of T-Labs, partnered with universities, identifying feasible ideas for future innovation. To empower employees, structure partnerships and make the creation of a network of partners easier, DT created an interactive tool called Magenta Connectivity. It empowered employees and decision makers to simulate a complete business model, filter partners, think about revenue sharing, and prepare simulations to negotiate and make things as transparent as possible with prospective partners.

Nevertheless, becoming a leader in digital couldn't be achieved just by lining up the right mix of start-ups as external partners: Steering into digital segments also required that DT internalize new roles and competences. It was thanks to a complete integration of key digital roles and skillsets into DT's own product and development processes that the telco was successful in growing revenue and upping the differentiation factor. Gradually, DT internalized the new roles for business intelligence, e-marketing, technology, e-category management and e-logistics, rather than outsourcing them, largely thanks to putting forward specific digital talent recruitment policies.

Throughout, DT actively used branding not only to capture users' imagination but also to represent its concerted foray from a traditional telco's bewildering complexity to a modern, digital-based, customer-friendly simplicity. The ubiquity of the magenta colour and the subsuming of older brands under a single 'T' brand emerged as powerful symbols of the company's drive towards strategic agility.

Needless to say, orchestrating a network of external partners is more complex than controlling one's own resources. There are risks of IP loss and the potential scenario of nurturing a future competitor to consider.

Open Innovation: Don't Go It Alone

In the past 15 years, the idea of open innovation, ie externalizing a company's R&D and innovation pipelines, has gone mainstream.[38] Companies in developed markets set in motion waves of outsourcing, particularly in IT. That trend produced its own set of challenges, from managing remote teams in different time zones to the 'not invented here' syndrome.[39] Often the larger and more successful a firm, the less it was drawn to nurturing a network of external partners. The GE-vs-Siemens comparison bears this out well. Siemens aggressively embraced the use of platforms, despite the considerable shift in control over data and apps to partners. By contrast, GE, as a long-standing market and thought leader in its traditional industry verticals, struggled to adjust to the co-creating paradigm.

Through open innovation, companies are increasingly operating an ecosystem of partnerships or cultivating start-ups through corporate incubators, accelerators and VC funds. Because corporate players in this space find themselves in head-on competition with private, independent investors, some corporates like BMW have pursued a 'venture client model', taking on start-up partners as fledgling suppliers rather than incubatees in the classic sense.[40]

There is More to Acquisitions Than 'Throwing Money at the Problem'

One of the ways companies continue to have to internalize new resources and capabilities is mergers and acquisitions. In 2019, McDonald's bought AI outfit Dynamic Yield, a start-up that specialized in personalized recommendations.[41] Of note is McDonald's emphasis on strategic KPIs as part of protecting its core business. Obviously, in today's digital landscape, a KPI may not be a simple number; it can be something as complex and tough to measure as 'This is a place I'm happy to bring my children.'

For strategic agility, acquisitions are a crucial piece of ammunition. The right approach to acquisitions allows greater sophistication in the way companies enter new businesses or develop new capabilities.[42] Timing, too, is essential; to be ahead of one's time is often tantamount to being wrong. According to John Chambers, Chairman of Cisco, picking a target should be done after the latter has already completed the development of the product but before it has made irreversible commitments about its go-to-market strategy.[43] In fact, the pace and rhythm of acquisitions has been shown to be a balancing act in its own right. Too many acquisitions may exert stress on a company's finances and learning capacity. With too few acquisitions, firms will not have the right integration routines in place.[44]

The Strategic Agility Canvas

Want to examine and evaluate how effective you are in developing strategic agility in your business? Use the Strategic Agility Canvas to find out what your business's strengths and weaknesses are in minimizing the five key trade-offs (Figure 3.3).

Figure 3.3 The Strategic Agility Canvas

	Your current strengths	Your current weaknesses	Your next steps	How you will do both
STABLE Protection and improvement of your core business				
NIMBLE Fast experimentation of next-market-creating businesses				
STABLE Disciplined planning and resource allocation process				
NIMBLE Fluid, experimental planning and resource allocation				
COMPLEX The portfolio is as diverse as necessary				
SIMPLE The portfolio is as focused as possible				
COMPLEX Ideation: Encouraging open and deviant thinking				
SIMPLE Execution: Ensuring collective commitment				
COMPLEX Orchestration of a network of external resources				
SIMPLE Orchestration of a network of key resources internally				

SOURCE Prof Stéphane JG Girod, IMD. Not to be used without permission

Conclusions

The search for strategic agility in today's disruptive business environment is more than just another stage in the evolution of strategy. In the past, the focus of strategy was to keep competitors from entering one's core business. It entrenched the status quo. Adaptive strategy was typically formulated along the lines of periodic strategic reorientations or renewals that punctuated long periods of stability. When ambidexterity was introduced, executives were told to explore for next business while exploiting the core business. Uncertainty and fast change render these approaches difficult yet underwhelming in their outcomes.

By contrast, strategic agility forms a core aspect of the ongoing reset of management. Today, strategic agility requires that a business should manage multiple contradictory demands (this study identified at least five) and reduce the scope of either/or trade-offs in order to achieve more flexibility. There will still be choices to be made, but the portfolio of experiments, for example, needs to widen and be more dynamic to accommodate uncertain futures.

Strategic agility internalizes uncertainty by opening new perspectives and bringing in more informed and expert stakeholders at different levels of the hierarchy and outside; by conducting fluid planning and resource allocation alongside the more formal processes; and by exploring multiple options for securing revenue streams.

In helping you create a state of continuous adaptation and building synergies between the What and the How of strategy, strategic agility is much more than survival. It's about playing to win by creating a more entrepreneurial business, better connected to external opportunities.

Table 3.3 summarizes what you should continue doing (evolution) and where you should build next practices (management reset) to achieve greater strategic agility.

Table 3.3   At the strategy level, why business agility is more than an evolution: It is a management reset

Strategy	
Evolution	**Management Reset**
• Pursuit of speed • Search for flexibility (eg through vertical integration) • Remember that strategy continues to be about differentiation and choices (but there needs to be flexibility in these choices, eg reversing them easily) • Continue to use scenario planning • Know when and how to buy external firms and how to integrate them successfully • Be mindful that ambidexterity, or the ability to explore next businesses while exploiting the core business, continues to be an important need • Continue to innovate dynamically in the core business	• Work towards a more continuous state of adaptation rather than occasional strategic renewals (usually when it's late) • Consider that there are more trade-offs to reduce than those that come with ambidexterity • Shift from either/or to both/and strategic decisions and ways of strategizing • Shift mindset from playing not to lose to playing to win • Shift from fixing detailed goals to fixing clear directions • Rely on bottom-up and top-down strategizing (formal planning as well as fluid planning) • Stretch your portfolio of exploratory next revenue streams (by unleashing the collective entrepreneurship power of the business) • Remember that digital creates new opportunities for strategists but also requires new types of strategy (eg platform strategies) • Make uncertainty an integral part of the strategy process • Increase cognitive diversity in ideation to broaden your field of possible futures (focus on the right questions more than the right answers)

Endnotes

1 Darrow, B (2016) At the ripe age of 105, IBM seeks to reinvent itself—again, *Fortune*, https://fortune.com/longform/ibm-105-anniversary (archived at https://perma.cc/BDM6-YJHD)

2 Redrup, Y (2018) Inside IBM: Struggling Giant reinvents itself for the AI, quantum and blockchain era, *Australian Financial Review*, 25 June, www.afr.com/technology/inside-ibm-struggling-giant-reinvents-itself-for-the-ai-quantum-and-blockchain-era-20180605-h10yyu (archived at https://perma.cc/LJ6D-2LM7)

3 Savitz, E J (2019) IBM completes red hat deal – the largest software acquisition ever, *Barron's*, 9 July, www.barrons.com/articles/ibm-completes-red-hat-deal-the-largest-software-acquisition-ever-51562700501 (archived at https://perma.cc/PMB5-G6SW)

4 Rumelt, R P (2012) *Good Strategy/Bad Strategy: The difference and why it matters*, Strategic Direction

5 Sull, D (2009) How to thrive in turbulent markets, *Harvard Business Review*, 87 (2), pp 1–10

6 Girod, S J G and Duke, L (2018) Digital transformation at GE: Shifting minds for agility, Case Study, IMD-7-2011, IMD International, Lausanne

7 Collis, D J and Junker, T (2017) Digitalization at Siemens, Case Study, HBS 717–428, Harvard Business School Publishing, Boston

8 Sakhartov, A V and Folta, T B (2014) Resource relatedness, redeployability, and firm value, *Strategic Management Journal*, 35 (12), pp 1781–97; Rumelt, R P (1978) Databank on diversification strategy and corporate structure, Paper MGL-55, Managerial Studies Center, Graduate School of Management, University of California

9 Ofek, E and Wagonfeld, A B (2011) Sephora direct: Investing in social media, video, and mobile, Case Study, HBS 511–137, Harvard Business School Publishing, Boston

10 Bornstein, J and McGinn, D (2014) How Sephora reorganized to become a more digital brand, *Harvard Business Review*, 92 (6), pp 1–4

11 CBInsights (nd) How Sephora built a beauty empire to survive the retail apocalypse, www.cbinsights.com/research/report/sephora-teardown (archived at https://perma.cc/WS7K-4WYS)

12 LVMH (2020) Record results for LVMH in 2019, www.lvmh.com/news-documents/press-releases/record-results-for-lvmh-in-2019 (archived at https://perma.cc/LWN2-DBCH)

13 Agnew, H and Copeland, H (2019) For Sephora, the store is core to its beauty, *Financial Times*, 24 July, www.ft.com/content/530db1bc-ae06-11e9-8030-530adfa879c2 (archived at https://perma.cc/RS9Q-SVKW)

14 LVMH (2020) Tiffany and LVMH modify merger price, www.lvmh.com/news-documents/press-releases/tiffany-and-lvmh-modify-merger-price (archived at https://perma.cc/EWX4-EXK5)

15 Mintzberg, H and Waters, J A (1985) Of strategies, deliberate and emergent, *Strategic Management Journal*, **6** (3), pp 257–72

16 Coleman, J (2017) The best strategic leaders balance agility and consistency, *Harvard Business Review*, **95** (1), pp 1–5

17 Slagmulder, R and Devoldere, B (2018) Transforming under deep uncertainty: A strategic perspective on risk management, *Business Horizons*, **61** (5), pp 733–43

18 Reeves, M and Deimler, M (2011) Adaptability: The new competitive advantage, *Harvard Business Review*, **89** (7–8), pp 135–41

19 Garton, E and Noble, A (2017) How to make agile work for the C-suite, *Harvard Business Review*, **95** (4), pp 2–5

20 Sull, D, Turconi, S, Sull, C and Yoder, J (2018) Turn strategy into results, *MIT Sloan Management Review*, **59** (3), pp 24–32

21 De Smet, A and Gagnon, C (2018) Organizing for the age of urgency, *McKinsey Quarterly*, 18 January, www.mckinsey.com/business-functions/organization/our-insights/organizing-for-the-age-of-urgency (archived at https://perma.cc/7X4T-MECT)

22 Stalk, G and Stewart, S (2019) Fast execution needs fast strategy, BCG Henderson Institute, 1 March, www.bcg.com/publications/2019/fast-execution-needs-fast-strategy.aspx (archived at https://perma.cc/XCF7-5YJU)

23 De Smet, A and Gagnon, C (2018) Organizing for the age of urgency, *McKinsey Quarterly*, 18 January, www.mckinsey.com/business-functions/organization/our-insights/organizing-for-the-age-of-urgency (archived at https://perma.cc/7X4T-MECT)

24 LaConceria (2020) Giorgio Armani: 'Luxury should stop imitating fast fashion', 9 April, www.laconceria.it/en/luxury/giorgio-armani-luxury-should-stop-imitating-fast-fashion (archived at https://perma.cc/Q3U8-HGTN)

25 Dawe, P, Edquist, L and Pichler, H (2014) Less can be more for product portfolios, BCG Global, 25 August, www.bcg.com/publications/2014/lean-manufacturing-consumers-products-less-can-be-more-for-product-portfolio-attacking-complexity-while-enhancing-the-value-of-diversity (archived at https://perma.cc/N99W-NG7L)

26 Schwartz, B (2018) *The Paradox of Choice*, Wiley

27 Weinberger, M and Hartmans, A (2020) Steve Jobs would have been 65 on Monday. Here's how the late Apple CEO saved the company from disaster and set it on the path to a $1 trillion valuation, *Business Insider*, 24 February, https://www.businessinsider.com/steve-jobs-apple-photos-2017-1?r=US&IR=T (archived at https://perma.cc/S3NL-3WCZ)

28 Rogers, C (2019) Is your brand portfolio fit for purpose? *Marketing Week*, 26 June, www.marketingweek.com/portfolio-fit-for-purpose (archived at https://perma.cc/6FXP-KGY9)

29 Wang, Y (2020) Store innovation: 7Fresh's Jonathan Wang's path to triumphal arch, JD.com, jdcorporateblog.com/store-innovation-7freshs-jonathan-wangs-path-to-triumphal-arch (archived at https://perma.cc/N3MQ-7KVW)

30 Arabian Business (2019) Rooms with a view: Accor CEO Sebastien Bazin, 3 June, www.arabianbusiness.com/travel-hospitality/421491-rooms-with-view (archived at https://perma.cc/7VCU-Z7FH)

31 Jordan, J and Sorrel, M (2019) Why you should create a 'shadow board' of younger employees, *Harvard Business Review*, **97** (3)

32 Lucas Jr, H C and Goh, J M (2009) Disruptive technology: How Kodak missed the digital photography revolution, *The Journal of Strategic Information Systems*, **18** (1), pp 46–55

33 Anthony, S (2016) Kodak's downfall wasn't about technology, *Harvard Business Review*, **94** (7–8), pp 1–5

34 Grant, A M (2017) *Originals: How non-conformists move the world*, Penguin

35 Achi, Z and Berger, J G (2015) Delighting in the possible, *McKinsey Quarterly*, 1 March, www.mckinsey.com/business-functions/strategy-and-corporate-finance/our-insights/delighting-in-the-possible (archived at https://perma.cc/GUR5-3HHZ)

36 Telekom (2007) *Connected Life and Work: The 2007 financial year*, www.telekom.com/resource/blob/329404/ef3dcf5b7b27daf df48127113e979617/dl-080304-2007-pdf-data.pdf (archived at https://perma.cc/8P5R-NMSU)

37 Telekom (2016) Deutsche Telekom continues aggressive business strategy: T-Systems breaks with conventional outsourcing models, www.telekom.com/en/media/media-information/enterprise-solutions/deutsche-telekom-continues-aggressive-business-strategy-t-systems-breaks-with-conventional-outsourcing-models-363256 (archived at https://perma.cc/2FL6-L32L)

38 Chesbrough, H, Vanhaverbeke, W and West, J (eds) (2006) *Open Innovation: Researching a new paradigm*, Oxford University Press

39 Antons, D and Piller, F T (2015) Opening the black box of 'Not Invented Here': Attitudes, decision biases, and behavioral consequences, *Academy of Management Perspectives*, **29** (2), pp 193–217

40 Gimmy, G, Kanbach, D, Stubner, S, Konig, A and Enders, A (2017) What BMW's corporate VC offers that regular investors can't, *Harvard Business Review*, **95** (4), pp 2–6

41 Kiron, D and Schrage, M (2019) Strategy for and with AI, *MIT Sloan Management Review*, **60** (4), pp 29–36

42 Brueller, N N, Carmeli, A and Drori I (2014) How do different types of mergers and acquisitions facilitate strategic agility? *California Management Review*, **56** (3), pp 39–57

43 Ebersweiler, C and Joffe, B (2018) 10 key lessons about tech mergers and acquisitions from Cisco's John Chambers, TechCrunch, 24 December, https://techcrunch.com/2018/12/23/twelve-key-lessons-about-tech-mergers-and-acquisitions-from-ciscos-john-chambers (archived at https://perma.cc/W5GL-J3NE)

44 Laamanen, T and Keil, T (2008) Performance of serial acquirers: Toward an acquisition program perspective, *Strategic Management Journal*, **29** (6), pp 663–72

04

Ramping Up Organizational Agility Without a Profound Overhaul of the Hierarchy

FIVE LESSONS FROM THIS CHAPTER

1 Are you creating adaptability and flexibility as a source of competitive advantage within your organization? The **Organizational Agility Assessment Test** will pinpoint your organization's starting position in developing organizational agility.

2 Discover the eight capabilities that can help you build organizational agility and resolve the tensions of stable vs nimble and complex vs simple.

3 Create an architecture of organizational agility that reflects and supports your business's unique operating circumstances.

4 Learn how 'Luxury SA' and Clarins Group achieved significant change within a short time span, without using agile methods and without overhauling their still recognizable internal hierarchy.

5 Discover how to use the **Organizational Agility Canvas** to start designing an organization for greater agility.

Organizational Agility: Choosing a Form That Fits Your Company's Circumstances

Chapter 2 explained that business agility is about reconciling stable-vs-nimble and complex-vs-simple tensions. Chapter 3 introduced the concept of strategic agility as a pursuit of embedded capabilities, mindsets and behaviours for greater flexibility. You may have identified that you have to tackle some areas of rigidity in your approach to strategy. Now it is time to examine whether you need to work on your organizational agility. Due to multiple sources of organizational rigidity and the persistent ambiguity of what agility means in practice, attempts at embracing flexibility often remain an uphill battle.

Start With the General Principles of Agility

Instead of dwelling on the methodology, companies should first understand the general principles of agility (Figure 4.1) and use them to adjust their organization's design. These principles are concrete manifestations of the nimble-vs-stable and simple-vs-complex continuums.

In the companies we have studied, principles 1–4 enabled large firms to become nimbler without becoming chaotic. With this way of approaching *what* to do, companies were better prepared for an uncertain future. Principles 5–8 enabled the firms to simplify without

Figure 4.1   Eight principles of organizational agility

becoming simplistic. As a result, they were more sophisticated in *how* they would respond to uncertainty. Instead of a piecemeal approach, it takes a holistic interplay of strategy, information systems and processes, structure, and people elements such as accountability rules, skills and incentives to bring these underlying principles of agility to life.[1]

Are You Challenged by Organizational Rigidity?

For every firm, there will be a starting point to building greater organizational agility. Typically, it will be anchored in the company's previous choices stemming from industry dynamics, level of uncertainty, past performance and even its response to crises. The shared goal is one of creating greater agility by enhancing the ability to adapt to fast and unexpected changes. The priorities may vary; they will range from accelerating the pace of innovation, improving its relevance and accuracy, and becoming more relevant to customers, to saving costs and boosting employees' creativity and engagement. Indeed, the level of uncertainty and speed of change may differ from business to business, even within a given company. As such, agility transformation itself needs to be flexible.

One way to assess whether you need to take action to resolve organizational rigidity challenges is to take the Organizational Agility Assessment Test (Table 4.1). It will also help you decide on the shape and form that agility should take in your organization. You may choose to take this test at the company, departmental, functional or business unit level.

Table 4.1   Where are your strengths and rigidities? The Organizational Agility Assessment Test will help you identify them

Diagnosis: How *nimble* is my organization?	Very Poor 1	Poor 2	Avrg 3	Good 4	Very Good 5
We make decisions quickly and we can reverse them quickly too					
We encourage collaborators to take risks and tolerate failure					

(continued)

Table 4.1 (Continued)

We continuously adapt our business practices to market conditions
We use and empower small cross-functional teams to self-organize and innovate
Our cross-functional teams innovate with and around the customer
We use agile processes to speed up innovation
In our innovation, we use small experiments, we learn and if successful we scale
Our structure is fully aligned with our customer journeys and pain points
Information flows transparently in our organization
Our budget allocation process is fluid enough to pursue new opportunities

Diagnosis: How *stable* is my organization?	Very Poor 1	Poor 2	Avrg 3	Good 4	Very Good 5
We use clear, short, easy-to-remember strategy statements					
Our leaders constantly tell our strategy story to empower employees					
Our employees have full knowledge of the company's direction					

(*continued*)

Table 4.1   (Continued)

Diagnosis: How *stable* is my organization?	Very Poor	Poor	Avrg	Good	Very Good
	1	2	3	4	5
We have set a few key strategic directions that provide our employees with a clear framework for innovation					
We use an appropriate set of KPIs to measure performance					
Our budget processes are sound; they enable the pursuit of a clear strategy and sound financial investments					
Accountability is precisely defined and we reward accordingly					
We pay attention to operational excellence and efficiency					

Diagnosis: How *simple* is my organization?	Very Poor	Poor	Avrg	Good	Very Good
	1	2	3	4	5
We favour a working product over comprehensive documentation					
We favour customer collaboration over contract negotiation					
We favour individual collaboration over comprehensive documentation					
We decentralize decision making as much as we should					

(continued)

Table 4.1 (Continued)

Everyone is measured
and rewarded on how
well they take up
ownership of their
business objectives

We reduce meetings,
committees, processes as
much as necessary

We cut down on silos as
much as possible

We simplify the
bureaucracy by limiting
the number of our
processes to a handful of
key and effective ones

«Your success is my
success» is a shared,
measured and rewarded
behaviour

Diagnosis: How *complex* is my organization?	Very Poor	Poor	Avrg	Good	Very Good
	1	2	3	4	5
We capture data and generate insights about the evolution in our environment, within and beyond industry boundaries					
We use digital technologies to empower our collaborators to make faster and relevant decisions					
We use analytics to simplify our internal functioning					
We give our collaborators constant opportunities for learning					

(continued)

Table 4.1   (Continued)

Diagnosis: How *complex* is my organization?	Very Poor 1	Poor 2	Avrg 3	Good 4	Very Good 5
We know when and where it makes sense to apply agile processes					
We remove hierarchical layers when it makes sense					
We simplify our bureaucracy when it makes sense					
Everyone gives regular feedback to each other and also absorbs it					
Learning from retrospectives is an important process					

SOURCE Prof Stéphane JG Girod, IMD. Not to be used without permission

Tailor Your Own Approach to Agility, One That Reflects Your Own Circumstances

Based on your findings from the Organizational Agility Assessment Test, consider these questions: Which form of agility suits your needs? What type of architecture will be conducive to growing agility in your organization? With an understanding of the underlying principles of organizational agility, executives can determine both the particular form of organizational architecture and the tools that will best serve them in creating a more agile organization. The next three chapters will help you calibrate the form of agility that suits your own circumstances. This chapter illustrates that, contrary to popular belief, large companies can design organizations for agility without automatically defaulting to agile methods like scrum. Chapter 5 examines in greater detail when agile methods could be useful for your business. Chapter 6 will walk you through some revolutionary organizational architectures for agility.

For many businesses, agility transformation was about making the traditional hierarchy simpler and nimbler but without using agile methods (Table 4.2, Cluster 1). This includes Clarins Group. It also includes global luxury company 'Luxury SA'. For the latter, agility transformation consisted of decentralizing power to its China division as a way of dealing more effectively with the unpredictable trends set by globe-trotting Chinese consumers. It did so by linking international operations more tightly with one another and standardizing processes and IT systems to serve those consumers better.[2]

A second cluster of businesses (see Chapter 5) went even further in their quest for simplification and nimbleness. What they did was introduce agile teams and methods in some divisions or in pockets within their organizations, always outside IT, typically in product development and other customer-facing operations. This is where GE, Lego, 'PharmaCo' and Deutsche Telekom, for example, rolled out agile methods such as scrum, lean start-up (FastWorks at GE) and design thinking.[3] The persistent challenge for this cluster had to do with bridging the gap between the traditional parts of the organization and the agile teams.

Table 4.2 A variety of pathways lead to organizational agility

Cluster	Approach to building organizational agility	Company cases	Book chapter
1	Traditional hierarchies that made modifications to their existing organization	'Luxury SA' Clarins	Current chapter
2	Traditional hierarchies that implemented agile methods in pockets or via hybrid approaches	GE Lego Deutsche Telekom 'PharmaCo' Danfoss Deutsche Bahn	Chapter 5
3	Companies that embraced radically new organizational designs and forms	ING Haier	Chapter 6

A third cluster of innovators (see Chapter 6) moved the furthest away from the traditional hierarchy in how they arbitraged the balance between stable–nimble and complex–simple. For ING Bank, battling to survive in a world increasingly dominated by digital giants and fintechs, agility consisted of scaling agile methods by implementing three archetypes of agile collaboration in every corner of its organization but with one common set of values and behaviours. In this organizational form, there are only 1.5 hierarchical layers left between the C-suite and the frontline. Increasingly copied by most European banks, ING reset the norm in its industry. China appliance-maker Haier, by contrast, follows the eight agility principles but without implementing or scaling agile. Its well-documented success is based on thousands of self-organizing teams governed by a few simple rules ('the Haier constitution'). Haier followed this approach to cope with the hyper-competitive conditions of the Chinese economy, a solution that also proved effective in dealing with crisis uncertainty.[4]

Figure 4.2   Decide where your business resides in the range of possible choices for organizational agility

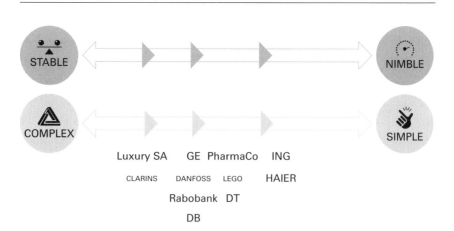

Use the Building Blocks of Organizational Design to Achieve Agility

To build organizational agility, companies deploy four building blocks of organizational design – ie strategy, structures, processes and people – in very different ways. (The four building blocks are reminiscent of the Star Model, a well-known framework for designing organization architectures developed by Jay Galbraith in the 1960s.[5])

- Strategy involves a company's strategizing process in addition to target markets, product portfolio and value proposition.
- Structures have to do with formal roles, reporting lines and power distribution across the organization.
- Processes range from business and management processes to metrics and KPIs but also include technology and data.
- The 'people' building block includes skillsets and career paths as well as values, behaviours and mindsets. Collectively, these building blocks form the culture of an organization.

Projected onto the stable-vs-nimble and complex-vs-simple tensions, these building blocks inform a decision-making instrument, the Organizational Agility Canvas (Figure 4.3). It is a design tool that helps you decide how to deploy the four specific elements of your organizational architecture – strategy, structure, processes and systems, and people – in order to resolve the stable–nimble and complex–simple tensions, thus increasing agility.

Because of their different needs, the companies in Figure 4.2 used the building blocks of organizational design very differently and their resulting degree of agility likewise varies. The cluster that is presented in this chapter includes Luxury SA and Clarins. These companies undertook significant change to become more flexible and adaptive in ways that suited their circumstances. Yet their traditional hierarchy remained highly recognizable.

Figure 4.3 The Organizational Agility Canvas

Your choices in the organizational agility canvas

My team, BU, department, company:	STABLE	NIMBLE	COMPLEX	SIMPLE
	• Clear, well-communicated purpose and direction • Disciplined, aligned and accountable execution	• Faster customer-centric experimentation/innovation • Small cross-functional teams, empowered with transparent information	• Differentiated choices (no one-size-fits-all) • Orchestration of networks for continuous learning	• Minimum viable bureaucracy • Minimum viable hierarchy (flatter, more collaboration)
Strategy • Markets and portfolio • Value proposition • Strategy process				
Structure • Power, authority • Reporting relationships • Roles				
Processes • Business processes • Management processes • Technology and data • Metrics and KPIs				
People • Skills • Incentives • Career paths • Values • Leadership styles				

SOURCE Prof Stéphane JG Girod, IMD. Not to be used without permission

How Luxury SA Adapted Its Traditional Hierarchy

Like most global players in the luxury segment, Luxury SA, the subsidiary of a leading luxury conglomerate, benefited greatly from the spectacular growth of China's appetite for luxury goods. Between 2012 and 2018, Chinese customers were the world's main luxury goods buyers, producing more than half the global growth in luxury spending.[6] To build its presence, Luxury SA set up several dozen retail outlets in China's tier-1 and tier-2 cities.

However, a traditional expansion in the company's bricks-and-mortar footprint proved woefully limited in tapping into the lucrative China market. The days of 'build it and they will come' turned out to be a thing of the past. With China's middle classes setting off a boom in international travel and with sticker prices on luxury goods up to 50 per cent higher in their domestic market, shopping for luxury goods became a predominantly overseas activity. In fact, pre-COVID, for every dollar spent on luxury, China buyers were spending another four dollars while travelling overseas – primarily in Europe but also in the rest of Asia Pacific, Japan and North America.[7] At home, international luxury vendors were pulling out all stops to court and reward loyal customers with innovative perks and services, including chauffeured transport and personalized events.

The large number of buyers whose preference was for overseas shopping created a number of unpredictable patterns for luxury brands such as Luxury SA. Through their sheer numbers, the Chinese set new trends in international travel and luxury shopping. Strongly influenced by social media and word of mouth, these shopping booms could vanish just as fast as they had materialized. Usually they were sparked by a combination of highly transient factors such as forex rates, travel trends, geopolitical developments and others. For instance, with anti-Beijing political sentiment growing in Hong Kong, once a magnet for Chinese buyers, the city quickly fell out of favour as a shopping destination.[8] Meanwhile, Europe fluctuated depending on China's latest fashion trends, price differences and purchasing propensities. For international brands like Luxury SA, this introduced extra volatility into pricing policies as well as inventory management. More importantly, keeping all of Luxury SA's new boutiques across China profitable became a challenge.

Travel was just one aspect that set Luxury SA's China customers far apart from buyers in other parts of the world. Technology fast emerged as a key determinant of customer behaviour and satisfaction. Chinese customers demanded an intricate mix of online and mobile information, services and support – before, during and after a shopping trip. In-store visits were the culmination of a long, information-intensive, tech-based process. Understanding the China luxury traveller therefore hinged on connecting with them – online and especially via smartphones. Failing this connection, the chances of attracting let alone retaining these customers became virtually nil. During in-store visits, they expected merchants to accept payments via apps like WeChat Pay and Alipay and to store all payment, receipt, warranty and other information on their phones using QR codes.

As with other domains of life, the China luxury shopper insisted on feeling comfortable socially before investing their personal trust in a commercial transaction. Therefore, communication had to be personal and direct (human-to-human) as well as facilitated through a convenient platform such as WeChat – a messaging, social media and mobile payment app developed by China tech giant Tencent and launched in 2011. Between 2019 and 2020, livestreaming emerged as one of China's top e-commerce trends.[9] Together, these developments left the China luxury market poised for the next phase where digital sophistication interacts with and enhances offline services such as flagship stores and experiential luxury.

Too Stable and Complex to Thrive in China's Consumer Segments

Luxury SA's starting point was one of inflexibility. Thriving on conservatism, its organization was stable and complicated. Luxury SA entered the China market because it promised growth. The company made sizeable investments into expanding its retail network and nurtured high employee commitment. But that's where the strengths ended, leaving Luxury SA very far from a nimble state. Physical presence was established but not leveraged well enough to build loyalty or to anticipate prospective buyers' travel and other propensities. Top-down decision making and a reactive supply chain left little room for predictive analytics and relevant local-language marketing content.

Luxury SA was also unprepared to nurture China-specific digital skills, digital partnerships and digital leadership. Its inability to react quickly or innovatively enough to changing consumer trends meant it was not nearly as locally relevant or technologically advanced as it needed to be. It found itself playing catch-up, inventing digital tools not only from scratch but also in a market that was very different from its established home bases.

Managers who challenged the reactive mode and started crafting a meaningful China presence for the company ran up against a complicated bureaucracy, over-reliant on reports, rules, approvals and authorizations. Highly centralized, the company stuck to a one-size-fits-all structure and standard ways of doing things. Although it was keen to learn from sister brands and fellow country offices within the parental conglomerate, knowledge sharing was sidelined by internal competition and jostling for attention. The dominant culture looked to the past rather than the future. 'Things have worked just fine in other markets, for more than 160 years. Why change them? Why in China and not Russia? Why now?'

Luxury SA's Response: Overcoming Rigidity

How did Luxury SA push the cursor from stable towards nimble and from complex towards simple?

In 2016, the company appointed a chief digital officer, working closely with a group transformation officer. Together, they set about building synergies across the entire group. At group level, a global partnership with China's WeChat was formed. Luxury SA then worked to devolve the partnership to regional levels within China as it learned that consumer preferences vary dramatically from one region or metropolitan centre to another. (The idea of a 'market of one billion consumers' was always misleading.) Luxury SA eventually opened a WeChat e-commerce store – a first of its kind for a company that previously was reluctant to display price tags online.

Internally, Luxury SA made significant investments into building employees' digital skills and profiles. It started collecting and analysing large pools of data points on local buyers and domestic as well as overseas shopping habits and preferences. The data, coupled with a system of online appointments, eased the long-standing pressures on operating processes such as stock management and mobility. Luxury SA then set up cross-functional teams of tech developers, web designers, digital storytellers and game engineers. Jointly, these teams developed compelling Chinese-language content and advertising campaigns while protecting the consistency of the brand image. The approach worked, and the brand was successful in gaining visibility in such crowded online spaces as the Baidu search engine – one of the world's largest internet companies. It was also ranked among top brands on WeChat Moments – no mean feat in terms of building customer intimacy, given that visitors are free to opt out of viewing the ads.

Reflecting the company's new omnichannel strategy, the outcomes of these developments extended to in-store experience – integrating IT systems with Chinese digital platforms, adjusting merchandising strategies to support local expectations and acknowledging that, in China, the buyer might be just as well or even better informed about specific product attributes than sales staff. Its centralized data lakes allowed the firm not only to shape the digital conversation with Chinese consumers but also to obtain a good gauge of its brand perception among different customer segments and to identify real influencers and key opinion leaders across media and communication platforms.

At a global level, Luxury SA launched a powerful and globally integrated customer relations management (CRM) system. Its roll-out allowed Luxury SA China to affirm itself as the group's global centre of expertise on China go-to-market activities. Responsibility was brought down to local level and hierarchy was streamlined, speeding up the clock of digital management processes. Good-quality CRM became an invaluable source of resilience in times of crisis. In April 2020, during an IMD webinar with executives of luxury players serving the China market, the consensus was that in the aftermath of the first wave of COVID-19, consumption levels were already resuming. The new CRM system also enabled staff at Luxury SA China to organize post-trip follow-ups and loyalty programme activities for customers who bought abroad and might have otherwise fallen off the radar. Virtual stock was made available across all channels.

Underlying these changes was a systematic effort to strengthen employees' commitment to the brand. To that end, training programmes included disruptive strategic planning based on war games that stimulated creativity and developed external hyperawareness. Equally importantly, incentive structures were reshuffled in order to let go of the old zero-sum-game mindset and engender a culture of 'my win is your win'. Consequently, staff who were involved in shaping a potential buyer's pre-travel choices would receive recognition even when the purchase was subsequently made overseas. Acknowledging and consciously connecting these seemingly disparate or unrelated parts of the customer journey went a long way in building staff motivation.

Luxury SA: A Late Starter, or a Company Transformed?

The brand largely succeeded in designing a level of agility by delivering a greater balance between centralization and decentralization. It gained speed and experimented (nimbleness), linking international operations much more strongly with one another (collaboration) and standardizing analytical processes and IT systems when they were disjointed (simplification) (Figure 4.4).

Luxury SA had to balance its quest for nimbleness with protecting a large measure of stability in its core business. The creative process in luxury industries is slow and focused on craftsmanship. Some parts of the process may lend themselves to acceleration but others don't. Maintaining global authenticity and prestige requires that marketing messages and brand integrity remain subject to careful control. Meanwhile, the firm's heritage and traditionally high margins served as cushions that protected it from severe disruption. Overall, the company was successful in conceptualizing and delivering change in proportion to what was necessary under the circumstances.

For multinationals that have successfully cracked the global-vs-local dilemma, Luxury SA's journey may not sound very inspiring. But for the company itself, it was little short of a revolution. Pushing

Figure 4.4 Luxury SA's choices in the Organizational Agility Canvas

	STABLE	NIMBLE	COMPLEX	SIMPLE
	• Clear, well-communicated purpose and direction • Disciplined, aligned and accountable execution	• Faster customer-centric experimentation/innovation • Small cross-functional teams empowered with transparent information	• Differentiated choices (no one-size-fits-all) • Orchestration of networks for continuous learning	• Minimum viable bureaucracy • Minimum viable hierarchy (flatter, more collaboration)
Strategy • Markets and portfolio • Value proposition • Strategy process	• Group Transformation Officer sets up global partnership with WeChat	• Luxury SA opens a mini e-commerce site on WeChat to test-sell limited editions for Chinese consumers	• Luxury SA develops its own digital strategy	• Group Transformation Officer and Luxury SA CDO align digital strategies • New Group-wide CDOs forum
Structure • Power, authority • Reporting relationships • Roles	• Appointment of Chief Digital Officer at Luxury SA • Luxury SA Marketing clarifies brand codes	• Small cross-functional teams of designers, storytellers, developers and game engineers develop China-relevant content	• No structural changes in other regions where key decisions remain centralized from HQ	• Decentralization: Luxury SA China becomes global centre of expertise for Chinese go-to-market activities
Processes • Business processes • Management processes • Technology and data • Metrics and KPIs	• New digital dashboard and KPIs to track delivery of set targets	• Analytics, click and collect, central CRM, appointments help stock mobility and loyalty building of Chinese consumers buying abroad	• Insights generated by analytics are shared globally, enabling adaptation of response to each customer	• End of analytics fragmentation by centralizing China-related analytics
People • Skills • Incentives • Career paths • Values • Leadership styles	• Luxury SA CEO as a storyteller of the brand's mission and purpose to integrate new digital talent in traditional luxury culture	• Growing digital culture with hiring of multiple new digital profiles and talents	• Cross-Maisons digital transformation programme with business schools since 2016 • Back-and-forth rotation of talents with digital commerce division	• New incentives: 'your win is my win'

SOURCE Prof Stéphane JG Girod, IMD. Not to be used without permission

and driving the change through culture consistently required top management to make tough choices. Manager attrition within the parent group swelled to one-third during this time, a clear sign that implementing the change was not without resistance. (It is worth pointing out that for companies that have been extremely decentralized, the journey to agility may well entail the reverse, ie balancing the decentralization with a degree of centralization.)

Clarins Group's Experiment During COVID-19

For Clarins Group, a global leader in the cosmetics industry, the 2020 COVID-19 crisis proved to be the trigger for bold experiments with organizational architecture, aiming for greater agility. Clarins Group, whose annual sales are estimated at $1.5–2 billion, operates two main brands globally: Clarins, founded in France in 1954, and My Blend, a bespoke skincare line. Clarins Group is a family-owned business that employs 10,000 talents around the world.

Clarins's Departure Point: Geographic Silos Slowing Down Modernization

The challenge facing Clarins Group's executives was how to negotiate more effectively the highly uncertain environment by transforming for greater agility. Pre-COVID-19, the company was making headway in transforming itself, particularly through digital adoption. It launched its own e-commerce sites and invested massively in a new CRM system. But there were rigidities to be tackled: The company's approach to customer relationships was still heavily reliant on intermediaries worldwide. It was slow to invest in new media – in an industry where start-ups and new brands were popping up everywhere. Organizationally, while the company was highly locally responsive, it tended to incur undue complexity due to entrenched geographic silos.

The Response: Global Squads Tackling Three Sets of Challenges

At the outset of the crisis, Clarins Group's senior management sensed that it was time to ramp up the company's modernization effort further. In a radical step, it rolled out a global network of teams to navigate the uncertainty of the crisis with flexibility. With no time for messy restructuring, management formed three types of virtual, cross-functional teams it called squads, in reference to agile terminology. The squads operated alongside the normal hierarchy, not as its replacement. Receiving on-demand support from employees, they generated great momentum and speed within the organization.

The first squad was composed of the executive committee including the CEO, the main functional heads, and the heads of the three business divisions plus a few other senior executives such as the security officer. It focused on the *What Now?* to ensure business continuity during the crisis. This squad had five missions: Protecting the health and safety of clients and employees; implementing home office; keeping morale high amongst employees; preserving the top line; and preserving cash. To boost efficiency, this squad made instant decisions applicable worldwide, short-circuiting internal bureaucracy and country managers' prerogatives. Meanwhile, digital changed the team's meeting culture. The team members, who met remotely, soon realized they needed a shorter, more decisive and continuous approach to meetings. They started to focus on information, problem definition, discussion, decision making and on-the-spot communication to the organization to give employees a sense of direction and create a basic sense of stability.

The two other types of virtual squads were small cross-functional and cross-hierarchical teams, liaising with consumers, public authorities, retailers, distributors, suppliers and other stakeholders. Their remit was to learn and continuously to adapt Clarins's responses accordingly. Each squad included digital talents. To ensure quicker and more locally relevant decision making, every country where Clarins ran a division formed a squad of each kind.

In the second type of squads, employees focused on the *What Next?* and took on two roles. First, they defined what the right conditions would be to resume operations in their country. These squads worked on questions such as defining the conditions for reopening physical stores, offices and plants; rescheduling new product launches; and rebalancing investments between conventional and digital media. Their second role was to update other squads, located in countries that were behind in terms of virus contamination. For example, what was learnt in Europe could be transferred to the Americas.

The third type of squads focused on *What If?* questions and prepared for various contingencies – defensive and offensive – that revolved around strong unknowns. Again, each squad had to share its insights with other squads globally. For example, what if the country does not reopen within three weeks? What if customers need to wear masks in stores? Will it reassure them or put them off altogether? What if 30 per cent of intermediaries disappeared? These squads were also scanning for more fundamental changes in consumer behaviour, competition and technology that would affect Clarins's strategy once the health crisis receded.

The experiment was an encouraging sign that organizational innovation, up to this point largely experimental, could bear lasting fruit. In addition, the company was able to strengthen its direct relationship with consumers and to protect some of its revenues by mobilizing the collective power of employees at all hierarchical levels. For instance, in Dubai, the local *What If?* squad decided at the outset of the lockdown to move all inventory from the now-closed stores to a temporary warehouse. In only three days, using the new CRM system, they were able to switch from store pick-up to home delivery and to secure resilience in online sales in the emirate. The team also started to stream regular personalized beauty advice to customers via Apple FaceTime and Microsoft Teams. As a result, the company's sales revenues in Dubai remained robust during the crisis.

Clarins Group did not adopt a specific agile method. Instead it organized around the fundamental principles of agility. To increase its nimbleness, it empowered employees through small cross-functional teams to experiment fast by learning from customers and the outside world more generally.

In the meantime, the *What Now?* squad was laying a foundation of stability to avoid chaos. Employees experimented within the framework of the clearly communicated collective purpose, preserving the top line and protecting the health of employees and customers. The company also carefully crafted new ways of working and defined the roles and responsibilities of the *What Next?* and *What If?* squads. It empowered them to collect evidence of market shifts with rigour and for the long run.

At the same time, Clarins gained flexibility by simplifying its internal mechanisms while allowing for the right level of complexity. It achieved this by short-circuiting the traditional bureaucracy and bypassing country silos. Yet, making locally relevant decisions, ie respecting the complexity of its global footprint, was equally essential. That was the purpose of the *What Next?* and *What If?* squads.

Clarins Group's organizational change sought to factor in another form of complexity, the orchestration of its organization-wide learning. Learning across a global network of teams was a complex but crucial task since it meant allowing for experiments and then consolidating them into common new practices, thus linking teams through knowledge sharing. Learning was both humanly and digitally enabled through tools, metrics and processes. Three teams of marketing integrators provided updates to countries and the centre. On the digital side, employees migrated to Microsoft Teams not only for meetings but also as a repository for sharing documents, which eased internal collaboration and learning. The high emphasis on learning and hyperawareness was critical to deal with the uncertainty.

Almost overnight, these adjustments helped the company make a three-year leap in digital sales and capabilities while cushioning its overall sales revenues.

In summary, Clarins did well in building on its prior good performance and finding a form or organizational agility that fit its circumstances (Figure 4.5). The company used a holistic alignment of strategy, information systems and processes, structure, and people elements such as accountability rules, skills and incentives.[10] There was no time during the crisis to start mastering specific agile methodologies. Nonetheless, by skilfully adjusting these elements, Clarins Group managed to bring to life the underlying principles of agility.

In terms of the impact on its operational systems, Clarins treated the current innovations as a pilot from which the organization will learn well into the future.

Figure 4.5 Clarins Group's choices in the Organizational Agility Canvas

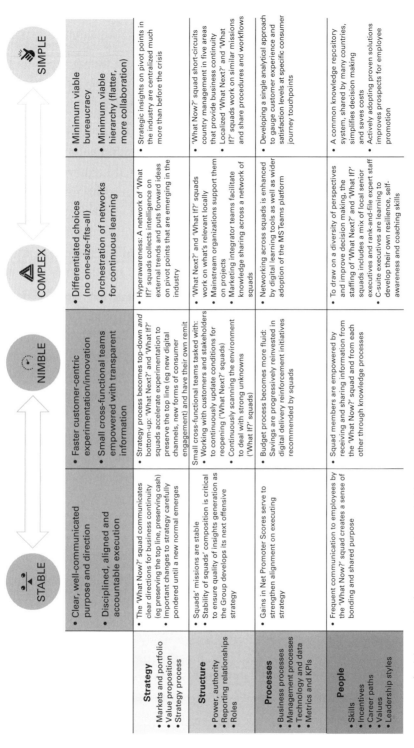

	STABLE	NIMBLE	COMPLEX	SIMPLE
Strategy • Markets and portfolio • Value proposition • Strategy process	• Clear, well-communicated purpose and direction • Disciplined, aligned and accountable execution	• Faster customer-centric experimentation/innovation • Small cross-functional teams empowered with transparent information	• Differentiated choices (no one-size-fits-all) • Orchestration of networks for continuous learning	• Minimum viable bureaucracy • Minimum viable hierarchy (flatter, more collaboration)
	• The 'What Now?' squad communicates clear directions for business continuity (eg preserving the top line, preserving cash) • Important changes to strategy carefully pondered until a new normal emerges	• Strategy process becomes top-down *and* bottom-up: 'What Next?' and 'What If?' squads accelerate experimentation to preserve the top line (eg new digital channels, new forms of consumer engagement) and have their own remit	• Hyperawareness: A network of 'What If?' squads collects intelligence on external trends and puts forward ideas on pivot points that are emerging in the industry	• Strategic insights on pivot points in the industry are centralized much more than before the crisis
Structure • Power, authority • Reporting relationships • Roles	• Squads' missions are stable • Stability of squads' composition is critical to ensure quality of insights generation as the Group develops its next offensive strategy	• Small cross-functional teams tasked with: • Working with customers and stakeholders to continuously update conditions for reopening ('What Next?' squads) • Continuously scanning the environment to deal with strong unknowns ('What If?' squads)	• 'What Next?' and 'What If?' squads work on what's relevant locally • Mainstream organizations support them on projects • Marketing integrator teams facilitate knowledge sharing across a network of squads	• 'What Now?' squad short-circuits country management in five areas that provide business continuity • Localized 'What Next?' and 'What If?' squads work on similar missions and share procedures and workflows
Processes • Business processes • Management processes • Technology and data • Metrics and KPIs	• Gains in Net Promoter Scores serve to strengthen alignment on executing strategy	• Budget process becomes more fluid: Savings are progressively reinvested in digital delivery reinforcement initiatives recommended by squads	• Networking across squads is enhanced by digital learning tools as well as wider adoption of the MSTeams platform	• Developing a single analytical approach to gauge customer experience and satisfaction levels at specific consumer journey touchpoints
People • Skills • Incentives • Career paths • Values • Leadership styles	• Frequent communication to employees by the 'What Now?' squad creates a sense of bonding and shared purpose	• Squad members are empowered by receiving and sharing information from the 'What Now?' squad and from each other through knowledge processes	• To draw on a diversity of perspectives and improve decision making, the staffing of 'What Next?' and 'What If?' squads includes a mix of local senior executives and rank-and-file expert staff • C-suite executives are learning to develop their own resilience, self-awareness and coaching skills	• A common knowledge repository system, shared by many countries, simplifies decision making and saves costs • Actively adopting proven solutions improves prospects for employee promotion

SOURCE Prof Stéphane JG Girod, IMD. Not to be used without permission

Conclusions

Under pressure to adapt to ever-faster and more unexpected changes, both Luxury SA and Clarins kicked off their agility journey with a decision to modify their organizational structures. Their stories illustrate the following:

1 **If you see a structural impetus for change within your organization, use it as a starting point.** That is what nudged Luxury SA and Clarins to accelerate successfully the pace of innovation, boost their relevance and accuracy vis-à-vis customers, reduce costs and energize employees' creativity and engagement. From structure, the companies moved quickly to embrace a holistic approach and deploy other elements of the architecture, thus avoiding misalignment.

2 **Select an architecture that is a good match for your company's circumstances.** You don't need to copy and paste Luxury SA and Clarins Group's exact trajectory. It is advisable, though, that you think deeply about these companies' decisions regarding organizational design. Their choices made sense not just at the time and in response to a specific challenge; rather, they inspired soul-searching throughout the global organization (and for Luxury SA, within the firm as well as across the parent group). Most importantly, their organizational design choices proved successful in embedding additional flexibility and resilience inside the firms' operations as well as partner networks. Can your teams emulate this thinking process in a way that is sensitive to your own organization's situation and environment?

The experiments – as that's what they were – that are described in this chapter should serve as a reminder: How a particular business designs its organization in order to balance stable–nimble and complex–simple needs to be tailored to its strategic, industry and performance conditions. Indeed, the level of uncertainty and speed of change might differ from business to business, even within a given company.

Many executives who are hopeful that agility will spearhead digital execution are likely to default to popular agile methods such as scrum, then work towards adopting them outside their IT department. But in reality it is easy for businesses to get bogged down by the intricacies of rolling out or scaling agile. In addition, while these methods may be useful, they cannot be assimilated quickly in a crisis like the COVID-19 pandemic. The big lesson is that an agility transformation itself needs to be flexible, not dogmatic.

3 **Before making any design choices, understand first the principles of organizational agility.** Does it feel like the journey towards organizational agility is thrust upon you by external factors rather than premeditated? That's okay, and it doesn't have to be an impediment. What you can observe from Luxury SA and Clarins is that both companies acted in their own ways to develop the eight characteristics of organizational agility.

Endnotes

1 de Smet, A, Lurie, M and St George, A (2018) Leading agile transformation: The new capabilities leaders need to build 21st-century organizations, *McKinsey & Company*, 1 October, www.mckinsey.com/business-functions/organization/our-insights/leading-agile-transformation-the-new-capabilities-leaders-need-to-build-21st-century-organizations# (archived at https://perma.cc/MJU3-KXW3)

2 Deloitte (2019) Global powers of luxury goods 2019: Bridging the gap between the old and the new, www2.deloitte.com/global/en/pages/consumer-business/articles/gx-cb-global-powers-of-luxury-goods.html# (archived at https://perma.cc/B6YW-NW90054)

3 Govindarajan, V and Immelt, J R (2019) The only way manufacturers can survive, *MIT Sloan Management Review*, 60 (3), pp 24–33; Girod, S J G and Duke, L (2018) Digital transformation at GE: Shifting minds for agility, Case Study, IMD-7-2011, IMD International, Lausanne

4 Hamel, G and Zanini, M (2018) The end of bureaucracy, *Harvard Business Review*, 96 (6), pp 50–59; Yu, H and Greeven, M J (2020) How autonomy creates resilience in the face of crisis, *MIT Sloan Management Review*, 61 (4)

5 Galbraith, J R (2011) *The Star Model*, Galbraith Management Consultants, Colorado, USA

6 McKinsey & Company (2019) *China Luxury Report 2019*, https://www.mckinsey.com/~/media/mckinsey/featured%20insights/china/how%20young%20chinese%20consumers%20are%20reshaping%20global%20luxury/mckinsey-china-luxury-report-2019-how-young-chinese-consumers-are-reshaping-global-luxury.ashx (archived at https://perma.cc/TS96-F7FL)

7 Lannes, B (2019) What's powering China's market for luxury goods? Bain & Company, 18 March, www.bain.com/insights/whats-powering-chinas-market-for-luxury-goods (archived at https://perma.cc/N9XB-UC3L)

8 Sun, N (2019) Hong Kong no longer a 'go-to place' for luxury shopping, *Nikkei Asian Review*, 31 December, https://asia.nikkei.com/Business/Business-trends/Hong-Kong-no-longer-a-go-to-place-for-luxury-shopping (archived at https://perma.cc/U94Z-9WMA); Cheng, E (2020) Luxury brands turn from Hong Kong to mainland Chinese consumers still eager to shop, CNBC, 9 July, www.cnbc.com/2020/07/10/luxury-brands-turn-from-hong-kong-to-mainland-chinese-consumer.html (archived at https://perma.cc/TU2P-D4ZK)

9 Jing Daily (2020) Next-level livestreaming: How luxury brands can profit from China's top e-commerce trend, https://jingdaily.com/livestreaming-china-luxury-report-covid-2020 (archived at https://perma.cc/AUD3-6TEK)

10 de Smet, A, Lurie, M and St George, A (2018) Leading agile transformation: The new capabilities leaders need to build 21st-century organizations, *McKinsey & Company*, 1 October, www.mckinsey.com/business-functions/organization/our-insights/leading-agile-transformation-the-new-capabilities-leaders-need-to-build-21st-century-organizations# (archived at https://perma.cc/G49Y-SVMK)

05

Intermediate Stage of Organizational Agility

Pockets of Agility, Powered by Agile Methods

FIVE LESSONS FROM THIS CHAPTER

1 Agile methods have become popular but have also raised unrealistic expectations. Often, they are amalgamated with the bigger project and capability of business agility.

2 Many companies have embraced agility in some parts of the traditional hierarchy they seek to rejuvenate, eg in product development or customer service. There are three main configurations you can choose from in deploying these methods.

3 You have to evaluate which agile methods your business needs. When using agile methods in pockets, companies tend to favour design thinking, lean start-up and scrum.

4 Adopting agile methods spurs the use of data, thereby facilitating digital transformation. Nonetheless, applications of agile methods can be extended far beyond software development.

5 Agile methods help businesses emulate start-up firms' characteristics and overcome some rigidity by pushing towards nimble and simple. The benefits of applying agile methods can be incremental – but they can also help support the exploration of radically new strategic horizons. It's a choice you have to make.

In your mind, are business agility and 'agile' one and the same? To many executives, they are. Agile has been their default starting point, a practical way of getting a handle on the long-term project of building agility. Conflating the two is a common misperception. Yet agile methods are not to be dismissed easily. If implemented well, they do help a business achieve certain benefits associated with agility.

Many freely available sources exist on 'how to do agile' (Table 5.1). This chapter considers agile in its wider context of an ongoing organizational and management reset and shares examples of agile implementations at large companies.

Table 5.1   Information resources on agile processes and methodologies: Industry associations/non-profits/community/education

Scrum Alliance	www.scrumalliance.org
Scrum.org	scrum.org
Agile Alliance	www.agilealliance.org
State of Agile	stateofagile.com
Association for Project Management	www.apm.org.uk/resources/find-a-resource/agile-project-management
Agile NYC	www.agilenyc.org
The Design Thinking Association	https://design-thinking-association.org
This is Design Thinking	https://thisisdesignthinking.net
The Lean Startup	http://theleanstartup.com
Lean Startup Co.	https://leanstartup.co
DevOps Agile Skills Association (DASA)	www.devopsagileskills.org

The previous chapter showcased Luxury SA and Clarins – traditional hierarchies attempting to implement agility transformation projects with minimal disturbance to their established order as multi-billion-dollar multinational players in the consumer goods segment and with no roll-out of agile methods. The companies presented in this chapter are less conservative but their transformation efforts weren't dramatic, either. In the emerging agility landscape (Figure 5.1), they occupy the middle ground – an agile methods-powered intermediary stage that is neither conservative nor radical (see Chapter 6 for these examples). Specifically, they used three configurations:

- Enclaves: Agile surrounded by non-agile divisions.
- Ad-hoc deployments: Selected methods are promoted but not mandated.
- Hubs: Small-scale showcases of agile ways of working, which borrow staff from traditional departments.

Figure 5.1   Agile methods adopters in the agility landscape

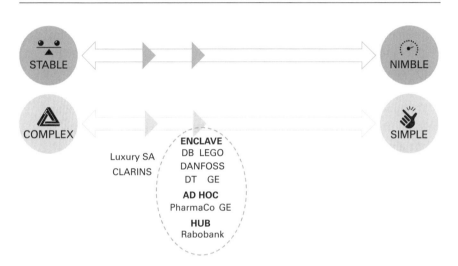

Agile Methods: Bridging the Old and the New

You may have heard of and possibly experimented with agile teams – small, cross-functional, customer-centric groups of employees that sprint their way through specific tasks, typically in software and other product development, and often pull work towards themselves rather than wait for assignments. Today's agile methodologies – scrum, lean start-up, design thinking and others – are not new. For decades, managers sensed that innovation couldn't be promulgated solely by top executives. There had to be a way to connect to the frontline, drawing direct inputs and insights from those parts of the company that were the closest to products and customers.

The tools and methods that originated from this thinking, such as lean and Kanban, resulted in so many efficiencies and quality improvements, particularly in manufacturing, that these largely became taken for granted in modern-day operations. In fact, their roots in product assembly lines (as opposed to software) are so overlooked that you often hear managers ask, 'Will scrum work in manufacturing?'

In **Kanban**, an old Japanese tool popularized in the 1970s for continuous improvement, you organize your work on a Kanban board. Every work item passes through columns from left to right. You pull your work items along through the *in progress, testing, ready for release* and *released* columns. You may have various *swim lanes* – horizontal 'pipelines' for different types of work. The only management criterion introduced by Kanban is the so-called work in progress (WIP). By managing WIP you can optimize the flow of work items. Besides visualizing work on a Kanban board and monitoring WIP, nothing else is needed for Kanban.[1] Today, the visualization tool is directly used in the scrum board, the socializing mechanism that underpins the sprints and organization of work in scrum teams.

These precursors of agile thrived in an environment of predictability and knowable risks. Their main benefits had to do with marginal improvements in quality. As innovation grew more complex, open and uncertain in its outcomes, businesses felt the need for a new set of tools, processes and methodologies. Tellingly, this new generation of agile tools was born in software development. Its aims were twofold: 1) strengthening experimentation and nimbleness; and 2) simplifying ways of working inside organizations. The new common denominator was speed – of product development, of making adjustments, and to market.

The 2001 Agile Manifesto (Figure 5.2) was a game-changer in that it proclaimed the primacy of people and their interactions over impersonal processes and tools; the idea of putting together an actual working product over painstakingly documenting every step, feature and parameter; the importance of involving the customer early on (even in the design stage); and, lastly, a culture of responding to change rather than sticking to and continuously following a plan.[2]

In some ways, agile is a just-in-time philosophy for the technology age. Teams should involve a few customer representatives and experiment on small parts of the product over short periods of time, gradually

Figure 5.2   The Agile Manifesto

We are uncovering better ways of developing
software by doing it and helping others do it.
Through this work we have come to value:

Individuals and Interactions	*over*	Processes and Tools
Working Product	*over*	Comprehensive Documentation
Customer Collaboration	*over*	Contract Negotiation
Responding to Change	*over*	Following a Plan

"While there is value in the items on the right, we
value the items on the left ***more***."

SOURCE http://agilemanifesto.org

making their way – through feedback loops – to a minimum viable product (MVP).[3] Customer collaboration ensures simplification and savings in an industry space where costs and time to market are paramount. (In the aforesaid May 2020 IMD webinar on managing extreme uncertainty with agility, 36 per cent of 550 participants ranked speed as the most important benefit of adopting agile methods.)[4]

Agile in Large Companies: Emerging Configurations

Before examining what agile can contribute to an organization's agility transformation, this chapter considers specific examples of companies that have introduced popular agile methodologies such as scrum, lean start-up and design thinking:

- Which agile methods, if any, does the company use?
- Why? What were the objectives?
- Where, ie in which parts of the organization, are they implemented?
- How do these methods work in terms of roles, processes, etc?

The next few pages define and describe three specific clusters of corporations that incorporated agile methods (Figure 5.3 and Table 5.2). Although their common denominator was the shared

Figure 5.3 Agility methods' place in the agility landscape

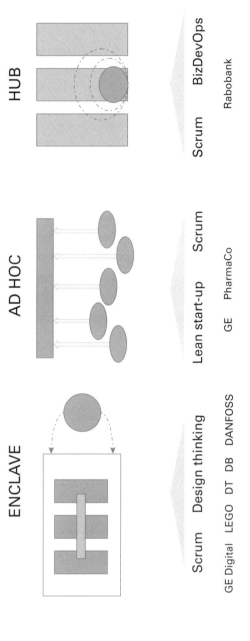

ENCLAVE	AD HOC	HUB
Scrum Design thinking	Lean start-up Scrum	Scrum BizDevOps
GE Digital LEGO DT DB DANFOSS	GE PharmaCo	Rabobank

Table 5.2 Main configurations of agile methods adoption

Cluster	Organizing style of introducing agile methods	Benefits	Company vignettes
1	Enclaves	• Ring-face, pilot, learn from an initial experiment • Pilot may be scaled • Progress is visible	Lego Group GE Digital Deutsche Telekom Deutsche Bahn Danfoss
2	Ad hoc	• Early adopters spread the word • Employees are empowered to choose what to do with the methods and where to apply them to add value	GE PharmaCo
3	Hub	• Transparency • Excitement in the workforce • Flexibility in the face of limited resources	Rabobank

goal of building speed and customer intimacy, each cluster chose a different organizing approach. Typically, the choice reflected the scope and style of innovation they were pursuing (radical vs incremental). This shows that every business can choose from a multitude of agile methodologies and processes, and each of these methods has a positive contribution to make. In addition, each scenario comes with its own set of benefits as well as implementation challenges (to find out more, see Chapter 9). Knowing this, you can make better choices.

Cluster 1. Enclaves of Agile Divisions Surrounded By Non-Adopters

The organizations in this cluster set up largely standalone showcases of agile to pilot and learn, to keep progress transparent and to demonstrate to the rest of the organization the appeal and outcomes of agile ways of working. Some experimented with scrum to expand their digital portfolio (Lego, GE Digital) or non-digital domains such as customer service (Deutsche Telekom). Others used design thinking to re-conceptualize their frontline service (Deutsche Bahn).

Enclave A: Scrum in divisions dedicated to digital offerings

Between 2007 and 2016, Lego Group, a family-owned manufacturer of play materials with global revenues of over €5 billion and a worldwide workforce of 15,000, built a successful enterprise platform which facilitated its international expansion, global supply chain processes and customer relationship management. In the 2010s, digital created new segments of toys, gaming, learning toolkits and hybrid products that provided a strong match with, and ample opportunities to extend and enhance, the company's traditional physical offerings. Lego was endowed with an army of customers, prospects and fans who were passionate about its products, immensely creative and technologically competent. Opening up its innovation pipeline and connecting continuously with end users was primarily motivated by opportunity, not a threat. It translated the new philosophy into a digital engagement platform.

Engagement entailed 24/7 connection with customers, disciplined data collection, omnichannel experience, rapid delivery of new functionality (coupled with brisk deleting of features and content whose popularity was waning) and the practice of eliciting a growing number of product and improvement ideas from fans.[5] As part of this new quality of engagement, Lego set up a crowdsourcing platform called Lego Ideas, allowing online customers and supporters to take over or eliminate entire chunks of product research, market sizing and prototype testing processes. Combined, these changes reduced the average length of product development from nearly two years to months, sometimes weeks.

Even a pocket of agile can act as a catalyst

In 2015, Lego's Digital Solutions division morphed into a team of teams. The teams were free to choose the agile methodology that suited them best. Most chose scrum but some transitioned to Kanban and other methods.[6] To enable teams to self-organize, embrace scrum and other processes, and work effectively together, Lego held a big-room planning session every eight weeks, addressing the relevant risks and dependences.[7] The benefits included time savings from reduced bottlenecks, work duplication and teams waiting for each other; easier planning including updating priorities; improved client trust thanks to shared visibility and a higher rate of achieving commitments; and improved motivation and fun factor not only for Digital Solutions but also for staff from other parts of the company who visited the team-of-teams meetings and were amazed by the level of energy and commitment they found.[8] Scrum was introduced in a specific pocket within the company, but it also acted as a catalyst, demonstrating its appeal to other parts of the organization.

Seventy-two per cent of firms that have adopted an agile method are using scrum.[9] First conceptualized in the 1980s, scrum has stayed true to its origins in the sport of rugby: With no time for sequential delivery or team members waiting for other members, scrum thrives on autonomy, built-in instability, overlapping work phases and playing to the team's strengths.[10]

Scrum is an agile process framework, originally used in software development, that structures work by emphasizing speed to market and cross-functional collaboration. Squads with up to nine participants form the smallest unit of a group and consist of a product owner and a scrum master in addition to a cross-functional development team. A product owner prioritizes what the team should do in terms of tasks and represents the interests of the client. A scrum master, on the other hand, focuses on how the team works, bears the methodical responsibility and serves to remove obstacles (Figure 5.4).

Scrum breaks down a complex work project into smaller, manageable chunks. Combining backlog visualizations with fluid updating of priorities, it enables disciplined, efficient time management and delivery. Teams hold daily stand-up meetings and work through short sprints, typically of one to two weeks. Scrum also sets aside room for retrospectives, so that members can learn from each sprint and improve their collaboration as they go into the next sprint. Thanks to trust and

Figure 5.4   The dynamics of scrum

'Scrum is a framework within which people can address complex adaptive problems, while productively and creatively delivering products of the highest possible value.' Scrum.org

Scrum has been deployed even in the most regulated industries.

Product Owner is responsible for managing the Product Backlog

Development Team is cross-functional and self-organizing

Scrum Master leads and coaches

confidence between team members, making mistakes is acceptable and contributes to a richness of learning. Scrum keeps team members on task and puts their collective intelligence to work. Teams are committed to testing small working prototypes. Similarly, they resolve disagreements through experimentation and feedback.[11]

With its inherent emphasis on transfer of learning, scrum, popular in software development, has also found a home in functions such as marketing and HR.

In 2015, GE launched GE Digital, a subsidiary tasked with developing GE's Predix platform of IIoT services, apps and analytics. This was a departure from GE's established focus on industrial equipment manufacturing. To nurture new paradigms of product development as well as a broader digital mindset, GE Digital employed agile methods. Scrum allowed the new entity to execute customer-focused strategic roadmaps in a series of small steps, thus giving the customer a clear idea of what was coming down the pipe.[12]

Viewing scrum as a process of general project management rather than software development is also leading to its growing popularity with marketing managers. Some have found it useful to play with the lingo, eg replacing 'product increments' with 'marketing micro-campaigns'.[13] According to statistics by Scrum Alliance, 42 per cent of marketers are using at least some parts of an agile marketing approach to manage their work – eg sprints, stand-ups, marketing backlog, retrospectives. On top of managing things faster, marketers are also reporting better innovation and greater ability to adjust to changing priorities.[14]

Enclave B: Scrum in non-software-dedicated activities

Like most leading telcos, with the advent of convergence and other digital trends, Deutsche Telekom (DT) saw tech companies and start-ups eating away at its business and disintermediating it. Annual revenue of more than €80 billion makes DT Europe's largest telecommunications provider. It is also the majority shareholder in T-Mobile, in 2020 the second-largest wireless carrier in the United States.[15] Facing commoditization trends in its established high-margin segments, the company started exploring new approaches to innovation. Erik Meijer, former member of DT's technology and innovation board area, explained, 'We were retooling the airplane in flight, piece by piece.'

To re-energize innovation, DT implemented agile values and principles, focusing on group innovation and customer service. It aimed to improve speed to market; deal more effectively with complex market environments like the rise of 'value vampires' – Skype and WhatsApp; reduce uncertainty through continuous learning and adaptation; and heighten customer satisfaction through customer-centric development processes.[16] DT used scrum to test different approaches to improving call-handling times, satisfaction ratings and other parameters, beginning in a single pilot site and eventually rolling out the most successful changes throughout its internal call centres.[17] Amidst intensifying competition from a multitude of new services and platforms, improved customer satisfaction and loyalty were of great benefit to DT. In 2020, the company used agile to migrate its consulting services online virtually overnight – moving 16,000 advisors from 50 service centres to homeworking, without any loss in efficiency for customers.[18]

Danish engineering multinational Danfoss opted for a mixed approach to agile vs waterfall processes in product development. Alongside using scrum to add software features to its products, it successfully applied agile methods to areas such as sourcing. In 2019, the company gave autonomy to an existing business unit – eSteering, the world's number-one developer of electrohydraulic steering solutions – to remove internal reporting lines and titles and become fully self-managed. Danfoss was not planning to implement this approach across the organization but hoped to learn from the experiment.[19]

Enclave C: Design thinking for driving more radical innovation

Deutsche Bahn (DB) Operations, the facilities management arm of one of the world's largest transport companies, started exploring agile methods including design thinking in 2016. The objective was to reinforce digitization and disruptive innovation – a tall order for a monopoly provider of Germany's train station infrastructure. With 70 per cent of train tickets sold online, DB executives were aware that the company's service counters were also the first instance of human-to-human contact with customers. Under the motto 'Let's try something new', DB Operations started conceptualizing a service counter redesign using design thinking sprints. To obtain feedback from passengers (including wheelchair users and visually impaired travellers) as well as employees and board members, it created a workshop inside an empty train station building on the outskirts of Berlin. It hired a set designer from the national opera to iterate the redesigned counter in cardboard. The service counter's final version included self-service terminals and other digital solutions.[20]

Much like total quality management (TQM), which combined specific tools (eg quality circles, Kanban) with frontline workers' insights to produce highly innovative outcomes, design thinking (DT) is a social technology that helps remove obstacles to innovation by directing creative energy to develop differentiated solutions. Design thinking challenges the focus on preserving the status quo and preventing mistakes. Known as human-centred design both because it places customers at the centre and because it is conducted by cross-functional or cross-competence teams of employees and external consultants, DT starts from what people desire, requiring empathy and reflection.[21] The initial immersive phases in the customer discovery process are sometimes referred as to 'painstorming' as opposed to brainstorming. The goal is to identify real pain points that are yet to be met, not to test hypotheses of possible business ideas. Immersion requires the presence of cross-functional specialists – market researchers but also psychologists, sociologists, artists – profiles that are not usually found or used in large businesses. Unlike traditional market research, it isn't based on focus groups, data reports and office work.

Greater speed is generally not the focus of this particular methodology. Customer discovery generates considerable data that needs to be refined into insights and then funnelled into concrete alternative ideas before a choice is made. To systematize and make sense of all this information, a common method is the gallery walk where entire teams of stakeholders walk through the findings, challenging each other on the most meaningful discoveries to avoid personal biases. Constructive dialogue is essential. Then, the teams focus on design criteria in the context of what is possible. With the list of design ideas in hand, the next milestone is to put together a portfolio of new ideas. Feasibility and viability are now used as the main selection criteria. Viability has to do with profits and costs, whereas feasibility determines what the company can technically and organizationally

Figure 5.5   Phases of the design thinking process

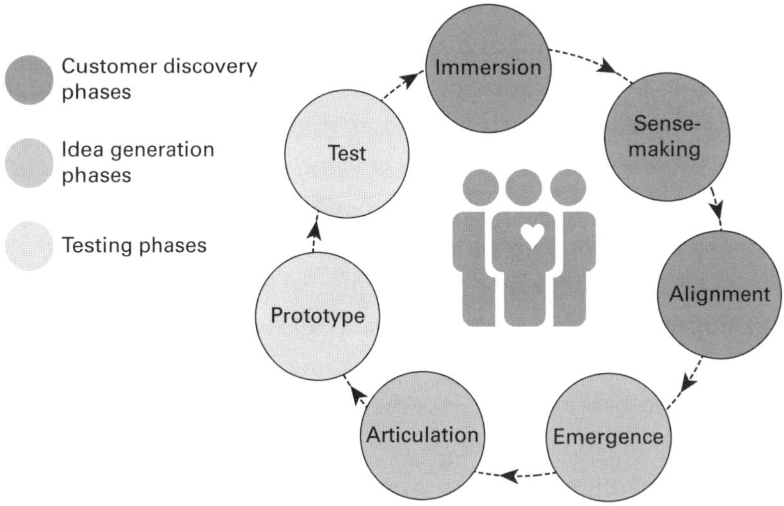

SOURCE Adapted from J Liedtka (2018) 'Why design thinking works', *Harvard Business Review*

achieve. This process is iterative. It is also an opportunity to debunk common biases such as stopping at the first solution, confirmation bias or over-optimism.

These stages feed idea generation followed by testing (Figure 5.5). Importantly, here the prototype that is tested is not a minimum viable product. It is a close simulation of the real solution, involving customers, real employees and real physical situations, as the Deutsche Bahn examples illustrates. Testing is collaborative and may involve role-play among staff whose resistance and fear of change dissipate as they become part of the solution.

Involving the end user intimately and early on is not a counter-intuitive concept, and yet in the old paradigm of scientific management it was virtually unheard of. As cross-functional agile teams apply design thinking, the outcomes – and effects on organizational but also strategic agility – are similar if oddly new. DT encourages team members to develop creativity and curiosity and become inquisitive.[22] It also teaches them how to ask and frame questions.

The benefits of applying an agile process to DB operations included improved quality and customer experience but also cost efficiency. This is one of design thinking's big draws: rooted in user empathy, its outputs appeal to minds and hearts. But the outcomes are not merely altruistic. In DB's case, design thinking sprints soon established that, for instance, queues often formed at train station counters because travellers had to ask for or verify the same information. By addressing this issue, the agile-inspired counter redesign and its digital features produced time savings and efficiencies for customers and staff, who were then enabled to add more value to station operations. Even more important was the impact that DB Operations created by promoting new ways of working by reaching out to IT specialists, civil engineers and other staff across the group. It was a timely step in its transformation from a traditional transport and logistics company to an innovative, digital mobility corporation.[23]

Cluster 2. Ad-Hoc Deployment of Agile Methods

The companies in this cluster consciously adopted elements of lean start-up methodologies (GE) and scrum (PharmaCo) in product development and in functions such as HR. The overarching goal was to learn how to disrupt the old and unwieldy, 'large conglomerate' way of getting things done, thus allowing teams and employees greater autonomy.

Ad-hoc setup A: Using a defined template, employees choose where to apply lean start-up

In the 1990s, GE innovated its business model from selling products to offering contractual service agreements. GE maintained equipment for 15 years and guaranteed the upside. In return, customers allowed GE access to data in order to assess how the equipment was performing. It was a hugely profitable business for GE as it entered the 21st century. However, by 2009, the contracts were maturing and customers were servicing their own equipment. The battle would be over who gets to control equipment throughout its lifecycle. Companies were talking about IIoT where sensors were built into machinery and analytics, and artificial intelligence and machine learning would be employed to reduce downtime and manage maintenance more effectively. For producers, this would mean higher profit margins due to associated revenue streams, increased customer loyalty and demonstrable continuous improvement.

Additionally, surveys revealed that customers found GE's bureaucracy and processes too complicated and inward-looking. This left GE vulnerable in its traditional businesses. To emulate new breeds of start-up and big-tech competitors and to inspire deep cultural change, in 2011 the company embraced the lean start-up methodology, enriched with elements of customer discovery and business model innovation. The programme was branded FastWorks. GE invested heavily in FastWorks and rolled it out across the verticals. In four months, 5,000 senior managers were trained and 100 projects were launched in the US, Europe, China, Russia and Latin America. The projects covered new gas turbines and disruptive healthcare solutions. Pre-FastWorks, an upgrade to a H-class gas turbine was a five-year, $500 million undertaking. Using FastWorks methodologies, the same job would have a proof of concept costing $25 million, with the whole project delivered in two years and for half the original cost.[24] More than 60,000 people across GE would experience FastWorks in some way, through formal training, projects or on-the-job coaching.

GE put in place a systematic corporate template but allowed employees to opt in or out. According to Janice Semper, former GE culture transformation leader who led the FastWorks initiative, 'We've learned that in today's world, there are so many different ways that people consume information that we wanted to have a number of different opportunities for people to learn… What we didn't want was people going through training and not using what they've learned. We wanted it to be applied when it made sense to apply it.'[25]

The lean start-up methodology challenged the idea of elaborate business plans as starting points in innovation projects and product development (and scaling). Its proponents maintained that much too often, customer appeal and revenue-generative potential did not measure up to the original (theoretical) assumptions. Lean start-up processes are built on a recognition that start-ups operate under conditions of extreme uncertainty. Therefore, these processes favour an outward-looking and hypothesis-driven approach to evaluating entrepreneurial opportunities.[26]

Figure 5.6   Lean start-up activities and resources

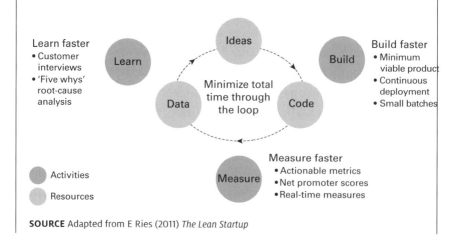

SOURCE Adapted from E Ries (2011) *The Lean Startup*

Using feedback from early adopters, a company can 'pivot', ie execute major changes in its direction – as opposed to the old way of doggedly persevering, no matter what.[27] This is why the method is called 'lean': Entrepreneurs have scarce resources, and they have to use them smartly.

The lean start-up methodology's near-cult-like popularity in many entrepreneurial circles signalled a shift from theoretical to practitioner concerns and fuelled a culture of accelerating processes, particularly speed to market. Lean's motto is to start small, fail fast, learn fast… but succeed faster, which is what many people forget. It legitimizes the idea of mistakes, provided we learn from them, but is not about glorifying failure. Lean inspired the rise of 'start-up consulting' targeting multi-billion-dollar corporations. As of 2020, organizations ranging from 3M and Telefónica to the US Department of Defense have embraced lean start-up.

Ultimately, lean start-up is a process, a set of principles that guides new product development. Its build–measure–learn loop is a learning cycle (to be repeated as many times as necessary), designed to turn ideas into marketable products as fast and efficiently as possible. The loop is built on a duality (Figure 5.6) of activities (build, measure, learn) and resources (code, data, ideas).[28]

GE intended to use agile as a catalyst for organization-wide change, not limited to product development. In HR, members of GE's learning and development function were organized into a global multi-functional team. Working closely with industry verticals and GE Digital, the idea was to define HR offerings such as training that would be more relevant to employees. It brought in staff from mergers and acquisitions, cyber-security and other divisions. Like any other scrum team, agile teams operate through daily virtual stand-ups and two-week sprints. According to Ann Johnston, former Digital Learning Transformation Leader at GE Digital, 'My core team is no longer bounded by an industrial image of a team that reports to me… We've killed more projects because they've failed than we've scaled. That's good because we are constantly saving money and leveraging resources. Our pace of work has increased hugely.'[29]

Ad-hoc setup B: Deploying agile methods in an exploratory bottom-up approach

In 2016, when bio-pharmaceutical company PharmaCo examined future trends, it was in a position of strength and had a strong track record in innovation. Yet with new entrants like biosimilars and digital disruptors flooding the market, the list of uncertainties and possibilities looked overwhelming. PharmaCo had to prepare for an uncertain future. Executives realized that the future was not going to be about *what* they do but *how* they do it. Since then, PharmaCo recast itself as patient-centred, value-driven and a pharmaceutical advisor rather than a seller.

Unlike GE, PharmaCo used no blueprint as a departure point in embracing agile processes. Nonetheless, letting different teams explore agile at their own pace triggered an avalanche of changes across the organization. In 2017, PharmaCo's central HR launched a leadership programme (running through mid-2019) where, starting with the top few hundred executives and cascading down, it asked leaders to imagine what PharmaCo's way of working should look like in this uncertain future. This sparked the creation of self-selected and self-organized (ie leaderless) teams, using various agile methods, where job descriptions were eliminated. From small experiments, big changes resulted. One team reduced the time to prepare a particular drug launch by a third, bringing drugs to patients several months early. Another team identified 30 per cent over-reporting on compliance, thus paving the way for simplifying the bureaucracy and cutting costs.

PharmaCo's adoption of agile processes was not confined to software-related activities. In 2018, it embarked on a 23-month HR process redesign to give employees an à la carte suite of HR services. In a push to develop a minimum viable product, PharmaCo invited employees to share input on which HR processes were value-adding and which were not. This allowed HR to prioritize building minimum viable products.

Cluster 3. The Hub Model: Staff From Other Departments Temporarily Attached to Agile Teams

The third cluster is about 'build it and they will come'. In this configuration, companies set up an agile workplace – strategically placed yet often modest-sized – as a showcase of how agile processes work and what they can accomplish.

In 2016, Rabobank, the Dutch multinational banking and financial services company with 43,000 employees and total assets exceeding €600 billion, centralized a number of its digital initiatives that had been scattered throughout the organization. The new entity was a 'digital hub' to be located inside the firm's retail domain. The hub brought together expertise on data and analytics, customer experience design and other offerings, including a mobile banking platform. This was in response to commercial banks across Europe moving away from the traditional high-street retail model to omnichannel offerings while also staving off competition from fintech players. In tandem, the bank promoted its head of fintech and innovation to chief digital transformation officer, aiming to make digital the main delivery channel, cutting across all customer segments. It sought to engineer a transition from DevOps-based IT development to BizDevOps, focusing on end-to-end customer journeys by involving data scientists, marketing, commercial and user experience specialists and compliance, legal and risk managers.[30]

Leveraging agile and lean principles and adding a focus on service and quality, **DevOps** is a set of practices that aim to involve operations in an agile lifecycle of software development. The result is additional value for customers, derived from faster and more reliable design, testing and operating of systems and applications. Taking the process one step further, **BizDevOps** integrates business alignment and market responsiveness directly into the development process.[31]

Alongside digital distribution and new revenue models, another key ambition in Rabobank's digital transformation was redesigning the bank's way of working. The adoption of agile methodologies was part of this multi-pronged initiative to infuse digital DNA into the company culture, emphasizing customer involvement and strengthening data-driven decision making. Agile methods, scrum in particular, were one of the components – along with boot camps, multidisciplinary teams and other innovative work structures – the bank embraced in order to sustain a vibrant work environment and attract fresh digital talent.

Launched in an official ceremony in early 2018 and housed in the company headquarters, the hub helped create a momentum towards accelerating Rabobank's digital transformation. With a skeleton team of six, occasionally supported by trainees and students, the hub populated its early squads (each working on a specific customer journey) with 10 people drawn from across the bank. Squad members were brought into the hub only on a temporary basis, through secondment arrangements with other departments, and depending on their availability. Squads worked to resolve straightforward customer pain points (eg losing a debit card) to create immediate impact and build momentum for agile implementation in the entire retail division.[32]

Agile Methods Come in Many Flavours, But They Share Underlying Qualities – and Benefits

Whatever the specific methodology behind them, the proliferation and popularity of agile methods has been driven by the rising costs and uncertainty of innovation mitigated by the direct and continuous customer involvement and feedback. In a transient, uncertain, tech-dominated marketplace, agreeing on a set of client specifications and then parting ways until the finished product is ready to be revealed is no longer viable. That is why, in 2020, the *14th Annual State of Agile Report*[33] and IMD's webinar on managing extreme uncertainty with agility both rated the ability to manage changing priorities as one of the top benefits of applying agile methods.

Overall, the 2020 IMD webinar's participants reported that 46 per cent of their companies had partially implemented agile methods in a single area such as software development, product development or IT; 27 per cent focused on a single area with full implementation; and 17 per cent were in the planning-to-implement phase. In the concurrent State of Agile survey, 44 per cent of companies said that less than half of their teams used agile practices; for 33 per cent, it was more than half; 18 per cent of companies had all of their teams adopt agile, while 5 per cent had yet to bring agile into any team.[34]

Agile methods have become increasingly popular as organizations, regardless of size and industry, private or public sectors, vie for greater customer-centricity and speedy delivery. 'Overcoming silos' was a mantra that never quite materialized in the corporate world. Agile processes not only made small cross-functional teams a principal building block, they also empowered them on the dimensions of What as well as How. Fewer superfluous specifications to track and hand-overs to manage, and more flexibility in roadmap planning due to short sprints resulted in better project success rates, particularly for larger and more complex projects, higher reliability of product delivery, and in overall cost reductions. In a 2013–17 report by the Standish Group, 42 per cent of agile projects were considered successful, compared to an 8 per cent failure rate. In contrast, classic waterfall projects saw a 26 per cent success rate, roughly equal to the 21 per cent failure rate. Large projects were twice as likely to succeed if run on agile processes.[35]

In addition to faster customer-centric experimentation and innovation, information sharing has become more transparent. From a cognitive standpoint, agile methods successfully mirror the human mind and imagination by tapping into intuition and repeated iterations.

Figure 5.7   The greatest benefits of introducing agile methods

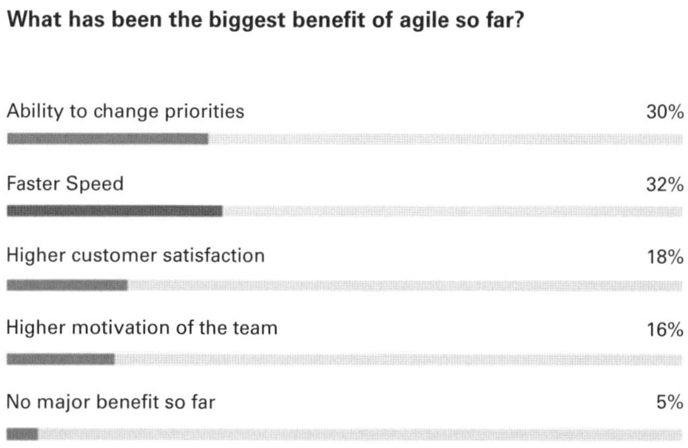

What has been the biggest benefit of agile so far?

Ability to change priorities	30%
Faster Speed	32%
Higher customer satisfaction	18%
Higher motivation of the team	16%
No major benefit so far	5%

SOURCE Managing Extreme Uncertainty with Agility. IMD webinar. May 2020

Involving the end user upfront has produced a parallel rise in customer satisfaction and employee engagement. Happier customers lead directly to higher team motivation – as evidenced by IMD's survey, where executives gave near-equal rating to both of these benefits of introducing agile methods (Figure 5.7). According to Deutsche Telekom, 'employees now see themselves as solvers'.[36]

What 'Agile' (ie Agile Methods and Processes) Can Contribute to Building Organizational Agility

Depending on whether they are well implemented (Chapter 9) and the scale of their deployment, agile methods have the potential to help foster wider organizational agility.

The companies in the above examples implemented agile into self-contained divisions; or widely but on an ad-hoc basis, or within a hub. None altered the broader organization's traditional hierarchy. On the stable-vs-nimble continuum, agile processes and the resulting pace of work naturally stimulate nimbleness through faster experimentation and continuous customer engagement and feedback. Some agile methods will translate this new quality of customer interaction into faster innovation and a speedier go-to-market process (Figure 5.8), such as

Figure 5.8   Agile vs agility: How adoption of agile methods stacks up against the main principles of business agility

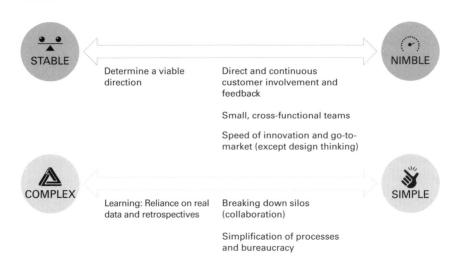

at Lego. In this context, agile methods are likely to create value for customers on top of additional efficiency for the company.

Imitating start-up dynamics, companies seek to become nimbler but without sacrificing the sense of stability and direction that have served them well. This is what Nick Jue, the former CEO of ING Netherlands, had in mind (Chapter 2) when he talked about elephants who are powerful but can also run fast. For Rabobank, getting the ball rolling, finding a simple starting point for squads and customer journeys, prioritizing between innovation goals, and staffing the agile teams with whoever was available, required strong leadership that could set a clear direction while charting unknown waters.

Similarly, PharmaCo was not pursuing speed for its own sake. The greater velocity and flexibility were achieved against a background of singular directions such as focus on patients and excellence in science, couched in the context of PharmaCo's core values. It was inconceivable that the company could discard these in exchange for a shorter time to market.

While all the firms aimed to simplify their hierarchy and bureaucracy, the characteristic mark of complexity in their organization was attention to learning, particularly when decisions are based on customer and real-world data. As Lego's CEO commented, 'We emphasize collaboration, cohesiveness and coherent choices to a very large extent – to such a large extent that many of our employees and leaders call it extremely complex.'[37]

Overall, the loose collaborative and reporting structures that prevail in agile teams, and the emphasis given to autonomy and creativity, naturally serve to up the nimble and simple factors. But they don't annihilate the opposing pole of stable when there is a clearly defined purpose, goals and long-term strategic planning. If properly understood, selected and implemented, agile methods can fundamentally embed a culture of curiosity, continuous learning and hyperawareness as natural attributes of the healthy level of complexity that comes with agility.

As diverse as they are, these trajectories show that introducing agile methodologies can be a useful step towards building a pool of improved skills and practices in areas such as customer intimacy, product development and speed to market. They encourage culture shifts of deepening empathy towards the user, collaboration, and accepting the viability and added value of challenging the dominant patterns of serving customers. Crucially, that added value has direct ramifications for both staff engagement (where happy customers equals happy employees) and the bottom line.

Conclusions

What does this diversity of methods and their applications mean for you and your business? Here are three main points to think about:

1 **Be clear about what it is you seek to achieve when you roll out agile processes.** Most companies discussed in this chapter use agile methods for continuous improvement. Agile processes promise a coherent set of benefits including better accuracy, reduction of waste (simplification), internal collaboration across disciplines and external collaboration by learning from and testing with customers. Yet nothing stops you from using them for more radical innovation in pursuit of your next revenue streams (Chapter 3). Deutsche Bahn was a good example of this approach. Meanwhile, industrial giant GE used agile as part of its search for a new innovation framework. Its goal was to endow the organization with the abilities of a start-up – launching but also killing projects quickly, making investment decisions based on hands-on validation and proven client and market traction.

   The issue is that unless someone specifies what the objective is, you will not arrive at those big breakthroughs by default. The majority of agile roll-outs turn out to drive incremental change. If you wish to be truly prepared for uncertainty, your approach will have to be bolder. In the end, you may well decide to roll out different methods to serve the two different purposes.

2 **Use agile to support digital execution.** Despite some of the unrealistic expectations of what agile methods can achieve, the link between agile and digital transformation appears well established and, in some

cases, robust: When PharmaCo plugged real-life data into virtual studies, it successfully accelerated the drug approval process. Access to transparent information also helps downplay managers' cognitive biases and tendency to act on an instinct. It nurtures a culture where employees have an affinity for, understand and appreciate data, and consistently leverage it to make decisions. That was Rabobank's aspiration in shifting to BizDevOps – tapping into data as a driving force for mapping and understanding end-to-end customer journeys.

Of course, agile is not limited to rolling out digital offerings. Agile methods have found application in HR, marketing and customer service innovation – with or without digital at the core.

3 **Pay attention to how you roll out agile.** It cannot be overemphasized that the benefits of agile methods are contingent on introducing them thoughtfully, with careful execution. However, this scenario is far from common: As many companies' experience bears out, jumping on the bandwagon simply because it's this year's buzzword is unlikely to deliver any of these improvements – and may in fact do more harm than good. The choice between the three configurations is eventful. The pitfalls and key success factors of implementing agile will be discussed in Chapter 9.

Endnotes

1 Anderson, D J (2010) *Kanban: Successful evolutionary change for your technology business*, Blue Hole Press

2 Fowler, M and Highsmith, J (2001) The agile manifesto, *Software Development*, **9** (8), pp 28–35

3 Rigby, D K, Sutherland, J and Takeuchi, H (2016) Embracing agile, *Harvard Business Review*, **94** (5), pp 40–50

4 Girod, S J G and Challagalla, G (2020) Managing extreme uncertainty with agility, www.imd.org/research-knowledge/videos/Managing-uncertainty-agility (archived at https://perma.cc/FF6F-C2UU)

5 Andersen, P and Ross, J W (2016) Transforming the LEGO group for the digital economy, Case Study, CISR WP No 407, Center for Information Systems Research, Sloan School of Management, MIT, Cambridge, MA

6 Sommer, A F (2019) Agile Transformation at LEGO Group: Implementing agile methods in multiple departments changed not only processes but also employees' behavior and mindset, *Research-Technology Management*, **62** (5), pp 20–29

7 Krush, A (2018) 5 success stories that will make you believe in scaled agile, *ObjectStyle*, 13 January, www.objectstyle.com/agile/scaled-agile-success-story-lessons (archived at https://perma.cc/S855-ZLWH)

8 Kniberg, H and Brandsgård, E T (2016) Planning as a social event: Scaling agile @ Lego, Scaled Agile Framework, December, www.scaledagileframework.com/wp-content/uploads/delightful-downloads/2017/09/LEGO_update.pdf (archived at https://perma.cc/7KTH-TT9R)

9 State of Agile (2020) *13th Annual State of Agile Report*, https://stateofagile.com/#ufh-i-613553418-13th-annual-state-of-agile-report/7027494 (archived at https://perma.cc/A2MT-H8CS)

10 Nijland, S, (2020) Why is scrum called scrum? *Medium*, 10 January, https://medium.com/serious-scrum/why-is-scrum-called-scrum-fac5315f6155 (archived at https://perma.cc/RJ2K-SPMS)

11 Maximini, D (2018) *The Scrum Culture: Introducing agile methods in organizations*, Springer International Publishing

12 Girod, S J G and Duke, L (2018) Digital transformation at GE: Shifting minds for agility, Case Study, IMD-7-2011, IMD International, Lausanne

13 Ackerman, S (2020) Does scrum really work in marketing? *Medium*, 12 July, https://medium.com/@stacey_41501/does-scrum-really-work-in-marketing-96c246ea6b28 (archived at https://perma.cc/ZVN2-U8BK)

14 Georgieff, M (2020) Agile marketing: Why marketers are going agile, Scrum Alliance, https://resources.scrumalliance.org/Article/agile-marketing-why-marketers-are-going-agile (archived at https://perma.cc/U7GW-ZUX6)

15 FitzGerald, D (2020) T-Mobile overtakes AT&T to become no 2 carrier, *Wall Street Journal*, 6 August, https://www.wsj.com/articles/t-mobile-overtakes-at-t-to-become-no-2-carrier-11596754162 (archived at https://perma.cc/TAK4-B6D7)

16 Telekom (2020) New working methods at Deutsche Telekom, www.telekom.com/en/careers/our-focus-topics/agile-working (archived at https://perma.cc/G246-V878)

17 BCG (2020) Deutsche Telekom gives customer service an agile makeover, 6 August, www.bcg.com/publications/2020/deutsche-telekom-gives-customer-service-an-agile-makeover (archived at https://perma.cc/7PQF-6CLH)

18 Weber, D (2020) Impact Of COVID-19: How does Deutsche Telekom react? Part 1, www.telekom.com/en/careers/our-focus-topics/center-for-strategic-projects/trafo-talk/impact-of-covid-19-how-does-deutsche-telekom-react-part-1-600466 (archived at https://perma.cc/MQ8G-94XQ)

19 Danfoss (2019) Danfoss unit goes beyond hierarchy, 11 September, www.danfoss.com/en/about-danfoss/news/cf/danfoss-unit-goes-beyond-hierarchy (archived at https://perma.cc/3WR2-8XLS)

20 von Schmieden, K and Bleuel, F (2018) Taking risks, earning trust and including co-workers: User-centred design at Deutsche Bahn Operations. This is design thinking, July, https://thisisdesignthinking.net/2018/07/design-at-deutsche-bahn-operations (archived at https://perma.cc/W7B4-9SJ9)

21 Black, S, Gardner, D G, Pierce, J L and Steers, R (2019) Design thinking, *Organizational Behavior*, OpenStax

22 Liedtka, J (2018) Why design thinking works, *Harvard Business Review*, **96** (5), pp 72–79

23 Wagner, M (2019). We're the good guys: Deutsche Bahn between tradition and innovation, Detecon Consulting, 25 September, www.detecon.com/en/knowledge/martin-seiler-were-good-guys (archived at https://perma.cc/CQ2B-9NYA)

24 *The Economist* (2014) General Electric: A hard act to follow, 27 July, www.economist.com/business/2014/06/27/a-hard-act-to-follow (archived at https://perma.cc/Y4DP-PKJA)

25 Girod, S J G and Duke, L (2018) Digital transformation at GE: Shifting minds for agility, Case Study, IMD-7-2011, IMD International, Lausanne

26 Nobel, C (2011) Teaching a 'lean startup' strategy, *HBS Working Knowledge*, pp 1–2

27 Ries, E (2011) *The Lean Startup: How today's entrepreneurs use continuous innovation to create radically successful businesses*, Currency

28 The Lean Startup (nd) Methodology, http://theleanstartup.com/principles (archived at https://perma.cc/VGE2-LN8W)

29 The Lean Startup (nd) Methodology, http://theleanstartup.com/ principles (archived at https://perma.cc/QY5K-MGZU)

30 Wade, M and Duke, L (2019) Rabobank: Building digital agility at scale, Case Study, IMD-7-2070, IMD International, Lausanne

31 Blueprint (nd) Agile and DevOps (and BizDevOps), www.blueprintsys. com/agile-development-101/agile-and-devops (archived at https:// perma.cc/P96W-GA6Q)

32 Wade, M and Duke, L (2019) Rabobank: Building digital agility at scale, Case Study, IMD-7-2070, IMD International, Lausanne

33 State of Agile (2020) *14th Annual State of Agile Report*, https:// stateofagile.com/#ufh-i-615706098-14th-annual-state-of-agile-report/7027494 (archived at https://perma.cc/D7U4-XAE8)

34 State of Agile (2020) *14th Annual State of Agile Report*, https:// stateofagile.com/#ufh-i-615706098-14th-annual-state-of-agile-report/7027494 (archived at https://perma.cc/XV22-UBAM)

35 The Standish Group (2018) New *CHAOS* report 2018, www. standishgroup.com/news/37 (archived at https://perma.cc/4K6U-JU55)

36 Girod, S J G and Duke, L (2018) Face-to-face interview with Erik Meijer, Group Innovation, Deutsche Telekom

37 Andersen, P and Ross, J W (2016) Transforming the LEGO group for the digital economy, Case Study, CISR WP No 407, Center for Information Systems Research, Sloan School of Management, MIT, Cambridge, MA

06

Organizational Agility

Pioneers of New Organizational Forms

SIX LESSONS FROM THIS CHAPTER

1 Bold organizational redesigns are occurring even in highly regulated industries including banking, and in once unwieldy state-owned enterprises in China.

2 Haier and ING took agility to higher levels by working in ways that not long ago were deemed unthinkable for very large companies. They emphasized radical customer-centricity and flattened the entire organization so that no more than two layers separate frontline workers from top management. At the same time, they placed innovative technology firmly in the hands of customers and partners.

3 Haier transformed into a network of autonomous microenterprises, proving that introducing measured elements of instability and stress into the organization can be conducive to flexibility and collaboration. Simultaneously, a leaner, flatter, ecosystem-focused architecture is a strong enabler of data-driven decision making. During a crisis, this use of live, real-world aggregate data is a source of great resilience.

4 'Scaling agile' is a misleading concept. It is not the only path to agility. Haier demonstrates that you can aim for organizational agility without using agile methods. What matters is that you focus

on the eight principles of organizational agility in designing the
organization the way you need it to be.

5 Haier and ING's ground-breaking organizational overhauls allowed
for the entire organizations to concentrate on customer needs and
pain points. They enabled resilient planning and adjusting of
priorities, customer insights derived from data, and stronger
employee engagement. These indicators directly translate into
improvements in the bottom line.

6 At the organizational level, discover what is evolution and what is
a management reset.

Chapter 5 illustrated that agile methodologies and processes may
serve as one of many stepping stones on the path to building business
agility. Adopting agile methods is not necessarily equivalent to or, in
many cases, even productive of agility. The majority of companies that
experiment with 'agile' are seeking to emulate start-ups, especially by
getting closer to the customer and speeding up product development.

The two company examples in this chapter are complete organizational overhauls, achieved through dramatic, deliberate self-disruption
(Figure 6.1). A leading European bank, ING, and Haier, the world's

Figure 6.1 Moving to a high level of nimbleness and simplification: Radical
organizational overhauls

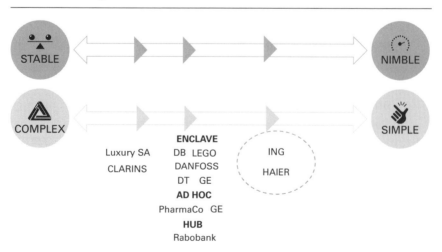

largest consumer appliance maker based in China, both deployed radically new organizational models to achieve agility – the former using agile methods, the latter not. Both show that cutting-edge experiments conducive of agility are no longer confined to the realm of start-ups and small firms. They are occurring even in the most regulated industries – a trend that is bound to continue shaping the 2020s business landscape.

Haier: Developing Agility Without Squads and Tribes

In 2019, Haier reported a global revenue of RMB 200.7 billion ($27.7 billion) and employed a workforce of nearly 100,000.[1] Set up in 1984, during the early days of China's economic reopening, Haier's origins were in the old centralized command-and-control, quantity-over-quality manufacturing sector. At the time, benchmarks or industry competition in the western sense were virtually non-existent. All of China's industrial enterprises were state-owned and primarily tasked with providing employment opportunities as well as political and ideological education and control. Today's CEO, Zhang Ruimin, was a government officer rather than a manager, appointed by the municipal authority to take charge of the failing factory.

Once China joined the WTO in 2001, reinventing the company became a matter of necessity and survival if it was to compete domestically as well as internationally. Haier had to orchestrate a thorough break with the legacy of its past. In 2005, it introduced a model named *rendanheyi* (人单合一) which was based on a synthesis of individual workers' interests with those of customers. From 2005 to 2009, the company set up new strategic business units, each assigned a set of quantitative performance goals directly linked to customers, and rolled out a slew of IT solutions.[2] By 2010, in a revolutionary move intended to support its networked strategy, it did away with formal departments, business units and divisions. Instead, it recast itself as a grouping of more than 4,000 autonomous microenterprises

(MEs), each containing about 9 to 15 workers. Of these thousands of MEs, 200 are customer-facing, 50 are incubating, and the other 3,800 MEs act as nodes – selling components, services and expertise to other MEs through a process of templated and facilitated but otherwise open bidding.[3]

MEs are integrated into industry platforms to ensure a minimum of coordination between MEs but enough alignment to execute Haier's strategy. The Shunguang platform, for example, is a community ecosystem that continually absorbs user experience data from urban and rural areas and even from MEs that operate inside trucks.[4] The focus of the Interconnected Factory platform is to achieve flexible mass customization by deploying intelligent technologies.[5] The U+ Smart Life platform allows users to connect with all smart-home terminals, including those powered by systems from other vendors, such as Apple's HomeKit.[6] A platform owner acts as a facilitator who brings ME teams together and helps them identify opportunities for collaboration. There is no further bureaucracy: The rest of the planning and execution is up to the MEs, whose members do not 'belong', let alone report to the platform owner in the classical sense.[7]

Haier replaced hierarchy with an open, entrepreneurial ecosystem where no more than two layers separate the frontline worker from the CEO. In effect, the entire organization became a wide network of empowered entrepreneurs, tapping extensively into an external source of ideas and business acumen from end users, suppliers, road show participants and other partners.[8] According to Haier's CEO Zhang Ruimin, 'Employees today should be encouraged to think for themselves. They should be cultivated to have an entrepreneurial, innovative spirit, and not just to implement orders.'[9]

The 'Network Strategy,' in place since 2012, empowers all nodes that interact in platforms to make decisions on what to do and how. It also gives them the freedom to choose their collaborators. That strategy directly informs and shapes the company's modular structure in which customer-facing MEs and node MEs constantly innovate with customers. As a ramification of this 'unfettered free market' microcosm that is mapped onto a corporate structure, nodes can go bankrupt and employees can fire their ME boss. There is also the annual contracting of node MEs – a process that creates room for experimentation and for open, even parallel innovation projects, but also entails establishing the metrics of success.

Viewed through the prism of the agility framework, Haier's actions come across as extremely nimble. Customer-centricity for innovation doesn't get much more pronounced than this. Simply put, customer-facing MEs will not survive unless they involve the customer in everything they do. User MEs have no access to central financing if their projects aren't developed in collaboration with users. Similarly, incentives are aligned with how big a share of innovation is based on customer feedback. The logic of open market dictates that node MEs which do not innovate and stay at the top of their game eventually run out of orders and die, since user MEs can choose suppliers outside Haier. This is what Zhang calls 'the principle of zero distance from customer', which applies to wherever one sits in the company, front office or back office.

Haier's CEO always maintained that 'an unsteady and dynamic environment is the best way to keep everyone flexible'.[10] Although Haier doesn't run scrums per se, all stakeholders come together at the outset of defining a product and then work side by side (including with external partners) in order to stimulate creative problem solving. Employees see their businesses as networks of collaboration, not linear processes. In addition to that, the company collects new ideas from internal as well as external pitches (such as countrywide roadshows). Meanwhile, migrating product development processes online has cut time to market by 70 per cent.[11]

When the COVID-19 outbreak in January 2020 caused widespread supply chain disruption across China, Haier's lean ecosystem of thousands of MEs allowed it to collect and analyse a wealth of live data, reroute orders to its factories overseas where necessary and make adjustments to its supplier and logistical planning. By late February, the company resumed running at full capacity, with a near-100 per cent rate of order fulfilment.[12]

Looking at this iconoclastic level of nimbleness, where does Haier find the sources of stability to mitigate and anchor its freewheeling organizational ethos? In large measure, the company equates stability with retaining high-performing employees. It has instituted an intricate system of team rewards, individual dividends, employee investment accounts and profit-sharing arrangements. Compared with western corporations, there is much less emphasis at Haier on formal and systematic employee development programmes; people adapt and learn because they have to. (Given the firm's paradigm of an open marketplace, it is only fitting that its stable attributes are mainly quantitative in nature.) Strategy is another source of stability, giving individual units the freedom to pursue what – in their own estimation – works and discard what doesn't, thus organically channelling resources in productive directions. As Zhang himself famously said, 'strategy is there to avoid temptations.'

In negotiating the tension between simplicity and complexity, Haier's chief impetus was to cut bureaucracy and hierarchy to a viable minimum. To this end, the company put forward standardized tools – known as Haier's 'constitution' – that facilitate: 1) strategy (MEs setting their priorities, forming internal and external partnerships); 2) people interactions (hiring and firing, defining working relationships, aligning individuals with job roles); 3) distribution (setting pay rates and awarding bonuses); and 4) internal negotiations (related to performance standards and profit sharing).

Nonetheless, Haier avoids a stifling emphasis on written rules. Sophisticated pragmatism often takes the upper hand. This is the principle that guided Haier's journey from a state-owned enterprise in a provincial setting to a world-class innovator. As such, incentives may be tailored, thus shifting the goalposts for product segments where Haier is not a category leader. Additionally, cutting across the seeming uniformity are meta-platforms that generate cross-business insights and predictive patterns to stimulate hyperawareness and organization-wide learning. The smart manufacturing platform conducts research on mass customization and advanced production tools. It sets the standards for the whole company. The marketing platform centralizes the customer Big Data analytics initiatives to unearth cross-business insights and build predictive models of emerging needs.

Without using agile methods or agile-related vocabulary, Haier aimed for organizational agility by focusing on the eight principles. It did so by deploying its strategy, structure, infrastructure and people in ways that could help it reconcile stable with nimble and complex with simple (Figure 6.2). Given China's cut-throat, fast-changing competitive environment, and because Zhang wanted an organization where

Figure 6.2 Haier in the Agility Canvas

	STABLE	NIMBLE	COMPLEX	SIMPLE
Strategy • Markets and portfolio • Value proposition • Strategy process	• Clear, well-communicated purpose and direction • Disciplined, aligned and accountable execution	• Faster customer-centric experimentation/innovation • Small cross-functional teams empowered with transparent information	• Differentiated choices (no one-size-fits-all) • Orchestration of networks for continuous learning	• Minimum viable bureaucracy • Minimum viable hierarchy (flatter, more collaboration)
	• Network Strategy since 2012 • 'Strategy helps in resisting temptation'	• All nodes are empowered on what to do and how; platforms have to create new business models	• Learning from outside: Generalized use of crowdsourcing and monthly China roadshows to scan new opportunities	• MEs can choose their collaborations inside and outside
Structure • Power, authority • Reporting relationships • Roles	• 50 platforms ensure alignment • Stable platforms in line with strategy (occasional new platforms for new big digital trends)	• Modular structure where customer-facing and node MEs constantly innovate with customers	• Special platforms disseminate learning on emerging technology trends	• Pancake-flat hierarchy (two layers between CEO and frontline) • 50 platforms leaders
Processes • Business processes • Management processes • Technology and data • Metrics and KPIs	• Contracting establishes metrics of success • Nodes can go bankrupt • Employees can fire their ME boss	• Online and parallel innovation projects • Annual contracting of node MEs allows for experimentation	• Annual agreement negotiation process between nodes and customer-facing MEs	• The Haier 'constitution' sets the four big rules for company processes
People • Skills • Incentives • Career paths • Values • Leadership styles	• CEO Zhang is the chief strategy storyteller • Multi-tier and generous reward system to retain good staff	• Zero-distance culture • Principle of 'everyone is paid by the customer' • Employees become owners	• Targets and KPIs tailored to each platform situation in the market	• Platform leaders have no formal reportees but hold budget and facilitate collaboration in and outside Haier

SOURCE Prof Stéphane JG Girod, IMD. Not to be used without permission

employees would behave like owners and entrepreneurs, Haier chose to push the cursor much further on nimbleness and simplicity.

ING's Agility Architecture: The Bank That Would Be a Tech Company

Established in 1991, ING, a Dutch multinational banking and financial services group with a workforce of 54,000, posted a 2019 revenue of €18.1 billion ($20.7 billion). An established player in a traditional and highly regulated sector, ING received a state bailout during the 2008 financial crisis. In 2008–14 it went through a tough restructuring. By 2014, ready to embark on a new growth chapter, the bank launched a new strategy named Think Forward, a blueprint for digital banking leadership. Its mission was one of 'Empowering people to stay a step ahead in life and in business.' It emphasized omnichannel convenience and cost leadership, passing efficiencies and savings on to customers in a zero-interest-rate environment.

Compared with 2008, customer expectations were profoundly different in terms of convenience, connectivity, time savings and instant gratification. The new banking clients were self-directed[13] and digitally fluent – eager to deal with banking the same way they booked flights and holidays, bought books and music, and shopped for groceries and other goods online. As Group CEO Ralph Hamers stated in 2014, 'The banking landscape is changing rapidly. Customer expectations are constantly changing, with clients becoming increasingly more mobile and willing to spread their business across multiple institutions. At the same time, technology is transforming the way in which we interact with our customers. Partly because of new regulation, all banks have been forced to re-think their business models and to assess where they can compete effectively and serve their customers best. In this new landscape, we need to be agile towards change, to ensure that our franchise remains sustainable and competitive.'[14]

Due to customer demand for digital ease and convenience, fast-moving fintech companies and other disruptors were gaining a strong foothold in financial services, with their increased focus on customer experience and continuous improvement. For example, PayPal allowed people to make payments without having a bank account and fintech companies such as Mint (aggregator) and Kickstarter (crowdfunding) were eating into banks' traditional businesses. In this context, for incumbents to stay relevant and avoid obsolescence, it was imperative to increase flexibility, customer-centricity and cost reduction and to accelerate innovation.

The Think Forward blueprint mandated that customers take centre stage, supported by new levels of operational excellence and a culture of enhanced performance. After visiting digital players such as Google and Spotify, ING Netherlands implemented agile ways of working in its product development organization. Betting on agile, ING hoped to keep pace with fintechs and other innovators in leveraging digital opportunities. As Group CEO Hamers (as of late 2020, UBS Group's CEO) put it: 'We want to portray ourselves as a tech company with a banking license.'[15] In late 2016, he announced an acceleration of the Think Forward strategy with a further €800 million investment in digital transformation to meet customer needs and achieve a €900 million annual cost savings by 2021.

To energize this new strategy, in 2015 ING proceeded with a 'Big Bang' organizational transformation of the Netherlands headquarters. It started with full implementation of agile in the core departments of product development, marketing, product management, channel management, data analytics and IT development. It invited all employees to re-apply for a job; 30 per cent were not reappointed.

Fulfilling the strategy entailed developing excellence in delivering banking services across channels, an initiative dubbed 'redesign into omnichannel' (RIO). The transformation was underpinned by the Orange Code, launched in 2014, which articulated desired values and behaviours, such as collaboration ('Your success is my success'), experimentation ('We challenge the status quo') and collective learning. These attributes were essential to support the new product development organization – where employees are only two layers of hierarchy away from top management.

Soon, 350 self-steering, autonomous squads – of nine employees each, representing a variety of backgrounds and disciplines – formed the backbone of ING's agile organization. Each squad held end-to-end responsibility for achieving its particular customer mission. For example, in the mortgage services tribe, one squad focused on continuously improving the customer journey for obtaining a mortgage, another optimized the search engine function related to mortgages. All squads used scrum to develop new products and followed the principles of lean start-up to experiment and deliver minimum viable products. This encouraged an intimate understanding of customer needs and pain points along with speedy experimentation.

Now, product modification could be performed in a fast and self-organizing manner. Coordination across squads between members of the same discipline took place in chapters, eg data analytics chapter, mortgage customer journey chapter, product management processes chapter. Chapters were in charge of continuous learning and functional development – what ING called the craftsmanship of its professionals. Chapter leads working across squads captured new practices and diffused them to optimize and create efficiencies but also to let experiments take place that would discover next practices. Finally, squads that were working on interconnected missions were grouped into one of 13 tribes, eg Securities and Private Banking, Mortgage Services, Business Banking Customer Experience, in order to ensure greater coordination, discipline and strategic alignment (Figure 6.3).[16]

Tribe leads represented one hierarchical layer. They aligned their 13 or so squads behind ING strategy and allocated quarterly budgets. Chapter leads formed the second and final layer. They conducted performance evaluation of employees across squads, zooming in on different areas of expertise. Nevertheless, about 60 per cent of their time was spent in their own squad. The hierarchy was flat but, importantly, there was still a hierarchy in place at ING, just as there was at Haier.

The heightened importance of proximity to customers reverberated through the company's processes. Tribes and squads were reorganized around and responsible for specific customer needs and journeys. At the same time, ING put cutting-edge fintech in customers' hands. For example, loans of as much as €100,000 for small businesses in France, Italy and Spain could now be evaluated in just 10 minutes via algorithms that analyse not only borrowers' credit data but also their Facebook and Twitter posts.

Figure 6.3 ING's product development structure

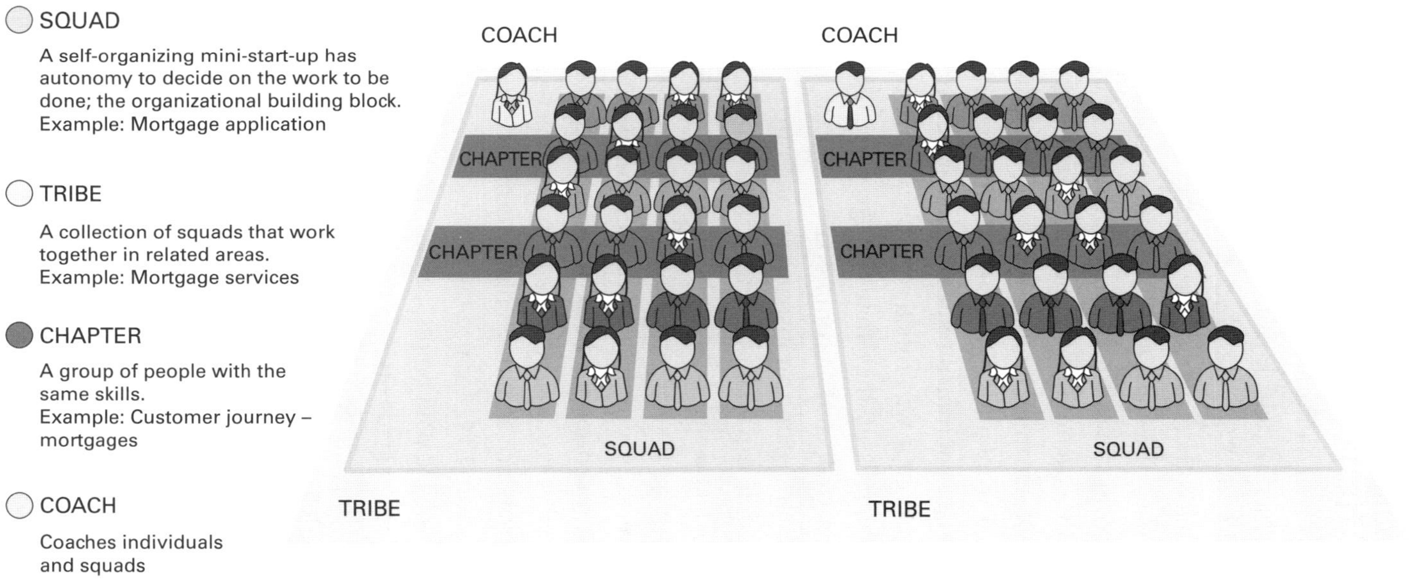

○ SQUAD
A self-organizing mini-start-up has autonomy to decide on the work to be done; the organizational building block.
Example: Mortgage application

○ TRIBE
A collection of squads that work together in related areas.
Example: Mortgage services

● CHAPTER
A group of people with the same skills.
Example: Customer journey – mortgages

○ COACH
Coaches individuals and squads

SOURCE S J G Girod et al (2018) ING: An agile organization in a disruptive environment, IMD case study

ING realized that having a single management process (called Quarterly Business Review – QBR) rather than a multitude of processes and rules was the best way to provide the organization with strategic alignment as well as fluid resource allocation. QBR is a process borrowed from Netflix, which believes that empowerment without information is nothing. With the freedom of empowerment comes the duty to know what others are doing. Under QBR principles, all squad members review their accomplishments in the previous quarter and lay out their objectives for the next, in support of the bank's overall strategy. QBR outcomes were publicly available for all tribes, thus permitting greater transparency and visibility. Empowerment necessitated learning from and with others to ensure strategic alignment. At ING, the budget continued to be multi-year and organized along strategic priorities but it was rolled over on a quarterly basis. This was to finance the squads as they made progress, reallocate budgets when priorities changed, and accommodate external uncertainty. In this way, QBR itself became an instrument of strategic agility.

As ING's agile capabilities matured, from 2016 agile was scaled further. HR, sales and service units went agile in early 2017, while other functions such as finance and risk management were deliberately excluded but were transformed into centres of expertise that were available to squads on a continuous basis. Simultaneously, ING recognized that squads and tribes would not work in its customer-facing retail branches and call centres since employees had to deal with customers on an ongoing basis. Instead, ING formed customer circles to capture and resolve customers' evolving pain points, passing on this information to the product development squads on a daily basis. This experimentation was part and parcel of implementing agile methods and finding out that they were a good fit with some business functions but not necessarily all. By 2020, the template was expanded to include Belgium, Luxembourg, Poland, Romania and Germany. The journey to adopting agile was itself an agile process rather than a cut-and-dry set of instructions (Chapter 10).

Benefits of Embracing Agile Ways of Working

ING leveraged digital to adapt its offerings to customers' changing needs and to develop an omnichannel customer experience. Previously, different IT systems, lack of connectivity across channels and siloed working resulted in slow and insufficient delivery of products and services to meet customer needs. By placing app programmers, product development and marketing colleagues at the core of each squad, agile remedied these shortcomings. Legacy systems were unified or closed down. Agile also improved performance in time to market and broadened the range of innovative product offerings. For example, instead of the previous five or six software releases a year, releases now took place every two or three weeks. The bank was able to react more quickly to observed customer trends and to ensure that client advice was relevant, proactive and timely.

ING outpaced its main competitors (Rabobank, ABN Amro) by offering innovative apps that allowed customers to manage their finances across multiple institutions in one mobile dashboard, moving closer to open platforms and digital ecosystems. In the Netherlands, ING was ranked number one in the rolling average of net promoter scores (NPS) which measure customer satisfaction and loyalty. Simultaneously, in 2019 ING Netherlands' pace of monthly content-delivery-as-a-service (CDaaS) applications going into production jumped from 280 before agile to 600 with agile.

Employees had to change their mindset to accept the release of non-perfect products. The quasi-instant loop that provided both positive and negative feedback inspired and pushed them to adapt and improve products. Teams could very quickly appreciate how their work impacted customers' journeys. Employee engagement improved significantly following agile implementation, reaching 93 per cent in some tribes. Feedback included comments such as 'I feel I make myself more useful and my work has a greater impact on the company' and 'I enjoy working in ING and contributing to shaping the future of banking.' Beyond learning by doing or by coaching, to support employee empowerment ING created employee guilds, encouraged participation in conferences and other industry events. It set aside a generous learning and development (L&D) budget to stimulate employees' continuous learning and to improve their chances of finding other work opportunities if their contract was terminated. Behind the human objective, there was a specific business objective: ING was clear that due to continued automation, future headcount reduction was likely.

'Fail fast and learn', based on a brisk roll-out of MVPs and quick responses to failures, produced considerable savings of time and investment.

Continuously analysing data in order to derive fresh customer insights propelled ING's product development towards establishing itself as fully data-driven. Working in tandem, agile and digitization produced cost reductions through a rationalization of the branch network. The thinning of the bricks-and-mortar network was compensated for by the high quality of service in the ING app. A total of 6,000 employees were committed to supporting the app and analysing its data flows.

Negotiating Tensions

On the simple-vs-complex continuum, ING's changes resulted in fewer silos, reduced bureaucracy and greater collaboration. Yet simplification also produced a greater level of sophistication as agile ways of working were adapted to what made sense and not implemented as a straitjacket. Although risk and finance staff weren't part of agile teams per se, they were expected to live by the Orange Code and rewarded for helping employees in squads to succeed. In other words, simplicity meant one common set of values and behaviours, even if the ways of working were differentiated.

Radical innovation was not favoured in the squads as they leaned toward short-term innovation. ING's radical innovation activities were located in a separate unit that focused on building an innovation ecosystem and forging partnerships with start-ups to access more disruptive ideas. As an example of ING's radical innovation efforts, the bank partnered globally with more than 65 fintechs and cooperated with several young companies working on video identification (Web-ID), photo transfers (Gini Pay) and payment verification by fingerprint (SmartSecure App by Kobil).

Exerting pressure on one main building block of ING's organizational design necessitated and helped produce change in the remaining blocks (Figure 6.4). As ground-breaking as the transformation was, it contained little room for making arbitrary moves or constantly reacting without focus. This inner coherence translated into company-wide optimization and getting in tune with an uncertain environment. ING's transformation achieved great strides in reconciling the tensions of stable vs nimble and complex vs simple. What made the revamped organization nimble was its emphasis on customer-centric experimentation, fuelled by a close-knit and empowered network of

Figure 6.4 ING in the Agility Canvas

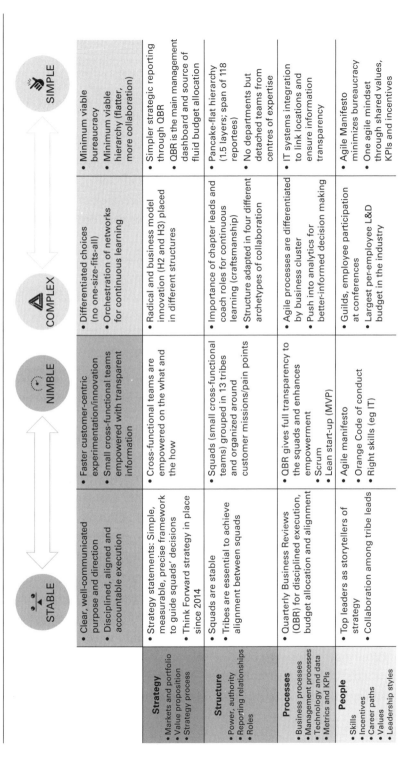

	STABLE	NIMBLE	COMPLEX	SIMPLE
Strategy • Markets and portfolio • Value proposition • Strategy process	• Clear, well-communicated purpose and direction • Disciplined, aligned and accountable execution • Strategy statements: Simple, measurable, precise framework to guide squads' decisions • Think Forward strategy in place since 2014	• Faster customer-centric experimentation/innovation • Small cross-functional teams empowered with transparent information • Cross-functional teams are empowered on the what and the how	• Differentiated choices (no one-size-fits-all) • Orchestration of networks for continuous learning • Radical and business model innovation (H2 and H3) placed in different structures	• Minimum viable bureaucracy • Minimum viable hierarchy (flatter, more collaboration) • Simpler strategic reporting through QBR • QBR is the main management dashboard and source of fluid budget allocation
Structure • Power, authority • Reporting relationships • Roles	• Squads are stable • Tribes are essential to achieve alignment between squads	• Squads (small cross-functional teams) grouped in 13 tribes and organized around customer missions/pain points	• Importance of chapter leads and coach roles for continuous learning (craftsmanship) • Structure adapted in four different archetypes of collaboration	• Pancake-flat hierarchy (1.5 layers; span of 118 reportees) • No departments but detached teams from centres of expertise
Processes • Business processes • Management processes • Technology and data • Metrics and KPIs	• Quarterly Business Reviews (QBR) for disciplined execution, budget allocation and alignment	• QBR gives full transparency to the squads and enhances empowerment • Scrum • Lean start-up (MVP)	• Agile processes are differentiated by business cluster • Push into analytics for better-informed decision making	• IT systems integration to link locations and ensure information transparency
People • Skills • Incentives • Career paths • Values • Leadership styles	• Top leaders as storytellers of strategy • Collaboration among tribe leads	• Agile manifesto • Orange Code of conduct • Right skills (eg IT)	• Guilds, employee participation at conferences • Largest per-employee L&D budget in the industry	• Agile Manifesto minimizes bureaucracy • One agile mindset through shared values, KPIs and incentives

SOURCE Prof Stéphane JG Girod, IMD. Not to be used without permission

cross-functional teams. Yet these attributes were balanced, due to the pre-defined components of the Think Forward strategy and the universal QBR dashboard. As such, nimbleness played out in concert with disciplined execution, budget allocation and strategic alignment.

Strategy and leadership played an important role to ensure a double focus on nimbleness and stability. Empowerment to experiment around the customer took place within a framework. As captured in the Think Forward strategy, 'We focus on being clear and easy, anytime, anywhere, and empowering customers to stay a step ahead in life and in business.'[17]

Does your company use such short and precise but broad, easy-to-remember strategy statements that give employees a clear sense of direction and purpose? Most companies do not. At ING, the tribe leaders' role includes tirelessly telling this story so that employees can stick to a strategy without feeling micromanaged.

Conclusions

On the surface, the ways ING and Haier set about developing their agile muscle don't have much in common. Yet on closer inspection, there is a great degree of similarity in terms of the levers they engaged and the tensions they addressed on the one hand, and risk management, delivery of strategy and accountability on the other. Both companies' behaviours can be described as transparent, enabling and collaborative in addition to putting customer first and making decisions based on data coming in from their flat but extensive ecosystems.

Haier and ING both achieved flatter organizations – closer to customer, attuned to market trends and quick to reshuffle internal resources as necessary. With these deep-seated adjustments in place, organizations gain the ability to (a) strengthen adaptability and resilience to unexpected changes; (b) enhance employee engagement; (c) heighten the accuracy and speed of innovation in response to digital; (d) continue reducing costs; (e) place customers at the forefront; (f) stimulate collaboration by removing boundaries and bureaucratic hurdles; and (g) make digital transformations stick.

What can you learn from the discussion of companies fighting to increase their organizational agility over the last three chapters? Similar to strategic agility, you will need to retain certain practices of the past when they make sense (evolution). But to be a real reset manager, you will need to embrace resolutely the next practices of organizational agility (Table 6.1).

Table 6.1   At organizational level, why business agility is more than an evolution: It is a management reset

Organization	
Evolution	**Management reset**
• Remember that hierarchy still exists, even if it has become much flatter • Continue to search for efficiency • Persist in shortening time to market and speeding up ways of working wherever necessary (but without becoming reckless; speed is not the essence of agility)	• Nimbleness: Recognize the power of end-to-end empowerment coming from small, cross-functional teams; working in an environment of trust, they can be a great source of bottom-up adaptation • Nimbleness: Accelerate the shift from customer awareness to customer-centricity. This can be achieved even in non-customer-facing roles • Place forceful emphasis on organizational learning including learning from failure by giving teams time to learn • Healthy stability: Within a clear framework of accountability, empower teams to deliver on strategy with a degree of predictability • Simplicity: Minimum viable bureaucracy and hierarchy. Look for opportunities to cut down on these two; it will help you identify transformative ways of working • Healthy complexity: Avoid the one-size-fits-all straitjacket. Orchestrate networks for continuous learning (learning becomes more important than knowledge). Use real-time data to strengthen innovation accuracy and reduce the surrounding uncertainty • See the roll-out of agile methods as a piece of organizational redesign rather than simply as a ritual that comes with the process • If deploying multiple agile methods, introduce them to employees as one set of tools rather than in silos • Recognize that the split between thinkers and doers is bound to erode with time

At organizational level, which practices add up to a management reset, as opposed to an evolution of existing trends?

- On the evolution side, studies show that large companies spent decades trying to eliminate layers of bureaucracy.[18] Likewise, the pursuit of speed and efficiency remains a constant. Since the 1980s and the emergence of local–global strategies and organizations, multinationals have created networks of divisions, countries and functions.[19] The 2020s continue to replace these with networks of small teams.

- The flattening of hierarchy, in the 10 companies we studied, is therefore part of the evolution. What is new is that this flattening can achieve much more if you compensate for the loss of middle management with clear strategic directions, team accountability aligned with quarterly rather than annual budgets, simpler and more transparent dashboards and – as shown in Chapter 7 – a reset of leadership styles.

The shift to organizational agility creates several rupture points, however:

- **From customer awareness to customer-centricity.** The shift to agility puts the customer firmly at the centre of organizations. Although as Steve Jobs used to say, 'I never ask the customers – they don't know what they want', and nothing should stop entrepreneurs from pushing ahead with a bold vision, agile methods can help test, learn about and scale big strategic bets while minimizing risk. In addition, customer-centricity as a design principle means that innovation accuracy goes up because you innovate with real-time data.

- **From knowledge management to continuous organizational and individual learning.** The 1990s saw the emergence of knowledge management and the distinction between codified knowledge and tacit knowledge – hard to replicate and therefore a source of superior competitive advantage.[20] In this new paradigm, knowledge still matters. What is even more important is the continuous need for unlearning and relearning at the organizational as well as the individual levels. Knowledge and best practices are one thing – but, as C K Prahalad said, next practices are even better.[21]

- **Blurred boundaries between thinkers and doers.** Traditionally, big companies tend to be loose in defining and storytelling their purpose, strategy and direction, tight in micromanaging employees on how and what to do, and loose again in transparency, collaboration and accountability. The 2020s management reset puts in motion a reversal of these priorities: As organizations build agility, they need to be tight in purpose and direction, loose in articulating a roadmap for how to get there, and tight again in ensuring accountability, collaboration and transparency.[22]

- **From corporate functions seen as cost centres to profit maximizers.** Because ING is now fully organized around the customer rather than by product, its corporate functions cease to be cost centres and become profit-adding centres of expertise. The new setup helps ING to link its products in boundary-spanning ways and customer journeys. As customers navigate through offerings more seamlessly, they are likely to bank with ING in more than one product segment. This helps the bank gain a bigger share of their wallet.

- **Do not fear loss of control.** Loss of control and operational risk are among the most common reservations executives express about agility. There are a number of ways to mitigate these risks. First, hierarchy does not disappear; it just becomes flatter. Second, the rules of accountability are frequently clarified. Third, peer pressure within smaller teams replaces leaders' pressure or the pressure of micromanagement. Contrary to what happens in steep hierarchies, in small teams there is nowhere to hide. Employees who underperform and don't contribute enough to the team are immediately noticeable. This is why ING was able to lift all limits on employees' vacation days – now decided by individuals and their teams. Fourth, agility is also a mindset – embedding in employees the spirit of ownership and the values of stewardship.

What you also learnt from the company stories is that agility is not just about speed. In addition, you need to choose the form and degree of organizational agility that suits your business; defaulting to agile is not the only option. The single most important thing to remember is: A creative design for organizational agility will go a long way in elevating adaptability as your next source of competitive advantage.

Endnotes

1 Haier Smart Home (2020) Haier strengthens industry-leading position with 9.05% revenue growth in 2019, Cision PR Newswire, 7 May, www.prnewswire.com/news-releases/haier-strengthens-industry-leading-position-with-9-05-revenue-growth-in-2019--301054597.html (archived at https://perma.cc/8U7M-X829)

2 Frynas, J G, Mol, M J and Mellahi, K (2018) Management innovation made in China: Haier's Rendanheyi, *California Management Review*, **61** (1), pp 71–93

3 Kanter, R M and Dai, N H (2018) Haier: Incubating entrepreneurs in a Chinese giant, Case Study, HBS 318-104, Harvard Business School Publishing, Boston

4 Haier (2018) IoT ecosystem brands – Shun Guang Platform: Creating an ecosystem of community interactions in the post-e-commerce era, Haier.com, 18 July, www.haier.com/global/press-events/news/20180718_142489.shtml (archived at https://perma.cc/VRJ8-KS8T)

5 Zhou, Y (2017) Exploration of interconnected factory mode: Haier Jiaozhou air conditioner interconnected factory, *Frontiers of Engineering Management*, **4** (4), pp 500–03

6 Haier Group (2015) Haier's cooperation with Apple reaps first fruits. Cision PR Newswire, 13 March, www.prnewswire.com/news-releases/haiers-cooperation-with-apple-reaps-first-fruits-300050162.html (archived at https://perma.cc/KX3Y-XKTP)

7 Hamel, G and Zanini, M (2018) The end of bureaucracy, *Harvard Business Review*, **96** (6), pp 50–59

8 Hamel, G and Zanini, M (2018) The end of bureaucracy, *Harvard Business Review*, **96** (6), pp 50–59

9 Zhang, R (2007) Raising Haier, *Harvard Business Review*, **85** (2), pp 141–46

10 *The Economist* (2013) Haier and higher, 11 October, www.economist.com/business/2013/10/11/haier-and-higher (archived at https://perma.cc/RR9U-SY2N)

11 Hamel, G and Zanini, M (2020) *Humanocracy*, Harvard Business Review Press

12 Lu, G and Mu, D (2020) Haier's adaptive strategy wins in the face of COVID-19 challenges, Forrester, 15 June, https://go.forrester.com/blogs/haiers-adaptive-strategy-wins-in-the-face-of-covid-19-challenges (archived at https://perma.cc/W7VA-XQH3)

13 Girod, S J G, de Pina, E P F, Svedjedal, S and Tanfour, M (2018) ING: An agile organization in a disruptive environment, Case Study, IMD-7-1852, IMD International, Lausanne

14 ING (2014) ING Bank Strategy Update: Think Forward, ING, 31 March, https://www.ing.com/Newsroom/News/Press-releases/PR/ING-Bank-Strategy-Update-Think-Forward-1.htm (archived at https://perma.cc/U5WR-VMFW)

15 Caplen, B (2017) ING's disruptive model: Interview with CEO Ralph Hamers, *The Banker*, 1 August, www.thebanker.com/Banking-Regulation-Risk/Management-Strategy/ING-s-disruptive-model-interview-with-CEO-Ralph-Hamers?ct=true (archived at https://perma.cc/4S9A-8KUH)

16 Girod, S J G, de Pina, E P F, Svedjedal, S and Tanfour, M (2018) ING: An agile organization in a disruptive environment, Case Study, IMD-7-1852, IMD International, Lausanne

17 ING (2016) ING strategy update: Accelerating Think Forward, ING Newsroom, 3 October, www.ing.com/Newsroom/News/Press-releases/ING-strategy-update-Accelerating-Think-Forward.htm (archived at https://perma.cc/TZ2P-ZWBV)

18 Rajan, R G and Wulf, J (2006) The flattening firm: Evidence from panel data on the changing nature of corporate hierarchies, *The Review of Economics and Statistics*, **88** (4), pp 759–73

19 Bartlett, C A and Ghoshal, S (2002) *Managing Across Borders: The transnational solution*, Harvard Business Press

20 Nonaka, I and Takeuchi, H (1995) *The Knowledge-Creating Company: How Japanese companies create the dynamics of innovation*, Oxford University Press

21 Prahalad, C K and Ramaswamy, V (2004) Co-creation experiences: The next practice in value creation, *Journal of interactive marketing*, **18** (3), pp 5–14

22 The authors wish to thank Telenor Group's Cecilie Heuch, Executive Vice President, Chief People and Sustainability Officer, and Thomas Øivind Andresen, Director, Culture Development and People Strategy, for pointing out this distinction.

07

Leadership Agility

FIVE LESSONS FROM THIS CHAPTER

1 In transforming for agility, leadership is more important than ever. Flattened hierarchies and revamped bureaucracies leave a constrained space for the traditional command and control. Therefore organizations that are successful in building agility demand a new, distributed type of leadership. This leadership is effective in addressing the tensions of stable vs nimble and complex vs simple.

2 Discover which elements of leadership should remain and what needs to change – both in degree and in kind.

3 You need to operationalize the four key competencies, or 4Cs, of leadership agility (Coaching, Cohesion, Connections, Cognition). Reconciling multiple leadership styles and competences is the essence of leadership agility.

4 While employees largely continue to be followers, they assume more leadership responsibilities. Discover what leadership means for them.

5 Tools: To diagnose your starting point, use the **Leadership Agility Assessment Test**. To craft your path forward you can explore the **Leadership Agility Canvas**.

The Time Has Come For a Reshuffle of Leadership Competences

Business agility is an embedded capability and a continuous process of addressing the tensions of stable vs nimble and complex vs simple. In strategy, legacy businesses aim to push back on the frontier of classic trade-offs. Embracing both/and choices, they play to win and to find new growth opportunities amidst uncertainty. At the organizational level, companies seek to flatten and transform their traditional hierarchies into networks of small teams that can test, learn and adapt fast. They work towards acquiring start-up characteristics such as flexibility and customer-centricity. They also capitalize on their scale, strategic direction, established power and influence, and achieve healthy complexity by differentiating their organizational choices. What connects these actions to the greater goals of building business agility is flexible behaviour and the willingness to embrace, rather than fear or ignore, the ongoing ambiguity and volatility of the outside environment.

Building strategic and organizational agility results in large-scale structural shifts. Power is transferred towards those who occupy positions of proximity to customers, such as product development teams and frontline service staff. Silos give way to diverse collaborative teams. Remote work is set to become the norm. Structures, systems and processes that used to form the lynchpin of the organization are now merely supporting the vision and the needs of self-organized units (Figure 7.1).

Figure 7.1   The new leadership space

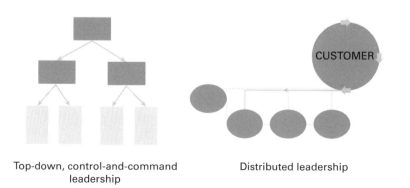

Top-down, control-and-command
leadership

Distributed leadership

These changes have redrawn the organizational map, sometimes beyond recognition. The ramification is that the physical space once occupied by leadership has suddenly vastly expanded. In a company whose frontline workers are just two layers of hierarchy away from the CEO, how much room is there for leaders? Is anybody at all left to lead? If everyone is a leader of some type, then who is the follower and why do we still talk about leadership? Could it be a case of 'Everybody is in charge, hence nobody is in charge'?

Building Agility Doesn't Eliminate the Need for Leadership

Not quite. Leadership is still present; it's just distributed across the organization. It takes place at executive and manager levels, among those who hold formal roles where leadership is expected, as well as among rank-and-file employees. The type of leadership that resonates with agility is a mix of formal and informal leadership. Informal leadership doesn't always coincide with job roles but occurs naturally in organizations that work towards a set of well-understood, transparently shared and continuously reviewed objectives.

A common source of rigidity in leadership is the gap between what is known as two icebergs of ignorance, frequently entrenched in large companies (Figure 7.2). Senior leaders have visibility into strategy but not into real customer and market situations. Studies show that CEOs

Figure 7.2   Icebergs of ignorance

Executives see **4%** of problems

Team managers see **9%** of problems

Team leads see **74%** of problems

Staff see **100%** of problems

Iceberg of ignorance

100%

5%
Strategy
understanding

SOURCE Adapted from Yoshida, 1989[2]

spend as little as 3 per cent of their time with customers and 72 per cent in meetings.[1] The reverse is true of the frontline. Middle managers – well, they are caught in the middle. As companies progress towards new forms of agility, becoming nimbler and simpler while streamlining their hierarchy, middle management is bound to shrink dramatically. Therefore, no shift towards organizational agility can manifest without teams and individuals at the frontline acting as leaders.

The objective of transforming leadership for agility is to create an organization that is flexible, resilient and innovative. From a leadership perspective, as hierarchies flatten they leave more space for internal (but also external, collaborative) networks and ecosystems. Another driving force behind distributed leadership is the blurred separation between doers and thinkers (Chapter 3). As individual employees contribute to their teams, strategy evolves through their daily choices rather than regular pronouncements by the C-suite. Once again, with power comes responsibility – at all layers of the organization.

To find out where you stand as a leader in this emergent, highly dynamic space, you can gauge your strengths, beliefs and capabilities in the Leadership Agility Assessment Test (Table 7.1).

Table 7.1   The Leadership Agility Assessment Test

Diagnosis: As a leader, how proficient am I in *Coaching?*				
My name:_____	Very Poor	Poor	Avrg	Good	Very Good
	1	2	3	4	5
I encourage collaborators to take risks and tolerate failure					
I do not hesitate to expose my vulnerabilities to create trust with my teams					
I accept that junior colleagues might have more expertise in some areas					
I give my collaborators regular, rather than infrequent, feedback					

(continued)

Table 7.1   (Continued)

Diagnosis: As a leader, how proficient am I in *Coaching?*					
My name:_____	**Very Poor**	**Poor**	**Avrg**	**Good**	**Very Good**
	1	**2**	**3**	**4**	**5**
I don't shy away from tough, personal conversations and I lead them constructively					
I am as comfortable with asking questions as I am with providing answers					
Based on facts, I can encourage a reversal of decisions quickly					
I role-model the behaviours I want my teams to embrace					
I regularly seek to improve the employee experience journey					

Diagnosis: As a leader, how proficient am I in creating *Cohesion?*					
	Very Poor	**Poor**	**Avrg**	**Good**	**Very Good**
	1	**2**	**3**	**4**	**5**
I have translated our strategy into simple, easy-to-remember statements					
I constantly tell our strategy story to empower employees					
My communication skills are as good as they should be					
I inspire purpose and show empathy					
I can distinguish team performance from individual performance well					
I take decisive action when performance is not there					

(continued)

Table 7.1   (Continued)

I make sure the rules of accountability are precisely defined					
I create the conditions for my collaborators to feel that they are stewards of the business					

Diagnosis: As a leader, how proficient am I in building _Connections?_	Very Poor	Poor	Avrg	Good	Very Good
	1	2	3	4	5
I make sure information flows transparently in my teams and organization					
I encourage the creation of communication tools that help us scout and collaborate better with external partners					
I encourage the creation of communication tools that help our employees collaborate					
I look for creating new synergies in and beyond my immediate realm of responsibility					
I spend as much time as I should dialoguing with customers					
I spend as much time as I should dialoguing with partners					
I make every effort to curb the politicking that entrenches unnecessary silos					
I am clear about when and where collaboration should take place. I have a good overview of the whole system to decide that					

(continued)

Table 7.1   (Continued)

Diagnosis: As a leader, how proficient am I in developing *Cognition?*					
	Very Poor	Poor	Avrg	Good	Very Good
	1	2	3	4	5
I strive to be more self-aware and to correct actions based on lessons learnt					
I have a complete focus on helping employees continually learn					
I am a keen learner and like to change my behaviour accordingly					
I keep the budget for learning and development as high as possible					
I make decisions based on facts and data and check that others do so too					
I spend all the energy and time I should scanning the external environment and making sense of changes, even if small					
I cultivate my listening skills with great care					
I encourage myself and others to shift from 'know it all' to 'learn it all'					
I encourage my collaborators to become thought leaders					

SOURCE Prof Stéphane JG Girod, IMD. Not to be used without permission

When the proper tools of leadership agility are in place, the result is a system that is adaptive and self-reinforcing:[3] Entrepreneurial leaders, typically concentrated at lower levels of the organization (Figure 7.3), create value for customers with new products and services. Collectively, they move the organization into unexplored

Figure 7.3   Adaptive, self-reinforcing leadership

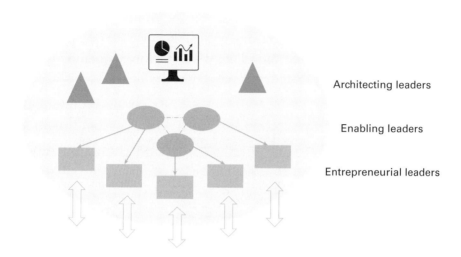

Architecting leaders

Enabling leaders

Entrepreneurial leaders

territory. Fewer but key enabling leaders, in the middle of the organization, make sure the entrepreneurs have the resources, knowledge and information they need. Architecting leaders, near the top, are tasked with monitoring the dashboard, particularly culture, high-level strategy, and structure.[4] Everyone keeps an eye on the external environment, although they scrutinize different horizons and facets of it and then make sense of it collectively, so that no pockets are overlooked. Haier (Chapter 6), for instance, treats employees like owners. They can exert as much change as necessary in order to keep the business relevant to customers. In this highly entrepreneurial internal ecosystem that resembles an open marketplace, there is very little that a top-down command from the C-suite, no matter how misguided, could derail.

What's Ahead For Leadership? Executives Share Their Views

In 2019 and 2020, 70 participants in several IMD executive education programmes were polled on the changes they expect to see in leadership. Their responses, which are captured in Figure 7.4, show that certain competences associated with top-down leadership are here to stay. In fact, fixing a clear direction and vision, along with communicating well, are perceived as more critical than ever. Similarly, customer-centricity and the emphasis on the frontline have pushed power, decision making and resources steadily down the organization. As such, the emphasis on controlling what employees do and how is likely to dissipate, replaced by a focus on achieving well-coordinated strategic objectives.

Figure 7.4   Executives' expectations of changes in leadership content

Remains the same	Different in quantity	Different in quality
• Tough conversations • Emotional support • Formulating strategy • Ensuring clarity of rules on accountability • Creating systems of collaboration	• Setting and communicating clearer direction • Stronger storytelling • Fewer formal leaders, especially in the middle ranks • Larger spans of control • Leading and doing at the same time (like in knowledge-based firms)	• Transparency • Coaching, enabling others • Emphasis on What, less on How • Servant leadership • Creating psychological safety • Reporting to, and/or including younger people • Digital acumen

Building Trust During Crisis: Clarins

During the 2020 crisis, Clarins Group took bold steps to short-circuit internal bureaucracy and empower employees by setting up three types of teams it called squads (Chapter 4): *What Now?, What Next?* and *What If?* Aware that once a certain degree of normality returned, the company might fall back on its old ways, executives at Clarins sought to sustain the change by continually adjusting how they lead themselves and others.

Organizationally, Clarins viewed the current innovations as a pilot from which to learn. Clarins scheduled a company-wide review post-crisis. Rather than dismantling the new squads, they will likely become a catalyst for a more substantive organizational redesign.

Individually, C-suite executives understand that for the transformation to stay the course, they must be the first to change. In many companies, senior executives' greatest fear about adopting agility is loss of power. The experience of Clarins Group demonstrates that this is unjustified. Its C-suite executives proved to be the champions of change by providing a sense of direction and stability and ensuring rigorous accountability. To create nimbleness, the leadership team had to learn how to create a secure base for employees to experiment and to support middle managers in building their own secure bases. By working on their self-awareness, comfort with ambiguity and vertical as well as lateral collaboration skills – all pre-conditions for building trust – Clarins Group's senior executives show what it is that needs to cascade down the organization in a sustained transformation.

Leadership to Juggle Different Styles and Competences

The old paradigm of leadership, reflecting Fordist and Taylorist scientific organization of work, was one of coercion. The prevailing style of leadership could be summarized as 'Do as I say'. Even the matrix organization serves to entrench this thinking. Impersonal and bureaucratic, it magnifies and reinforces status differences and boundaries between management and employees.[5] Inevitably, employees experience alienation from their work and start to engage in defensive behaviours.[6] This directly feeds organizational rigidity and an anti-learning culture of 'If it ain't broke, don't fix it'.

In today's uncertain world, leaders need to learn to use multiple leadership styles simultaneously. Our research reveals that leadership agility consists of reconciling four competences (4Cs) of distributed leadership. The 4Cs framework captures the ways in which leadership agility contributes to the reconciliation of the tensions between stable vs nimble and complex vs simple. Figure 7.5a looks at what is expected from formal roles of leadership, Figure 7.5b at the employee level. Collectively, the 4Cs crystallize the next practices of leadership to reinforce strategic and organizational agility.

In this framework, Coaching and empowering of individual employees helps them improve speed and customer intimacy (which is a link to nimble). It is balanced with Cohesion, which gives rise to shared purpose for achieving higher performance through a set of

Figure 7.5a   The 4Cs framework of leadership agility: Formal leaders

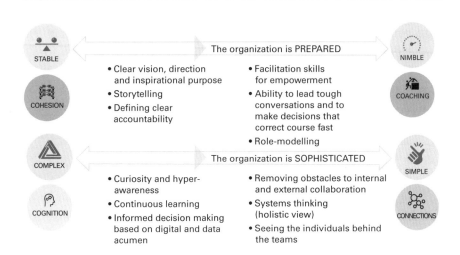

Figure 7.5b   The 4Cs framework of leadership agility: Employees

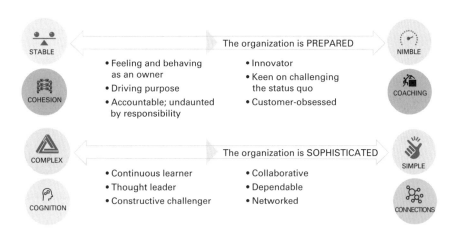

clearly communicated directions and a sense of stewardship (as a link to stability). Connections – the managing of the company's internal network and external ecosystems – aim to foster collaboration and commonalities where needed (boosting simplicity). Connections are balanced with Cognition, which is leaders' ability to stimulate their own and others' curiosity; continuously unlearn and relearn by looking at facts; and constructively challenge each other (which develops healthy complexity).

Underpinning Each of the 4Cs: A Leader's Self-Awareness

A key aspect of leadership agility that permeates the framework is self-awareness. This is undeniably the toughest part of building leadership agility. Surveys consistently point to lack of self-awareness as one of the main obstacles to agility transformation.[7] Discarding a long-standing control orientation[8] and confronting, possibly for the first time, one's own psychological processes[9] are equally painful to the majority of seasoned executives. More hassle than it's worth, then? Far from it: In a 2018 worldwide CEO study of 400 corporate leaders conducted by Egon Zehnder, 79 per cent of respondents said that a company could only undergo successful transformation if the person at the helm also engaged in self-renewal.[10]

There are parallels to be drawn with cross-cultural communication: The consensus is that it is nearly impossible for people to step outside their own cultural conditioning.[11] It is a programming developed in childhood and long turned into an iceberg, with 90 per cent of it submerged and therefore inaccessible to conscious examination and enquiry.[12] The same can be said about leadership. Managers and executives who for decades thrived in a command-and-control culture are unlikely to embrace a coaching, mentoring and facilitating leadership style overnight.

Despite that, honing self-awareness is useful and many of the skills and competences leaders acquire in the process can indeed be transferred. As the CEO role transitions from CEO as captain to CEO as steward, employees and other stakeholders expect to see a strong measure of empathy and personal vulnerability. CEOs are no longer know-it-alls. On the contrary, they are open about not having all the answers. They understand that exposing their weaknesses will go a long way in generating trust. They also accept that younger experts may be better informed, particularly about what goes on in the digital domain. From former Xerox CEO Ursula Burns to Microsoft's Satya Nadella, CEOs who speak candidly about their minority or immigrant backgrounds, childhood privations and parenting challenges are perceived as strong, authentic leaders.[13] As IMD's professor of leadership George Kohlrieser puts it, responsible leadership starts with the leader as a person – their integrity, values, mission, personality and life experiences.[14]

4Cs: Coaching and Creativity

'Taking people with you' in the 2020s business environment requires that formal leaders provide employees with guidance and support rather than instructions.[15] This coaching and facilitating style of formal leadership builds resilience in teams as well as individuals and allows them to operate with confidence. It also speaks to the needs of the millennial workforce, accustomed to receiving frequent feedback and encouragement. Leadership agility is built on relating to others, not demanding from them.[16]

The coaching style is empowering in that it allows for candid and specific feedback including criticism. Combined with a sense of personal caring, these tough conversations produce what Kim Scott, a former executive at Google, Facebook and Apple, calls 'radical candour'.[17] In the bureaucratic order, managers often tried their best to sidestep these 'personal' and 'uncomfortable' conversations, keeping the peace but often at the cost of preventing individual employees from learning and growth. In the world of responding to disruptive change with agility, you don't have that luxury anymore. Connecting with individuals on a deeply personal level is what it takes to overcome the legacy of impersonal, cog-in-the-wheel people management.

As a result, coaching as a leadership competence is a great source of organizational nimbleness. Leaders who are competent coaches don't just empower their staff and then tell them, 'Go forth and prosper.' Importantly, these leaders are able to correct the course of teams' actions where necessary by making tough decisions. Until late 2020, Herman Tange was in charge of marketing and customer experience for ING's business banking. He encouraged his tribe to explore and quickly kill new ideas that were not panning out. At the same time and in keeping with the company's QBR (Chapter 6), he retained the leeway to reprioritize budgets and investments away from unproductive experimenting.

Coaching-competent leaders know how to build the psychological safety that employees need to experiment, ie to fail often, learn and succeed faster. When empowering others, formal leaders shouldn't underestimate employees' anxiety as the 'comforting' hierarchy is abandoned. Creating a secure base requires setting up non-threatening spaces and contexts where no questions are out of bounds and learning from failed experiments is encouraged. It is also about accepting ideas and the influence of junior colleagues. In some contexts, an agile leader's best contribution to the organization and its innovativeness will be to follow others.[18]

It's not just employees who may be afraid of the transition. Amongst formal leaders, there are two types of fears. Senior leaders, having previously micromanaged everything, fear loss of control. For middle managers, who are typically younger, fear comes from competing with junior talent. In a flatter organization, middle managers who are scrambling to get a leg up the (now much shorter) ladder are less prepared to encourage and coach their sometimes more talented younger colleagues, or for that matter to collaborate with one another. These managers will resist empowerment and delegation. Senior leaders who are more secure in their experience and career might not harbour the same degree of resistance. This is why agility transformation requires addressing the politics of organizations through self-confidence building and extreme attention to career progression for the middle.

Finally, coaching-competent leaders role-model the critical behaviours they want their teams to adopt. For example, T-Mobile's John Legere embodied the service-oriented, customer-centric behaviours he expected from his workforce. His colourful, over-the-top personality made a segment once full of opaque practices and customer frustration look vibrant and exciting again, for customers as well as the young frontline staff who interacted with them. Legere spent many hours daily on social media, poking fun at competitors. His willingness to steer clear of bland corporate speak and to court controversy only reinforced the message.[19]

Among Employees, Coaching-Style Leadership Translates into Creativity and Innovation

Coaching-style leadership creates an environment that enables and supports certain behaviours in others. Some scholars go as far as to describe it as an operating system.[20] While the label may be new, outstanding companies have used their own version of 'leadership OS' for decades. In an interview for the 1986 book, *Kaizen*, Eiji Toyoda, chairman of Toyota Motor Corporation, commented, 'Our workers provide 1.5 million suggestions a year, and 95 per cent of them are put to practical use. There is an almost tangible concern for improvement in the air at Toyota.'[21]

Companies that build leadership agility will attract and nurture employees who feel energized by solving customer problems and are unafraid to challenge the status quo. Staff at companies like Haier, ING and Deutsche Bahn have long internalized the notion that new products and services won't 'fly' unless employees address specific, tried-and-tested customer needs and pain points.

Many agile companies come to the realization that what they achieved in customer-centricity works just as well with internal customers, ie employees. So do marketing and market research tools such as journey maps and persona development. As your business nudges towards agility, doesn't your human capital deserve the same attention that you accord to customers? It does, and that's why mapping and designing employee experience is now a valid and vibrant aspect of leadership agility.[22]

4Cs: Cohesion

Although coaching facilitates an organization's bottom-up narratives and informal leadership, agile organizations don't discard top-down mechanisms altogether. On the contrary, when sensitively applied, the qualities and practices grouped in the 4Cs Cohesion pillar are a source of great stability and contribute to empowering employees within a solid framework. Cohesion provides a counterbalance to the nimbleness gained through a coaching style of leadership. It creates alignment behind a common direction and purpose. A 2018 BCG survey involving more than 200 companies showed that addressing purpose, leadership and culture is at the heart of the transformation effort and can increase odds of sustained impact by 50 per cent.[23]

Agile leaders achieve this alignment by setting clear goals and communicating them through appealing yet strategic internal story-telling. For business agility to work, leaders are expected to engage in a lot more storytelling than in the past. Thus, part of John Legere's choice of cultivating a consistently eccentric image, presence and media footprint (as the action-hero 'un-CEO' of an 'un-carrier') served as a daily reminder to the company's workforce that T-Mobile was actively disrupting its industry, not just responding to disruption. In a 'medium is the message' style, he further galvanized support from customers as well as staff through his Sunday morning podcasts and social media challenges. These communication strategies weaved together a sense of shared purpose with motivation and emotion. Having employees throw an ice bucket on their CEO may be viewed as a cheap stunt, but in the context of the US wireless industry it symbolized T-Mobile's commitment to pushing the envelope and continually reinventing itself. Similarly, ING captured the strategy dimension of its transformation in punchy, memorable and broad but specific-enough statements, such as its promise to customers to 'make banking clear and easy, available anytime and anywhere and to em-power them to stay a step ahead in life and business'.[24] This is an example of leadership agility that draws on simple rather than hard-and-fast rules.

Indeed, simple rules can work wonders in cohesion. But they have to be acted on every day, not to mention with accountability and dis-ciplined execution. Successful agile leaders have a clear sense of who is responsible for what.[25] Coaching-style leadership creates room for freedom, but that freedom has to be balanced with control if a certain amount of formal planning remains important (Chapter 3). As the old adage goes, with freedom comes responsibility – or, in the agility con-text, accountability. Figure 7.3 illustrates this balancing act. It shows that the bulk of a CEO's ammunition will always come from setting a decisive direction – especially when it comes to sharing resources; fac-ing crushing uncertainty; articulating clear rules; bringing them home through effective storytelling; and demanding accountability through KPIs and other metrics. Coaching may give some leeway to underperformers, but true leaders will step in and call the shots.

Cohesion and Employee-Driven Leadership

Employees in an agile organization are not freed from disciplined delivery and a sense of ownership, or encouraged to concentrate their effort on playful, open-ended innovation only. Workers who believe in and identify with the company's purpose will be undaunted by the responsibilities that agility has placed upon them. Distributed leadership releases the power of employees' inner commitment. Also known as intrinsic motivation – an expression of the innate human need for self-actualization[26] – it has been shown to work better than external rewards such as bonuses.[27] Empowered employees believe that their contribution can make a difference. The outcome is a greater sense of stewardship of the company. Formal processes, eg quarterly business reviews, help enhance this trait by holding employees accountable.

Companies undergoing agility transformation, such as GE and Deutsche Telekom, know how to tackle this accountability. On shared digital spaces, their employees post tutorials, videos and other stories about their experiences and accomplishments – for instance, in using agile ways of working and training their peers in these new methodologies. T-Mobile has similarly embraced employee-driven, bottom-up narratives and storytelling. Its social media content pushes the idea that 'heroes' are not just mythical creatures. They include the carrier's young frontline workers who diffuse problems on a daily basis, entertain irate customers and steadily build their employer's reputation as a service leader among US mobile operators.

4Cs: Connections

The Connections pillar is about removing obstacles to internal and external collaboration. Fundamentally, it is about managing across silos. On the complex-vs-simple continuum, it pulls the organization towards simplicity by uniting collaborators, both internally and externally in the ecosystem. By 2020, with the digital vortex in full force, legacy companies like Siemens and GE had to reinvent themselves as platform businesses. The proliferation of digital dictates that executives' focus be external as much as internal.[28]

Increasingly, forging connections goes hand in hand with developing strategic agility. Deutsche Telekom's Magenta Connectivity tool (Chapter 3) encapsulates DT's effort to link internal collaboration (by executives and employees) with external partners including clusters, incubators and app developers. At Haier, the platform leader leads by influence and focuses on sharing knowledge as well as brokering internal connections with transparency. Because leaders do not set objectives for the microenterprises who are part of their platform, they have more time to help microenterprises work through issues and find commonalities and synergies. Haier platform leaders also help their platform members source ideas from clients in regular roadshows. This T-shaped role encourages learning from the fringe. In 2017, John Chambers, then CEO of Cisco, told other CEOs at Harvard, 'a decade or two ago, CEOs could be in their office with spreadsheets, executing on strategy. Now, if you're not listening to the market and catching market transitions… if you're not understanding that you constantly need to reinvent yourself every three to five years, you as a CEO will not survive.'[29]

'Collaborating across silos' is an old mantra. Yet silos are not automatically detrimental to agility – after all, every organization needs deep pockets of knowledge in order to excel. Only when silos operate independently and don't share the created value do they become an obstacle to achieving agility. ING's formal leaders (tribe leads and the C-suite) think strategically about which parts of the company should be connected so that value creation and capture can be amplified throughout the bank. Call centre and branch staff must be incentivized to share insights with product development, for instance. Alongside incentives, fostering this connection may take new processes and communications tools. Moreover, agile leaders work to strengthen the organization's resilience by getting those parts of the company that are under stress supported by those whose capacity and bandwidth are stretched to a lesser extent. Similarly, the edgy new squads at Clarins were time-poor and juggling a mass of tasks – but they were also free to marshal resources from the mainstream organization as necessary.

Seeing the Individuals Behind the Teams

Managing and measuring performance amidst agility transformation is a work in progress for many businesses. In that context, facilitating the right connections also applies to individuals as opposed to teams: Excessively prioritizing teamwork at the expense of the individual, an organization that is transforming for agility runs the risk of developing a totalitarian approach.

In the initial stages of their transformation, companies like ING focused on team outcomes. With work roles yet to be properly defined, individual performance was deemed too fine-grained and slippery to handle. Soon enough, however, these organizations were reminded that they could ill afford to exclude individual employees from the equation. If they did, employees not only showed a loss of motivation, they also started falling back on the old top-down, waiting-for-instructions thinking and behaviours.

Despite what is said about the power of teams – especially diverse, multidisciplinary, customer-centric teams – in developing agility, agile transformations are not solely about teams. They must make room for individuals and their talents, aspirations and contributions. It is people who do the heavy lifting in any organizational change. The idea of an organization's vision and mission always presupposed there was more to leadership than coercion (telling people what to do) or transactional exchange (buying their time). Individualized consideration has been considered one of the hallmarks of transformational leadership since the 1990s.[30] Correspondingly, leadership agility needs to make space for individual employees and identify the goals that provide them with job satisfaction, competitive compensation rates, and appealing career development opportunities.

Yesterday's bureaucracies and hierarchies, in their quest for 'modern', ie rationalistic, management, depended on impersonalizing the worker. In the context of 2020s' proliferation of AI, Big Data, online work, surveillance and other digital tools, it is important that companies do not revert to the same paradigm, reducing individual employees to a number on a screen. As an agility architect, it is your responsibility to prevent this kind of dystopian workforce future, one that is dominated by the tyranny of technology and data.

Connections and Employee-Driven Leadership

Meanwhile, employees also exercise leadership by building connections in ways that are similar to fraternizing outside work – open, networked and collaborative yet dependable. In rigid, siloed companies, these connections will often fly under the radar. As a matter of fact, employees may feel no sense of obligation whatsoever to help someone from a different part of the organization. In other words, employee leadership will only thrive in collectives that share a holistic understanding of the system and how their joint efforts contribute to higher goals.

4Cs: Cognition

Cognition is about how leaders recognize and perceive facts, trends and causal relationships. In an agile company, cognition primarily takes the form of continuous learning and informed decision making. As fast change and turbulence are the norm, the focus is shifting from a knowledge-based to a learning-based organization. Leaders at companies that have transformed for agility, such as ING, are the ones who institute the industry's highest learning & development budgets. In addition, they set up clear leadership roles to govern expertise and craftsmanship development.

Agile leaders are also committed to building data-driven organizational cultures. Increasingly, data cultures are set to replace hierarchical, relationship-based ('old boy networks') and ego-driven organizational cultures. Building a data culture means that leaders understand, appreciate, decide and act on data much of the time, instead of seniority, routine, precedents or anecdotal evidence. A data culture generates insights that allow companies to balance simplicity with diversity in their product portfolios, the way China's 7Fresh chain of supermarkets keeps the stock in its outlets physically simple yet richly tailored to its customers' actual preferences as captured via digital.

A rebel like John Legere is a good example of this new quality of knowing and sensing as a facet of leadership agility. Ostensibly a 'shock jock', Legere stimulated organizational agility by energizing the workforce, deploying new elements of strategic agility and personally embodying attributes of leadership agility. These changes had a very real effect on the bottom line: Between 2013 and 2019, T-Mobile captured 80 per cent of the US wireless industry's post-paid phone growth.[31] Despite militating against the 'system' (in his case, a moribund industry ecosystem where handset manufacturers were hiding behind carriers and jointly denying consumers any extent of power, autonomy or transparency), he was a meticulous observer of what was happening in that outside environment; a doer as well as a hyperaware thinker.[32] His complex, multi-layered persona illustrates the importance of leaders' self-knowledge as a gateway to learning.

Satya Nadella's predecessor (2000–14) at Microsoft, Steve Ballmer, thrived on public self-aggrandizement, cultivated a larger-than-life CEO persona, and opposed open-source innovation. By 2014, Microsoft's share price stalled and the company was heading for a decline. Nadella, on the other hand, upheld empathy as the foundation of reinventing Microsoft's culture and spent much of his first year as CEO listening to and learning from others: 'Listening was the most important thing I accomplished each day, because it would build the foundation of my leadership for years to come.' At the same time, he put forward a vision of empowering users and organizations to 'do more'.[33] Much of the impetus behind the cultural change Nadella effected at Microsoft had to do with turning the company's complacent, 'know-it-all' engineers to, in his words, 'learn-it-alls' who could propel Microsoft into a leadership position in cloud.[34]

Employees As Continuous Learners

In an agility transformation, learning isn't confined to classrooms or training courses. Adult learning is said to work best when triggered by an actual need. Therefore, employees take charge of their own learning needs, filling their metaphorical 'backpacks' with relevant new knowledge and skills. In contrast, 75 per cent of information that isn't applied in the real world will be lost within days – a phenomenon scholars describe as the forgetting curve.[35]

With support and encouragement from the employer, self-directed learners can become established as thought leaders. ING staff, for example, are known to publish research papers and present at conferences and other industry events. Naturally attracted to peer learning and teaching, thought leaders help employees learn how to listen to others and challenge their colleagues in a constructive way. With a strong cohort of thought leaders among employees, a data culture isn't limited to the executive suite or even middle management. The frontline is where data analytics can truly flourish, almost in a social movement-like fashion.[36] It is where data gets operationalized and becomes an agile business's key capability. Eventually, curiosity about how digital shapes other segments and industries leads to learning that will help inform company strategy.

Sense-making

Although rarely acknowledged as a leadership capability, sense-making brings together a diversity of perspectives to arrive at an understanding and then test and refine it, or dismiss it if necessary.[37] Managers who are involved in sense-making can be located anywhere within the organization. Sense-making leads to hyperawareness as a precondition for leadership agility. Leaders who are hyperaware can better assess the need for changes of direction. Strategic agility, particularly its embrace of both/and thinking and decision making, likewise emphasizes sense-making as a way of accepting diverse points of view. These are incorporated into sources of deviant creativity as well as leadership unity. Sense-making is not just the domain of formal leaders: Increasingly, it draws on insights from junior managers who are unafraid to step out of the office and map out stakeholder pain points, consult non-traditional sources, uncover patterns and, importantly, revise their own assumptions as necessary.[38]

Conclusions

How should you make sense of these developments?

1 Learn to be comfortable with a more distributed leadership model. Transforming for agility changes both the parameter of the space where leadership plays out and the actual content of leadership. In highly flexible organizations, leadership becomes distributed. Employees at every level of the organization can take initiatives and lead, particularly in the context of resolving customer requirements and navigating unforeseen external developments. This means some leadership competences and roles are more devolved at the employee level. But hierarchical, position-based leadership for middle and top management remains equally important.

2 **Become proficient in multiple leadership styles and master the relevant competences.** In addition to capturing these new dynamics, the 4Cs framework of leadership agility will guide you as you address the organizational tensions at the heart of agility transformation: (a) releasing the leadership capability and personal potential in managers and employees throughout the organization while at the same time nurturing and reinforcing what they share – the company's purpose and direction; and (b) learning how to manage self, others and the organization's network – particularly the new forms of open innovation and external as well as internal collaboration that are powered by digital.

Throughout, it is worth bearing in mind that leadership agility increasingly deals with paradoxes and contradictory demands (Table 7.2) and involves a range of leadership styles and skills. Among these, the competences you inherited from the old command-and-control system may still stand you in good stead – for instance,

Table 7.2 The paradoxes of leadership agility[39]

Enabler ⟷	Disruptor
Curiosity, learning, collaboration, transparency	Thoughtfully decisive, digitally literate, questioning the status quo, creating new ways of thinking, close to customer trends
Influencer ⟷	Target of influence
Sense-making, setting direction, energizing others	Examining own assumptions, understanding and managing self, learning
Incremental learner ⟷	Transformative learner
Open to new insights, particularly from customers and networks	Challenging the status quo, stepping outside one's own expertise

SOURCE S Hayward (2018) *The Agile Leader: How to create an agile business in the digital age*, Kogan Page when it comes to injecting a sense of cohesion into your leadership. Granted, leaders in the 2020s are expected to be authentic – to empathize, inspire and show vulnerability and to face the market head-on with a personal brand of charisma and magic. But the instrumental, operating elements of their role haven't gone away.

What links all the 4Cs is a sense of self-awareness. Holding up one's deepest assumptions to scrutiny – by self and others – is painful and uncomfortable but very necessary. There is an array of tools and techniques available that will help you gauge and direct your leadership style. To establish yourself as a decisive, visionary and courageous leader, you will have to put in the hard work of introspection, flexibility and taking up new habits and behaviours.

3 **Learn where you really need to change as a leader.** Some aspects of formal leadership remain the same while others change – both qualitatively and quantitatively. Table 7.3 shows which components of leadership agility are merely undergoing evolution and which ones characterize the next practices of a management reset.

4 **Use the Leadership Agility Canvas to craft your path ahead.** The Leadership Agility Canvas (Figure 7.6) starts with your strengths and guides your approach to becoming a more agile leader. Where relevant, you will need to consider how to be simultaneously better at command-and-control and coaching-style leadership. The outcomes, if applied effectively, will give a great boost to the long-term project of transforming your business for agility.

Table 7.3 At leadership level, why business agility is more than an evolution: It is a management reset

Leadership	
Evolution	**Management reset**
• In leading yourself and others, be aware of multiple leadership styles • If you are in senior or middle management, you need to communicate directions clearly • Continue to improve your storytelling and communication skills	• In leading yourself and others, be proficient in multiple leadership styles: coaching, cohesion, building connections, cognition • Distinguish between positional and non-positional leadership: in a distributed model, employees assume some leadership responsibilities

(continued)

Table 7.3   (Continued)

Leadership	
Evolution	**Management reset**
• Continue to work on your self-awareness • For those in senior and middle management, it is important to inspire people with purpose and direction • Stick to precise rules of accountability	• Learn to lead in a flatter hierarchy by emphasizing direction, resolving bottlenecks and shifting attention to controlling outputs rather than inputs • As you keep paying attention to rules of accountability, give as much attention to individuals as you give to teams • Prepare for the changes ahead by going beyond the command-and-control style of leadership. Instead, know when to listen; stimulate the right questions; accept that you don't have all the answers; learn from junior colleagues • Develop your digital acumen and be rigorous in applying data to fact-based decision making • Build the secure base that will give employees the confidence to experiment, even if they fail • Make sure transferrable learning takes place after failures as well as successes • Learn to navigate the paradoxes of leadership agility (eg being an influencer and a target of influence) • Role-model a collaborative, boundary-spanning leadership style

Figure 7.6 The Leadership Agility Canvas

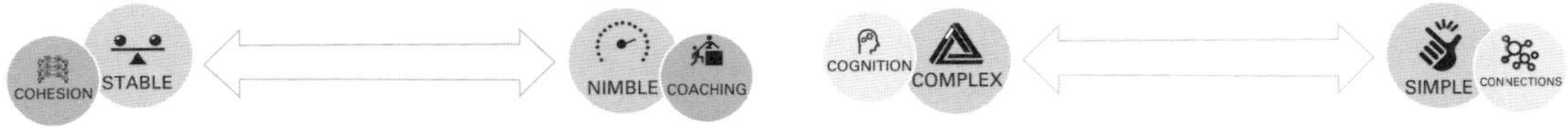

	COHESION / STABLE	NIMBLE / COACHING	COGNITION / COMPLEX	SIMPLE / CONNECTIONS
	• Defining vision, direction and purpose • Storytelling capabilities • Holding individuals and teams accountable	• Facilitating • Ability to lead tough conversations and to change course fast • Resilience	• Curiosity • Self-awareness • Systems thinking	• Digital acumen • Removing obstacles to internal and external collaboration • Seeing the individuals behind the teams
Your current strengths				
Your current weaknesses				
Your next steps				
How you will do both				

SOURCE Prof Stéphane JG Girod, IMD. Not to be used without permission

Endnotes

1 Porter, M E and Nohria, N (2018) How CEOs manage time, *Harvard Business Review*, **96** (4), pp 42–51

2 Yoshida, S (1989) The iceberg of ignorance, *International Quality Symposium*

3 Whiteley, J and Whiteley, A (2006) *Core Values and Organizational Change: Theory and practice*, World Scientific Publishing Company

4 Ancona, D, Backman, E and Isaacs, K (2019) Nimble leadership, *Harvard Business Review*, **97**, pp 74–83

5 Winter, R P, Sarros, J C and Tanewski, G A (1997) Reframing managers' control orientations and practices: A proposed organizational learning framework, *International Journal of Organizational Analysis*, 5 (1), p 9

6 Ashforth, B E and Lee, R T (1990) Defensive behavior in organizations: A preliminary model, *Human Relations*, **43** (7), pp 621–48

7 Lovich, D, Beauchene, V, Hunke, N and Goel, S (2020) Is leadership your agile blindspot? BCG, 26 May, www.bcg.com/publications/2020/leadership-agile-blindspot (archived at https://perma.cc/6K2U-57PN)

8 Kofman, F and Senge, P M (1993) Communities of commitment: The heart of learning organizations, *Organizational Dynamics*, **22** (2), pp 5–23

9 Haslam, S A, Reicher, S D and Platow, M J (2010) *The New Psychology of Leadership: Identity, influence and power*, Psychology Press; Brunklaus, M, Chim, L, Lovich, D and Rehberg, B (2019) Do you have the courage to be an agile leader? BCG, 3 January, www.bcg.com/publications/2019/courage-to-be-agile-leader (archived at https://perma.cc/6DGA-F6PE)

10 Ensser, M and Najipoor-Schütte, K (2018) *Harvard Business Manager*: Command and control is obsolete, EgonZehnder, 19 April, www.egonzehnder.com/what-we-do/ceo-search-succession/news/harvard-business-manager-command-and-control-is-obsolete (archived at https://perma.cc/528B-NBKP)

11 Lewis, R (2010) *When Cultures Collide: Leading across cultures*, Nicholas Brealey Publishing

12 Schein, E H (2010) *Organizational Culture and Leadership*, vol 2, John Wiley & Sons

13 Nadella, S, Shaw, G and Nichols, J T (2017) *Hit Refresh: The quest to rediscover Microsoft's soul and imagine a better future for everyone*, Harper Business

14 Kohlrieser, G (2006) *Hostage at the Table: How leaders can overcome conflict, influence others, and raise performance*, vol 145, John Wiley & Sons

15 Ibarra, H and Scoular, A (2019) The leader as coach, *Harvard Business Review*, 97 (6), pp 110–19

16 Hipp, R, Bellm, E and Geck, T (2018) The success formula of winning corporate transformations: 7 recommendations to get your organization ready to transform, Porsche Consulting, https://newsroom.porsche.com/dam/jcr:56f99787-4f20-4681-b72d-f309585f5fe9/20181031_The%20success%20formula%20of%20winning_A%20Porsche%20Consulting%20Paper_(C)_2018.pdf (archived at https://perma.cc/YY84-2783)

17 Scott, K (2019) *Radical Candor: Be a kick-ass boss without losing your humanity*, St Martin's Press

18 Ancona, D, Backman, E and Isaacs, K (2019) Nimble leadership, *Harvard Business Review*, 97, pp 74–83

19 Legere, J (2017) T-Mobile's CEO on winning market share by trash-talking rivals, *Harvard Business Review*, January–February, https://hbr.org/2017/01/t-mobiles-ceo-on-winning-market-share-by-trash-talking-rivals (archived at https://perma.cc/RY2R-LFAV)

20 Kinley, N and Ben-Hur, S (2020) *Leadership OS*, Springer International Publishing

21 Graban, M (2013) Eiji Toyoda, credited with developing TPS and expanding Toyota into North America, passes away at 100, Lean Blog, 20 September, www.leanblog.org/2013/09/eiji-toyoda-credited-with-expanding-toyota-and-tps-into-north-america-passes-away-at-100 (archived at https://perma.cc/7J3W-T829)

22 Henretta, D and Chopra-McGowan, A (2017) 5 ways to help employees keep up with digital transformation, *Harvard Business Review*, 27 September, https://hbr.org/2017/09/5-ways-to-help-employees-keep-up-with-digital-transformation (archived at https://perma.cc/C396-9BG5)

23 Hemerling, J, Kilmann, J and Matthews, D (2018) The head, heart, and hands of transformation, BCG, 5 November, www.bcg.com/publications/2018/head-heart-hands-transformation (archived at https://perma.cc/K4UX-A2WK)

24 ING (nd) Purpose and strategy, www.ing.com/About-us/Profile/
Purpose-strategy.htm (archived at https://perma.cc/84QW-DET9)

25 Lange, K, Joseph, F and Karner, M B (2019) Leadership capabilities:
Transforming your organisation for the digital age, SMU, 25
November, https://cmp.smu.edu.sg/ami/article/20191125/leadership-
capabilities (archived at https://perma.cc/H8TS-WYLJ)

26 Maslow, A H (1971) *Self-Actualization*, Big Sur Recordings

27 Ben-Hur, S and Kinley, N (2016) Intrinsic motivation: The missing
piece in changing employee behaviour, *Perspectives for Managers*,
(192), p 1

28 Hipp, R, Bellm, E and Geck, T (2018) The success formula of winning
corporate transformations: 7 recommendations to get your
organization ready to transform, Porsche Consulting,
https://newsroom.porsche.com/dam/jcr:56f99787-4f20-4681-b72d-
f309585f5fe9/20181031_The%20success%20formula%20of%20
winning_A%20Porsche%20Consulting%20Paper_(C)_2018.pdf
(archived at https://perma.cc/YY84-2783)

29 Groysberg, B and Gregg, T (2020) How tech CEOs are redefining the
top job, *MIT Sloan Management Review*, **61** (2), pp 21–24

30 Avolio, B J, Waldman, D A and Yammarino, F J (1991) Leading in the
1990s: The four Is of transformational leadership, *Journal Of
European Industrial Training*, www.emerald.com/insight/content/
doi/10.1108/03090599110143366/full/html (archived at https://perma.
cc/B4UF-6S3S)

31 T-Mobile (2020) T-Mobile completes merger with Sprint to create the
new T-Mobile, www.t-mobile.com/news/un-carrier/t-mobile-sprint-
one-company (archived at https://perma.cc/BES2-AMSC)

32 de Vries, M F K (2010) *Reflections on Character and Leadership: On
the couch with Manfred Kets de Vries*, John Wiley & Sons

33 Ibarra, H, Rattan, A and Johnston, A (2018) Satya Nadella at
Microsoft: Instilling a growth mindset, Case Study, HBR case no.
LBS128, Harvard Business School Publishing, Boston

34 Ibarra, H, Rattan, A and Johnston, A (2018) Satya Nadella at
Microsoft: Instilling a growth mindset, Case Study, HBR case no.
LBS128, Harvard Business School Publishing, Boston

35 Glaveski, S (2019) Where companies go wrong with learning and
development, *Harvard Business Review*, 2 October, https://hbr.
org/2019/10/where-companies-go-wrong-with-learning-and-
development (archived at https://perma.cc/R2CX-PCZH)

36 *Harvard Business Review* (2020) How to lead a data-driven culture, Webinar, 24 June

37 Ancona, D, Williams, M and Gerlach, G (2020) The overlooked key to leading through chaos, *MIT Sloan Management Review*, 8 September, https://sloanreview.mit.edu/article/the-overlooked-key-to-leading-through-chaos (archived at https://perma.cc/2HBG-ETSC)

38 Ancona, D, Williams, M and Gerlach, G (2020) The overlooked key to leading through chaos, *MIT Sloan Management Review*, 8 September, https://sloanreview.mit.edu/article/the-overlooked-key-to-leading-through-chaos (archived at https://perma.cc/2HBG-ETSC)

37 Hayward, S (2018) *The Agile Leader: How to create an agile business in the digital age,* Kogan Page, London

PART THREE

How to Transform for Agility Successfully

By now you have a better understanding of:

- The Why of business agility: A response both to uncertainty and to a business world where traditional, 20th-century hierarchy and bureaucracy have outlived their usefulness.

- What is business agility: An ongoing, open-ended process of embedding new capabilities, recognizing built-in tensions and reconciling, through both/and solutions, competing (even paradoxical) demands in strategy, organizational design and leadership. Reducing these tensions enables flexibility in the face of high uncertainty. In turn, the extra flexibility translates into stronger entrepreneurship and innovation. You are now playing to win, not just to stay in the game.

As outlined in Chapter 1, managers who are lacking clarity on the Why and the What share many misgivings that surround the concept and the importance of business agility. Typically, they are either sceptical or they confuse agility with 'agile' in its aggressively peddled meaning of specific agile methods like scrum or lean start-up.

We hope you are now amongst the executives who 'get it' – those who are on board and enthused with the richness, ambition and long-term goals of developing business agility. As you read this, many are out there in the trenches, redesigning their own businesses, redefining strategy and nurturing new mindsets within the workforce. Learning on the go, what is it they are grappling with the most?

Executives who take part in IMD's programmes raise questions such as, 'What should agility look like for us?' Or, 'Agility is a tool, not a goal. How can I make everyone in my organization understand what the goal is?' They find that the way their firms approach change has to change. They find that developing agility is not a one-off initiative that can be ticked as 'Done' by June 30 or December 31. It's about creating a state where adaptation and entrepreneurship can happen when needed, without creating chaos and loss of direction.

Most importantly, they discovered that, although dismantling the old system (bureaucratic, hierarchical, removed from customer…) can't happen fast enough, that system cannot be replaced with 'nothing' – a free-for-all of no rules, no job scopes and no accountability. A sense of stability, direction and leadership – even a degree of top-down control – are still necessary. But the quality and the underpinning logic of this new type of leading, organizing and strate-gizing are vastly different from their old selves. Therein lies the ex-citement as well as the challenge, and it is not without its own fears and hesitations. It was never going to be easy.

This is what brings us to the last piece of the puzzle: The How of agility transformations. There are several things to note:

- First, this is a journey, not a quick fix. Nonetheless, to achieve results, the journey should have specific milestones and at least an outline of a resolution.

- Second, the journey isn't always a sequential change management programme. It often consists of testing, piloting, learning and iterating; it's about being creative and inventive. Incidentally, this doesn't prevent you from 'copying ideas with pride'.

- Third, although strategic and organizational agility transformations have their own specificities, both entail learning how to reduce tensions between seemingly contradictory objectives and priorities.

08

Managing the Trade-offs of Strategic Agility

FIVE LESSONS FROM THIS CHAPTER

1 Many executives fail to identify the key trade-offs they need to minimize as the first step towards greater agility. When they do, they may not be decisive enough to address the resulting tensions for fear of challenging the status quo or because they don't know how to resolve them.

2 Learn how to reduce the inherent tensions in strategic agility and address the challenges decisively.

3 With the right mix of organizational and leadership elements that are suited to your company's context and aspirations, you can successfully leverage the mix to tackle the tensions of strategic agility.

4 The tensions need to be reduced comprehensively. Companies that pay attention to some but not to others will not be as strategically agile.

5 Digital is not just a source of disruption that firms are yet to come fully to grips with. Increasingly, digital is also the missing link that minimizes trade-offs and allows you to integrate competing demands in building strategic agility.

The five trade-offs that characterize strategic agility need to be minimized holistically. This presents executives with its own set of challenges and roadblocks. For instance, you may well ask yourself:

- 'We've got to try launching new ventures. But how do we make big-enough money from them?'
- 'Wouldn't it be quicker and less costly to outsource the creation of digital capabilities, or enter into a partnership?'
- 'It's great to have the autonomy to experiment. But how do we combine that experimenting with a top-down strategic direction?'

How to Optimize For Both the Core Business and the Next Businesses

Innovating in the core business and simultaneously experimenting with next businesses creates tensions that need to be managed well if it is to continuously propel your business forward.

Priorities, political power, attention, money and rewards typically reside within the core business. Executives are under pressure to protect these resources by delivering on their P&L in the here and now. In consequence, the odds are stacked heavily against next businesses. To make things worse, next businesses are often blamed for diverting (or outright 'stealing') resources. On top of that, large listed entities can be averse to the very idea of a business starting small.

Many companies choose to create a structural separation between the two types of businesses to shield the next business from this pressure. What they often neglect is to build bridges between the two, including the formulation of a joint strategy. In practice, what companies that are strategically agile have in common is a strong governance focus on orchestrating the bridges. Without it, the tension between the core and the future may turn out destructive to rather than productive of agility in your company.

Governance Over Structure

Chapter 3 contrasted GE and Siemens as two competitors and their very different approaches to reducing the tension caused by the need to protect their core business (industrial machinery) and nurture the next ones (data platforms and predictive analytics). GE placed the brainchild of its radical business model innovation in GE Digital as a separate entity, whereas Siemens opted to embed it in its existing business. Both paths were valid; neither was doomed to fail from the start. But transforming for agility requires that both of these worlds be linked early and decisively enough. As GE discovered, in the absence of tangible links, the outcomes become unpredictable.

GE spotted very early on that commodification processes were afoot in its established industrial verticals. It realized that value was shifting to those who could control predictive analytics through connected data platforms. That is how GE Digital was born, a separate Silicon Valley mover and shaker, running on scrum and handing out stock options rather than sales quotas and bonuses. Predix was GE's opportunity to become a leader in IIoT. The platform would enable the company to become the orchestrator of an ecosystem of apps and analytics, not only those built by GE but also, with open source, other developers and equipment manufacturers. Over time, however, GE found that its Digital initiative was slow to fire up the imagination of its workforce as well as its clients. The vision may have been crafted logically and meticulously but the core business in its current shape was proving resistant to that vision. Attempting to disrupt itself, GE pushed itself to be nimble but lost touch with some of its realities.

Siemens's strategy was to uphold governance over structure. The company was aware that Mindsphere, its cloud-based IIoT-as-a-service solution, was a disruptive force, redrawing customer relationships, scope of offerings (including from products to services and solutions), ecosystem boundaries and profit formulas. For Siemens, digital transformation meant creating a connection with the core business today, as opposed to a distant tomorrow, by linking businesses through a common governance mechanism. CEO Joe Kaser, in collaboration with the CSO, appointed a transformation board that included the CSO, the chief transformation officer, and the heads of the nine divisions. As part of this governance mechanism, the leading divisions would extend help to the laggards. An important outcome of this approach was that industrial leaders steered the digital transformation strategy towards areas with deep industrial know-how and applications that big digital giants would not master, thus keeping them at bay.

Within the divisions, it was possible to create separate special task forces for the most radical new businesses, but the whole governance push was towards collaboration. Having an overarching governance body also meant that Siemens could find synergies to create a common digital vision.

The agility mindset is about empowering employees to become co-creators of their future. All Siemens businesses became co-creators of the digital present and future. Splitting off this responsibility and giving it to new separate businesses runs the risk of telling core business employees that innovation is not their responsibility, which is the opposite of nimbleness. The nature of digital is such that progress on long-term projects can immediately feed into strengthening the core business. Therefore if those connections are not revealed fast enough, there is a strong chance the core business will reject the change.

In the Siemens governance model, all businesses were held accountable, quarter after quarter, for progress on all three horizons of the digital strategy. That included showcasing progress with digital KPIs, presenting ideas and business cases about what digital meant for their own business and how it would spur growth; deploying initiatives such as digital twins for development and virtual factories; advanced divisions helping the laggards; and making internal processes faster, smarter and more efficient.

The Siemens CEO was omnipresent in driving the effort, evangelizing about the importance of digital and pushing for collaboration and accountability through new digital-focused KPIs. The governance mechanism helped build effective bridges between the three strategic horizons.

Increasingly, it is Digital That Provides the Missing Links

Connecting the core and the next businesses through digital enabled Siemens to pursue cost leadership, product excellence and customer intimacy at the same time – despite management lore telling firms to excel in one of these three value disciplines and stick to it.[1] Flexibility prevailed over either/or choices. Digital twins and factories helped the company reduce costs for customers. On the product excellence front, analytics made it possible to predict machine downtimes with greater accuracy, which made Siemens's machines perform better.

In terms of customer intimacy, Mindsphere opened the doors to the practice of users developing and fully customizing their own industrial applications.

There is another way a digital platform strategy can help you link tomorrow's business with today's. For example, Ford partnered with Starbucks and Amazon to enable in-car orders of Starbucks coffee via Alexa, Amazon's voice-controlled virtual assistant.[2] For Ford, the platform is not a next revenue stream yet. However, it comes with an app – which means digital traffic and eventually a wealth of data on how customers use the Starbucks ecosystem. This will allow Ford to learn about consumer propensities and behaviours from novel perspectives and from non-competing vendors.[3] In time, these lessons may help Ford come up with ideas for new revenue streams.

Next Practices for Exploring Next Businesses and Protecting the Core Business Simultaneously

Our research also revealed that, to reduce the tensions between exploiting the core business and exploring next businesses, companies need to develop multiple next practices focused on strategy itself. They need to support those with organizational and leadership agility next practices (Table 8.1) – examples of which you discovered in the previous chapters.

Once your company has set up the links between the core and the next businesses, drawing on all three manifestations of agility, you

Table 8.1   Optimizing for both the core business and the next businesses: Next practices

Agility focus	Next practices
Strategy	• Use governance over structure • Rely on a portfolio approach to next businesses • Adapt next-business KPIs but ensure clear delivery and progress • Collect data on future businesses; observe whether they are expanding or cannibalizing the core business. If expanding, use it as an argument to overcome resistance inside the company

(continued)

Table 8.1 (Continued)

Agility focus	Next practices
	• Use digital as a link between core and next businesses, as well as an enabler of pursuing cost leadership, product excellence and customer intimacy (ie all three value disciplines as opposed to one)
Organization	• Ensure that the practice of employees reflecting on and transferring lessons from new businesses to the core business (collaborating across silos) is second nature
	• Foster inclusiveness: business units should be involved in setting next directions, especially on scale vs customer intimacy
Leadership	• If you are a senior leader, champion the new direction day in, day out
	• Communicate, communicate, communicate why this is important for the business's future
	• Ensure that management intensify their digital acumen through shared training; co-create common digital vocabulary for the whole business; articulate how to transform own business
	• Rely on the creativity of digitally savvy and motivated employees and make sure they contribute to the full

will find that the tyranny of the core business is starting to recede. In its place, your company will learn to maintain a vibrant portfolio of options and skilfully navigate between multiple horizons (Chapter 3). Your business will emerge as more flexible and entrepreneurial.

How to Optimize for Both Disciplined and Experimental Planning: Resource Allocation

Building powerful links between core business and next businesses allows a company to prepare for multiple uncertain futures by giving itself options that extend well beyond today's business. There is a similar impetus behind reconciling traditional, top-down planning and resource allocation with an experimental, bottom-up, issue-based approach. In every company's strategy, particularly as related to next businesses, there are areas that won't fit under the umbrella of disciplined, conventional planning and will require a different tack.

Pursuing both can be difficult. Even perfect information will not eliminate poor decisions. What matters is spotting and correcting those decisions. For companies that are faced with extinction in their core segment, experimental planning and resource allocation may be a matter of life and death. For instance, in June 2020, Fujifilm announced a $928 million investment in a Danish biologics facility – a move the media described as the former camera-maker's 'pivot' towards healthcare.[4] But too much conservatism, such as avoiding big bets altogether, won't help either. Research suggests that companies that avoid taking big bets tend to fall behind the marketplace.[5]

Fluidity of Ideas Must Be Matched By Fluidity of Resources

Strategic agility dictates that a company's business portfolio as well as resource portfolio be kept as nimble as possible. Companies that have handled this effectively know how to free up resources often and in a fluid fashion, and how to apply them to where value is created in core and in next businesses. When IBM sold its PC business to Lenovo in 2005, it wasn't just to 'get out' of a segment the vendor didn't see as the best fit for its capabilities. The proceeds gave IBM some time to define its future and contributed to financing its next core strategy in cognitive sciences and AI. Similarly, by 2013, GE fully exited the media and entertainment segment to refocus on IIoT.

Market sentiment can be a good gauge for where the future action is. Unfortunately, too many companies hold off on divesting assets to a point where these are of little value not only to the seller but to prospective buyers as well. Poor timing, in addition to misreading industry trends, can prove costly. An early (2003) investor in online retailer Net-a-Porter, luxury conglomerate Richemont pulled out in 2015 after Net-a-Porter's merger with Yoox (creating YNAP), only to buy 95 per cent of the combined entity's shares in 2018. By then, thanks to YNAP's global presence and wealth of data analytics, its price tag had gone up to €2.8 billion.[6]

Agility in planning can also be achieved through internal budget allocations. Longer-term, three-year plans coupled with quarterly budgets (within the QBR framework) was how ING managed to reconcile stability with executing adaptive initiatives. The practice reflected the company's understanding that annual goals are too tactical and long-term goals too abstract to provide concrete guidance.

The 'follow the money' philosophy can yield results with a lot of accuracy but there are also elements of organizational design and leadership that may help balance the imperatives of standard vs experimental planning. The early instalments of LVMH's DARE hackathons (Chapter 3) ran into follow-up problems as the initial excitement waned and day-to-day demands took over. LVMH responded by bridging DARE's experimental spirit of bottom-up innovation with actual goals in personal development. What started as a three-day exercise would gain real champions and sponsors to see the novel ideas through to fruition.

The Missing Link: Approach Big Bets as Small Bets Through Agile Experiments

Big bets are essential but they don't have to start with big financial commitments, although the size will vary by industry. In segments like consumer goods, working with real data and fast testing allows specialists to validate and iterate ideas such as value proposition and website designs with tens of thousands of social media users in a record few hours. The outcome is shaped in real time and through live market input, thus removing much of the guesswork, weeks of meetings and unnecessary costs.

Combining digital with elements of agile methods allows companies to take an experimental approach to strategic bets and initiatives. Big bets can be hedged by starting small, learning fast and scaling safer, with continuous learning throughout. As such, executives can pull the plug on new initiatives quickly and without incurring ruinous bills. The 'test fast, learn fast' process enables businesses to create portfolios that involve new markets and new technologies, then decide which opportunity is or isn't worth pursuing.

Next Practices for Managing the Competing Demands of Conservative and Experimental Planning and Resource Allocation

Successfully linking conventional and fluid planning means breaking out of the status quo instead of pursuing incremental changes. Companies at ease with a more fluid allocation of resources will also become adroit at aggressively entering new markets and rapidly scaling up new businesses. Underpinning this process is a pioneering mindset of 'be proud of your past but remember that the past is not your future'.[7]

Nevertheless, different industries and product segments face different urgencies as far as experimental planning is concerned. GE's or Sephora's timelines need not be the same as Kodak's. Likewise, in automobile, electric vehicles proliferated quickly whereas the even more disruptive self-driving cars remain a thing of a relatively distant future.

Table 8.2 details how companies such as IBM, ING and LVMH drew on the next practices of strategic, organizational and leadership agility to bring together elements of conservative and experimental planning.

Table 8.2 Optimizing for both experimental and conventional planning: Next practices

Agility focus	Next practices
Strategy	• Be aware of strategic blind spots as they evolve over time. Make sure to run experiments on each of them
	• Channel resources (cash, talent, time) to where they will create value
	• Maintain nimble portfolios of businesses as well as resources
	• Recognize the speed at which you might be disrupted to decide how much fluid planning and resource allocation you need
Organization	• Lean start-up approach: test fast, learn fast, kill fast if necessary to start big bets as small bets
	• Reversibility of investments: can you partner rather than make or buy?

(continued)

Table 8.2   (Continued)

Agility focus	Next practices
	• Give top management scrum-board-like visibility into priorities, bottlenecks
	• Support experimental teams with resources and time after hackathons
Leadership	• Link experiments and issue-based planning to personal development
	• Define clear rules on who makes the tough calls

An important implication of conducting stable as well as fluid planning processes is the pressure it exerts on corporate functions. A more fluid budgeting framework, such as ING's QBR, calls for changes in finance. In an otherwise conservative luxury sector, LVMH's DARE creates a secure base for trial and error but that needs to be reflected in performance management. What about manufacturing? What are the implications of a fast ramping up or shutting down of an experiment there? These examples illustrate that, increasingly, functions including HR, finance, budgeting, risk, compliance and production need to adapt and collaborate. Increasingly, companies should overcome the old idea that functions are cost centres. They are also profit maximizers in more collaborative models.

How to Optimize for Both Diverse and Complex Portfolios

The 7Fresh story (Chapter 3) is proof that a simplified portfolio can be vibrant and sophisticated enough to speak to consumers' fast-changing tastes and preferences. The balance 7Fresh finds between simple and complex portfolios earns it a disproportionate amount of revenue. How do you go about emulating such companies' flexibility, thus giving your growth a boost? Does your firm need to be a digital pioneer to thrive on personalization?

Netflix teaches us that strategic agility can stem from placing a different emphasis on each portfolio type (business, country, product, customer). Netflix made sophisticated choices regarding complexity vs simplicity: It runs a simplified product portfolio (large in number but global in scope) combined with a high number of diverse customer segments.

For Netflix, fine-grained customer segmentation proved to be a source of customer-centricity and relevance. Thanks to its analytical and AI capabilities, the high number of customer segments didn't inflate the number of products in the Netflix portfolio to unmanageable levels. Instead, Netflix became an expert on what types of media content in its global library viewers prefer, how to optimize its recommendation engines for them and what kind of marketing they respond to. Global distribution also means more revenue and economies of scale in production. Additionally, the company embraced the long tail[8] of customer profiles and built customer intimacy with each. Using technology, it reconceived viewers' end-to-end experience,[9] essentially treating every customer like a market of one.[10]

The Missing Ingredient: Data Granularity

On its own, slashing your offerings and country-specific portfolios will not take you very far. The result will be simplicity for simplicity's sake, rather than a real impact on your top line. It is fine to start with a complex portfolio; in fact, it gives you a large pool of data to examine and analyse. What companies need to learn is how to go through that data thoroughly, separating the wheat from the chaff the way Netflix does – the chaff being the commodified, undifferentiated offerings that don't add value.

In a number of industries, fine-grained data combing is known as de-averaging. Traditional businesses love to look at averages such as sales by country, by category, etc. But what do the averages actually tell us about real customers and emerging trends? The answer is, not enough. The resulting broad-brush approach results in budget misallocations and unidentified – or simply unserved – growth opportunities.

How do you escape the averages trap? First, your company will need to start collecting, continually and consistently, lots of real data from business lines, countries and product categories. That pool of near-real-time, frequently updated data can then be mined for patterns, including predictions. A keenly analytical, granular view will bring into sharp relief what is viable and what isn't. Based on that information, companies are in a position to simplify, credibly and systematically, the content of their product and country portfolios.

What Will Yield That Type and Volume of Granular Data? A Shared Data Pool Enriched With AI

At companies like Amazon and Netflix, each business line collects its own data, increasingly stored in the cloud. Crucially, the data is then centralized in a shared data pool that allows the companies to run powerful analytics and use machine learning (Figure 8.1). As straightforward as it sounds, even at Amazon this data centralization didn't happen overnight; it took considerable discipline and a firm mandate from Jeff Bezos himself.

The central data platforms enable these players to perform better algorithms and quickly trace undetected patterns, as well as support partner ecosystems. Giving instant access to third parties to develop and improve applications greatly enhanced the virtuous cycle Amazon calls the flywheel effect: Customer interactions with AI systems generate data; with more data, machine learning algorithms perform better, which leads to better customer experiences; better customer

Figure 8.1   Amazon's strategy of successive data centralization

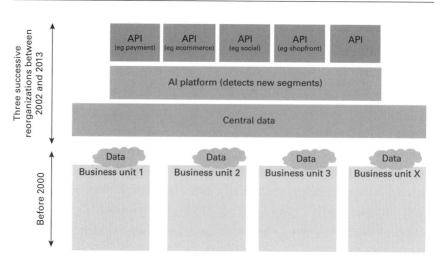

experiences drive more usage and engagement, which in turn attracts more vendors and generates more data.[11]

The good news is that you don't need to be a digital native like Amazon to put this strategy into practice. Nike's AI-run mobile dashboard feeds sales performance data by outlet to management on an hourly basis. It is a capability not unlike guerrilla warfare, as the company can change course and make tactical moves nearly instantly.

Next Practices to Manage the Competing Demands of Simple and Complex Portfolios

The Luxury SA story (Chapter 4) illustrated that standardization and centralization can be make-or-break factors in building agility. Smart complexity of a company's product portfolio will not be achievable without effective simplification of its bureaucracy. The organizations we highlight made smart choices about how to centralize data and analytics and institute shared practices throughout the company. To bring your strategy to a new level of agility, you also need organizational agility.

Table 8.3 summarizes the next practices that sustain a dual focus on simple as well as complex portfolios.

Table 8.3   Building simple and complex portfolios simultaneously: Next practices

Agility focus	Next practices
Strategy	• Make data-driven decisions • Use insights from real, live data to inform planning and to recognize fine-grained patterns and segments • Leverage a machine learning-based approach to customer segmentation
Organization	• Gain simplicity by centralizing data and standardizing data management practices (eg openness, data architecture) • Reduce unnecessary silos and increase cross-business collaboration • Deploy a common IT infrastructure (it can be cloud-based)

(continued)

Table 8.3   (Continued)

Agility focus	Next practices
Leadership	• Role-model a culture of informed decision making • Promote a style of leadership that draws on digital and data acumen • Develop a clear vision of what can be done with data and for what purpose • Be decisive in building a data-driven culture

How to Optimize for Both Divergent Thinking and Leadership Unity

Scouting for new growth paths yet ensuring disciplined execution requires both creative, 'outlier' thinking and leadership unity. Can managers handle both? Or could the obvious solution be to set up two separate camps within the organization's management: Creatives vs Operators; Left-brained vs Right-brained? Empirical evidence shows that this won't work. Senior executives are not necessarily resistant to change, but they are overwhelmed by the number of strategic (and operational) initiatives. Meanwhile, managers who were not involved in conceptualizing the change initiative and the sense-making that preceded it will, consciously or unconsciously, resist it and may attempt to derail it. If anything, as Chapter 7 showed, companies pushing towards agility see the boundaries between doers and thinkers blurring or disappearing altogether.

Nurturing Good Quality (Not Just Quantity) of Future Strategic Directions

With a history stretching back to 1288, Stora Enso, a Helsinki-headquartered €10 billion global business (2019) with 26,000 employees, bills itself as the world's oldest limited-liability company. The advent of digital in the 2010s was not kind to its traditional core market of paper products. The company's leadership sensed that, given the urgent need to reinvent the business, approaching the process like a standard restructuring, headed by the same cohort of senior executives, was not the way forward. Bringing in consultants could also be hit-or-miss, as what was really needed were new, fresh perspectives but steeped in the firm's history and legacy. Deciding in the end to tap its own, reenergized workforce for answers, from 2011 to 2016 Stora Enso partnered with IMD to launch a learning and development programme called Pathbuilders.

Working to ambitious six-month deadlines, teams of 14 employees from across the ranks each collaborated with one C-suite member to analyse and redefine the firm's pressing challenges. These ranged from purpose and values through strategy to areas such as accelerating sustainability. The missions were defined by top management but only in terms of broad directions and objectives. Similarly, the teams' C-suite sponsors mostly lent their expertise, cross-company networking and other contacts. Importantly, the applicants who joined the Pathbuilders teams weren't randomly thrown together; they received IMD training in strategy, structured thinking, innovation, digital and leadership. The end result was a set of unconventional yet implementable ideas and recommendations that helped recast Stora Enso from a traditional paper maker to a renewable materials company. The approach proved a success: By 2018, new growth segments contributed 76 per cent of revenues and between 2011 and 2017 the company's share price doubled.[12]

Pathbuilders turned out to be an effective way of sourcing and promoting new talent. Up to a fifth of the programme's participants had not been on the firm's radar as up-and-coming leaders before. At the same time, the initiative strengthened the unity of the senior leadership team who, despite initial reluctance, became keen to contribute ideas and proposals to the path-building missions.

Whatever the transformation, it is important to ensure good quality and control as well as to limit the quantity of initiatives before management fatigue and resistance set in. Figure 8.2 provides executives with a tool for estimating and weighing a change programme's potential value against the risk involved.[13]

Figure 8.2   Managing innovation fatigue

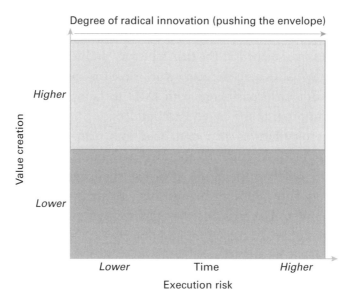

SOURCE P Strebel (2003) *Trajectory Management: Leading a business over time*, John Wiley & Sons, p 135

The Missing Link: Applying Principles of Organizational Agility

Empowering small teams the way Pathbuilders did allows C-suite executives to re-allocate their time to more value-creating activities. Instead of focusing on as many operational details as possible, organizational agility principles help executives build strong internal and external connections. According to one survey, when C-suite executives work in this way, leaders can quadruple the time allocated to strategy (from 10 per cent to 40 per cent) by reducing time spent on operational management.[14] This revised distribution of roles also helps senior executives to build hyperawareness by paying more attention to weak signals.

Pathbuilders relied on a new management structure and on processes rooted in multidirectional learning. The company gave cross-functional and cross-hierarchical teams full ownership of and

Table 8.4 Optimizing for both divergent thinking and leadership unity: Next practices

Agility focus	Next practices
Strategy	• As a top team, embrace divergent thinking to come up with the next sources of growth • Ensure clear timelines and disciplined follow-up • Learn how to prioritize initiatives
Organization	• Communicate clearly the strategic direction but let employees find the right map to get there • Ensure information transparency • Foster internal collaboration aided by agile work processes • Prefer small, cross-functional and cross-hierarchical teams
Leadership	• As a top manager, use your coaching style (facilitation, empowerment) • Use your connection style: remove obstacles to internal collaboration • Use your cohesion style: develop the sense of ownership among employees; develop purpose-driven accountability • Use your cognition style: Senior management accepts to learn from junior colleagues

accountability for their mission, as well as close attention from stakeholders. This enabled the teams to experiment, test hypotheses and pivot or pursue as necessary. The CEO personally ensured transparency of each mission's progress, meeting with the teams regularly and nudging all C-suite executives to keep the programme on their radars and gradually get involved. Over time, peer pressure kicked in.

Organizational agility principles also help deal with the problem of initiatives bloat by making clear what the ultimate criterion should be – customers. Customer-centricity, an agility principle, helps here because it's the customers, or stakeholders, that will dictate what is really adding value and should be prioritized.

How to Optimize for Both Internal and External Competences and Resources

By 2025, it is likely that 30 per cent of global corporate revenues will be generated through digital ecosystems.[15] How do you know when to keep (or bring) resources and capabilities in house and when to partner with other companies? What is the formula for doing both well? In what ways do the two approaches inform and influence each other?

Needless to say, orchestrating a network of external partners is more complex than controlling your own resources, because there are risks of IP loss and even the scenario of nurturing a future competitor to be considered. Relying on both internal and external sources of innovation requires the right approach to scouting for partners; structuring the resulting partnerships in ways that create win–win value yet protect the company's IP; instituting the right learning processes; internalizing core digital capabilities; and incorporating acquisitions into an overarching strategy.

Siemens deliberately looked for intra-industry, customer-intimate digital applications that would be difficult to replicate by big tech vendors. Early on, Siemens determined who was friend vs foe and how to steer clear of 'no-fly zones', ie scenarios that carried too much risk in terms of IP leaks and inadvertently birthing the next competitor. Paradoxically, the company went as far as spinning off Siemens Information Services (a €4.5 billion business), a generic IT provider, and merging it with French company Atos in order to create a complementary, non-competing partner.

By contrast, GE adopted a more generalist approach. It poured billions of dollars of its own cash into its Predix platform, sourcing software from paid partners and internal business units.[16] This left the company vulnerable to disruption, including through copycat tactics from other tech giants, because the applications were not industry-specific enough to protect the know-how. A long-standing market and thought leader in its traditional industry verticals, GE struggled to adjust to the co-creating paradigm.

It is precisely by understanding your current and next sources of competitive advantage that you will be able to reconcile the need for orchestrating complex external networks of innovation and partners and decide what should stay inside the firm. Once this is clear and properly communicated, you can empower employees to scout for and nurture the right partners.

The Missing Link: Sourcing (Through Digital) Ideas From Outside But Internalizing Their Execution

This is not to say that daring experiments have no place in the partnering game. Some global firms forsake the relative simplicity of their established operational models. They dabble in radical, cutting-edge complexity – for instance, by using the virtual environment and the power of the crowd to solve issues and to test and pilot new business models.[17] Haier's ground-breaking organizational strategy extends into areas like digitally powered idea crowdsourcing. By posting calls for improvements and new business opportunities, Haier receives hundreds of inputs each time. External researchers, scientists and even individual consumers are encouraged to submit innovation ideas. Haier absorbs this feedback to supplement rather than override its in-house processes and outputs. Yet the company's leadership finds the crowdsourcing mechanism appealing, partly because the risk of IP breach is considerably lower when collaborating with enthusiasts as opposed to other corporations.

Collaboration With External Partners: Where Do Employees Fit In?

The quality of connecting what's inside the firm with what's outside also hinges on trust-building and collaboration among employees. The GE Digital example showed that tribal mentalities of who's in and who's out are hard to eradicate even within the same company. That doesn't mean, though, that tearing down all boundaries between collaborating firms is purely beneficial. Studies show uncontrolled external knowledge sharing to be detrimental to radical innovation.[18]

According to Accenture, companies that outperformed peers say they encourage employees to be proactive in building relations with external stakeholders, compared with just over one-third of underperformers.[19] What is necessary is for ecosystem leaders and partners to create shared mechanisms and understandings of purpose, working methods, conflict resolution and incentives. Approaching these areas on an ad-hoc basis or working with tools that aren't in any way managed by the employer will quickly add up to failure. Leaders and partners need to discuss systematically and regularly how to design connectivity into their activities.[20]

Bringing IT Capabilities in House

In digital transformation, which is where many non-digital legacy firms have struggled, the choices have become even less intuitive than before. Not too long ago, IT roles could simply be outsourced. Today, areas such as programming and analytics are where the next core competences come from, and as such are best developed internally. The emergence of digital distribution strategies and business models has led many companies to view digital as their core capability, one that is well worth keeping in house.

Once again, to optimize the choices between internal and external resources and competences, you need to embrace next strategy practices and combine them with those of organizational and leadership agility (Table 8.5).

Table 8.5   Optimizing for both internalized and externalized resources and competences: Next practices

Agility focus	Next practices
Strategy	• Clearly define your next source of competitive advantage by reflecting on how the next game will play out
	• Reverse the trend of technology outsourcing for those competences that will give you a competitive advantage
	• Seek out intra-industry content that will be tough to replicate by non-industry specialists
Organization	• Communicate clearly the strategic direction
	• Extend new forms of organizing to external collaborations, eg through crowdsourcing of ideas, global hackathons
Leadership	• Empower employees to identify partnerships of value based on clear rules, principles
	• Set up clear frameworks and rules for people-to-people collaborations across company boundaries

Conclusions: Management Evolution vs Management Reset

This chapter drilled deeper into the dynamics and emerging next practices of flexible and reversible decision making based on 'both/and'. It presented pragmatic guidance, not only on how to build and sustain the pairs of seemingly contradictory strategic choices that are at the heart of the tensions of strategic agility (conventional vs experimental, disciplined vs fluid), but also how to handle the competing demands effectively. As the examples illustrate, with the right approach the energy that stems from reconciling the two poles results in agility.

At their best, evolutionary forms of management were limited to identifying the tensions that were relevant to a company's flexibility and the trade-offs you had to make to maintain that flexibility. The 2020s management reset revolves around knowing what strategic agility is and why it matters. Crucially, whereas traditional managers recognized but accepted trade-offs, the reset – as captured in this book – minimizes the trade-offs. Post-reset, organizations can innovate in both their core and their next businesses; their ideation processes can be both disciplined and experimental; they can optimize both internal and external competences.

The reset also involves a better understanding of the effects and impact of digital technologies and ecosystems, essential for developing strategic agility. Digital can be daunting because it comes with its own demands; it gives strategists new tools but also requires new types and a new quality of strategizing. Nonetheless, in the context of agility transformations, digital and especially data analytics are precisely the types of capabilities that can help a business redefine its decision making and gain new sources of and spaces for flexibility, collaboration and learning.

Finally, the reset – brought on by reducing the tensions in making choices, thus giving rise to strategic agility – is about ceasing to play not to lose, and instead playing to win. The process of change becomes more accurate both in terms of what to achieve and when and how to change. The level of entrepreneurship and calculated risk-taking rises. Executives and employees suddenly see a larger game where the pie actually grows bigger.

Figure 8.3   The reset mindset

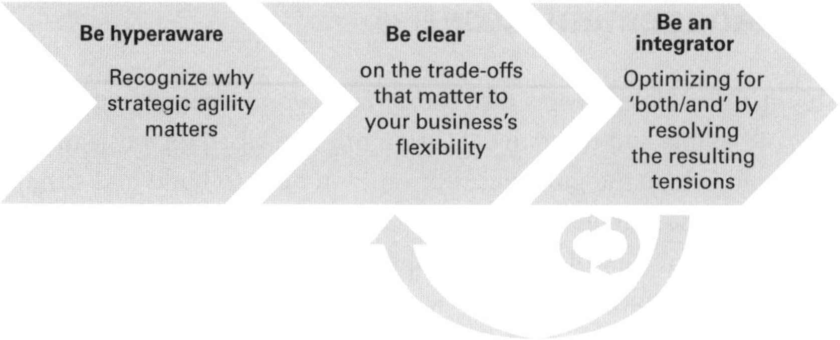

If you choose to embrace the reset mindset, consider structuring your thinking in a new way. You will need to:

1 Understand why strategic agility matters.

2 Recognize which inherited strategic trade-offs are impeding flexibility in your business.

3 Step forward and take on the role of an integrator – addressing conflicting demands and relating next practices back to conventional practices, all the while acting as a thinker as well as a doer.

4 Consciously and consistently optimize your company's strategy-making as an ongoing, dynamic process by adopting a perspective of both/and rather than either/or choices (Figure 8.3; and Chapter 3).

5 Continually review and verify that you and your teams are addressing the right trade-offs; and that you trace the progress of optimizing for both/and over time.

Endnotes

1 Treacy, M and Wiersema, F (1993) Customer intimacy and other value disciplines, *Harvard Business Review*, **71** (1), pp 84–93

2 Kinsella, B (2017) Ford drivers can order Starbucks with Amazon Alexa, Voicebot.ai, 23 March, https://voicebot.ai/2017/03/23/ford-drivers-can-order-starbucks-with-amazon-alexa (archived at https://perma.cc/36DA-4FMB)

3 Subramaniam, M and Piskorski, M J (2020) How legacy businesses can compete in the sharing economy, *MIT Sloan Management Review*, **61** (4), pp 31–37

4 Reuters (2017) Japan's Fujifilm to spend $928 million to double capacity of Danish drug facility, 12 June, https://ca.reuters.com/article/instant-article/idUSKBN23H0C3 (archived at https://perma.cc/U8PT-6ZCK)

5 Sull, D, Turconi, S, Sull, C and Yoder, J (2018) Turning strategy into results, *MIT Sloan Management Review*, 28 September, https://sloanreview.mit.edu/article/turning-strategy-into-results (archived at https://perma.cc/57HK-CFNN)

6 McDowell, M (2019) Yoox Net-a-Porter CEO: 'We sit on a gold mine of data', *Vogue Business*, 3 July, www.voguebusiness.com/companies/yoox-net-a-porter-ceo-federico-marchetti-ynap (archived at https://perma.cc/3QH9-MWF5)

7 Yeung, A and Ulrich, D (2019) *Reinventing the Organization: How companies can deliver radically greater value in fast-changing markets*, Harvard Business Press

8 Elberse, A (2008) Should you invest in the long tail? *Harvard Business Review*, **86** (7/8), p 88

9 Charan, R (nd) The new corporation: Reimagining organizations in the age of Amazon, *Corporate Board Member*, https://boardmember.com/corporation-reimagining-organizations-age-amazon (archived at https://perma.cc/8JJ6-D2KA)

10 Taneja, H (2018) The end of scale, *MIT Sloan Management Review*, **59** (3), pp 67–72

11 Rossman, J (2016) *The Amazon Way on IoT: 10 principles for every leader from the world's leading internet of things strategies*, vol 2, Clyde Hill Publishing

12 Enders, A and Haggstrom, L (2018) How the world's oldest company reinvented itself, *Harvard Business Review*, 30 January, https://hbr.org/2018/01/how-the-worlds-oldest-company-reinvented-itself (archived at https://perma.cc/NP2Z-7K4R)

13 Strebel, P (2003) *Trajectory Management: Leading a business over time*, John Wiley & Sons

14 Rigby, D K, Elk, S and Berez, S (2020) The agile C-suite, *Harvard Business Review*, May–June, pp 64–73

15 Catlin, T, Lorenz, J T, Nandan, J, Sharma, S and Waschto, A (2018) Insurance beyond digital: The rise of ecosystems and platforms, *McKinsey & Company*, 10 January, www.mckinsey.com/industries/financial-services/our-insights/insurance-beyond-digital-the-rise-of-ecosystems-and-platforms# (archived at https://perma.cc/383Q-HXXZ)

16 Digital Adoption (2019) What to do when your digital platform is actually the problem, not the solution, 7 April, www.digital-adoption.com/digital-platform (archived at https://perma.cc/L6X4-KTZY)

17 Reeves, M and Deimler, M (2011) Adaptability: The new competitive advantage, *Harvard Business Review*, **89** (7–8), pp 135–41

18 Ritala, P, Husted, K, Olander, H and Michailova, S (2018) External knowledge sharing and radical innovation: The downsides of uncontrolled openness, *Journal of Knowledge Management*, **22** (5), pp 1104–23

19 Accenture Strategy (2015) Ecosystem collaboration: New engines for growth and competitiveness in the digital age, www.accenture.com/us-en/~/media/Accenture/Conversion-Assets/DotCom/Documents/Global/PDF/Strategy_6/Accenture-Ecosystem-Collaboration-Infographic.pdf (archived at https://perma.cc/Q2TM-A935)

20 Harrington, K (2017) Entrepreneurial ecosystem momentum and maturity the important role of entrepreneur development organizations and their activities, *SSRN Electronic Journal*

09

Navigating the Challenges of Agile Methods

FIVE LESSONS FROM THIS CHAPTER

1 To use agile methods effectively, you need to master the processes and apply them properly. Many companies stumble because they underestimate or misapply the methods.

2 Agile methods do not exist in a vacuum. Companies take frequent missteps because they focus on the methods to the exclusion of other organizational design elements – in particular the softer ones such as people, leadership and rewards.

3 Pay attention to the journey your company will take when deploying agile methods. Discover the implications of the three implementation configurations that were highlighted in Chapter 5.

4 It is likely – at least temporarily – that the level of complexity will actually go up. This chapter identifies and describes specific next practices that will help you anticipate and navigate those challenges.

5 Drawing on the pioneering experience of large companies that implemented agile methods, this chapter will help you plan and execute agile at scale.

Chapter 5 introduced agile methods and processes that help businesses discard their rigidity. When properly implemented, these methods help companies emulate start-up dynamics by strengthening experimentation, speed of innovation, continuous engagement with and feedback from customers, and simplifying ways of working inside the organization. In the overall context of building agility, that will push the cursor towards nimble and simple. Indeed, researchers who studied specific implementations of design thinking, for instance, reported benefits that accrued to employees, product quality, systems and stakeholders – as well as improved implementation of change management initiatives.[1] In a 2019 study by Forrester, some mature design thinking practices achieved an ROI between 71 per cent and 107 per cent.[2] Those are impressive value-adds in a world where about two-thirds of large-scale corporate change efforts are deemed unsuccessful.[3]

However, many agile methods adoptions likewise fail. In the *14th Annual State of Agile Report*, 48 per cent of respondents rated general organizational resistance to change as the main challenge in adopting and scaling agile. This was followed by insufficient leadership participation (46 per cent) and inconsistent processes and practices across teams (45 per cent).[4] According to the UK State of Project Management Survey, only 45 per cent of organizations say they maintained a good agile development track record.[5] A 2019 McKinsey study shows that many companies are off to a good start, then get derailed when scaling up to go beyond a few pilots.[6] Other criticisms of agile include placing teamwork on a pedestal, expecting staff to give their best at all times (something we revisit in Chapter 10) and mandating rather than nurturing customer empathy.

It is not the aim of this chapter to replicate existing manuals on agile teams' recruitment, composition and training. Instead, we focus on the overlooked considerations related to organizational design and how companies configure and scale agile (journey considerations).

Pitfalls That Come With Adopting Agile Methods and Processes

Most managers think agile is about methods and processes. Indeed it is. Having employees mastering the methods is critical. What they forget are the other key components of organizational design, notably the softer, people-related elements. As a result, many companies solely train their staff in 'agile'. The strong emphasis on the methodology itself often overlooks or underestimates the importance of the other parts of the equation. This is not just a new type of product or software that employees learn to use. In other words, it's not just a skill. It requires a big change in people and in the organization. It involves creating new ways of working, collaborating, communicating, leading – within teams, with managers, suppliers and customers. Yet very often, the blueprint for adopting agile is copied-and-pasted wholesale from elsewhere, regardless of the company's circumstances and overall context.

Research also shows that agile processes work best with at least moderately experienced staff. On the other hand, senior staff and MBAs sometimes resist the underlying approach of learning by doing.[7] Other poor practices include treating agile methods as a quick fix; subordinating, in a rush to develop, everything to speed; or allowing creative input to be hijacked by constant rational explanations and justifications to the rest of the team.[8]

In the hurry to learn the How, the people component – particularly the Who – is often skipped (Figure 9.1). Nevertheless, it is the one most

Figure 9.1   Many organizations focus too narrowly on the process components of agile methods

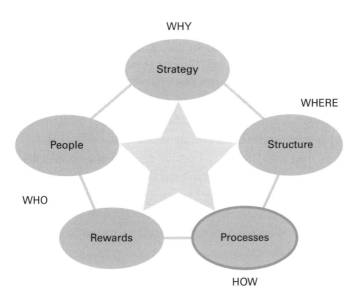

SOURCE Adapted from Galbraith's Star Model

likely to turn into an iceberg that will sink the entire initiative. Will people embrace a build-test-learn approach? Product development staff may have a natural affinity for such new ways of working – but what about middle management? Will they be able to self-organize, experiment, learn from failure?

Properly Implementing Agile Methods is an Exercise in Organizational Design

In general, many companies adopt the practices of agile but not its values and principles. What is sorely needed is a holistic perspective. A framework as simple as Galbraith's Star Model[9] will instantly highlight the fallacy of going straight to the process and its mechanics – en masse – and ignoring the direction (in other words, purpose), people, structure and rewards dimensions of the exercise. Without this holistic view in place, the outcomes may be almost comically dysfunctional, as the common phenomenon of 'faux scrum' or 'dark scrum' proves.

A **faux scrum**[10] (or **dark scrum**) is a scrum implemented for all the wrong reasons – largely as window-dressing to cover up persistent organizational issues, politics, even personal vendettas. It typifies a 'lifeless' agile process, ie going through the motions, such as when organizations describe a scrum master as 'basically a project manager' – a death knell for meaningful agile implementation. Ultimately, it serves to enhance tensions rather than resolve them. That said, in an 'antimatter' fashion, it provides a useful glimpse into the backdrop of agility transformation. It also underscores the fact that agile transformations occur at an intersection of technological and cultural change.

Overall, a faux scrum shows that half-hearted approaches don't sit well with agile. Just like agile won't work in a siloed environment, trying to micromanage within an agile framework, apportioning blame or expecting perfect execution from every task will lead to a 'weaponized' form of agile. Employees then feel that the new methods are used against them.

The direction, strategy and purpose of adopting agile methods need to be communicated constantly. Why are we doing this? What will it achieve? What are the objectives? How will it reposition the company? What happens if we fail? In some cases, if the answers are not wholly clear, it can also be about making people aware of the challenges ahead.

It is worth pointing out that agile methodologies are not applicable to all contexts. There are many industry segments where product specifications are truly etched in stone from the start and involving the end user in development is unnecessary. The same is true about tasks like compiling a balance sheet or a P&L statement – they are regulated by laws, carry no ambiguity and, as such, there is no need to involve the end user. Other tasks are complex and cannot be broken up into smaller batches to suit scrum, for example.[11] Under those circumstances, what agile methods represent – rapid experimenting, iterating, adjusting and learning – will not be useful. Therefore, it is a good idea to ask, 'Where does it make sense to implement agile processes?' 'Are the teams likely to outperform the traditional top-down structures?'

Where agile methods do add value is in helping staff to think critically, to test hypotheses, to come up with alternative solutions and to prioritize. The learning process should go beyond trial-and-error experimenting and bridge the gap between data-driven and opinion-driven, between analysis and synthesis.[12] At their best, agile process implementations create spaces for learning excellence where competence becomes mastery.[13]

The people dimension of agile roll-outs requires a redesign of the structures, processes and technology at individual and organizational levels (aligning people, customers and business processes as well as physical and digital working environments).[14] Underlying that redesign are new ways of relating to work, outputs, customer specifications and co-workers. These need to be reflected in recruitment policies, promotions, rewards.[15] The new skillsets that are required include soft skills in areas such as social interaction and customer communication.[16]

Many of the leadership paradoxes of building agility persist (Table 9.1) and need to be addressed in agile methods implementation.[17]

Table 9.1   Implementing agile methods: Leadership paradoxes

Ensure control while simultaneously giving up control
Acknowledge individual achievement while encouraging team efforts
Create a secure base for employees to learn, even at the cost of (calculated) failure
Encourage diversity while maintaining uniformity of team norms, values and goals
Achieve a strong sense of purpose but allow for team and individual creativity and expression
Emphasize the collective yet uphold individuality

The role of middle managers is particularly critical. The top expects results, not additional costs caused by failure. As promotion considerations to move up the hierarchy kick in, middle managers do not feel comfortable relaxing control. We found six ways you can mitigate this issue (Table 9.2).

Table 9.2   Bringing middle management on board with agile methods

✓ Encourage and role-model frank conversations to build trust across leadership ranks (cascading down the remaining hierarchy) so that middle managers feel the support of their more senior managers
✓ Help middle management understand that some control still exists, provided that the strategic directions are clear and performance and accountability are transparently measured
✓ If employees know they have the backing of middle management, they will more easily accept and trust that they have been empowered to experiment. This is where agile methods truly deliver value. Because if the idea was to play safe, then why use them in the first place?
✓ Tailor new leadership training priorities. Programmes and exercises should help middle managers learn how to avoid micromanaging what the teams do and how, so long as they achieve the end results. Explore and learn specific coaching and facilitation styles
✓ Encourage 360-degree feedback to help middle managers monitor how they are doing
✓ Align incentives to reward middle managers who have facilitated growth through collaboration and innovation in the deployment of agile methods

In transformations, many companies focus on changing the work-force because they think employees don't have the skills. But perhaps it is the ways of working that don't allow workers to reach their full potential. Agile methods, if applied well, can resolve that, even though learning the methodologies will continue to be important.

Can Workers Take Part in Agile Processes Remotely?

There are indications that companies with agile practices embedded in their operating models managed the impact of the 2020 COVID-19 crisis better than their peers.

Because agile processes thrive on prioritizing and transparency, agile business units responded better than non-agile units in terms of customer satisfaction, employee engagement and operational performance.[18]

At team level, however, agile methods were always about bringing a raw energy to a room by co-locating team members. This was accentuated through rituals such as daily stand-up meetings to discuss backlogs and workloads. With the onset of the health crisis, agile teams found that transferring this group chemistry to online collaborative tools takes some experimenting and adjusting.

Our research revealed some of the important next practices for enhancing the success of agile methods (Table 9.3). Many of them are common across methods – for example, the need to mitigate interdependence issues that will surface with non-agile parts of the organization. Vocabulary is another recurring consideration. If necessary, companies should make the terminology their own, like GE did with FastWorks.

Some practices are method-specific. For example, new research shows that the skills required to engage in design thinking may well be so specialized, it makes more sense for some companies to buy the service rather than do it themselves.[19]

Table 9.3 Deploying agile methods successfully: Next practices

Strategy	Structure	Processes	Incentives	People
• **Objectives** of what teams have to accomplish need to be crystal clear (creating the right framework for empowerment) • Defining **where** we need agile methods and which one(s) • DT: **Buy-or-do** decision (it's expensive, skills)	• **Roles**: Effective composition of cross-functional teams • S: In IT needs more programmers than project managers • S: T-shaped product owners • DT requires talents who can practise live immersion in customers' lives • S: Separation of roles (what and how)	• **Start** with intensive **training** • LS,DT: Both require **customer involvement** in the fast-testing iteration stage • DT: When engaging customers, the final solution is not an MVP • DT: **Data:** How to condense large data sets into smaller data sets	• S: Use rewards to get over the initial **fear of empowerment** • If strategic, make **adoption mandatory** through new incentives and career progression rules • DT,S: **Balance** team and individual rewards • Feedback becomes a personal incentive • If leaders take accountability, it will liberate the teams	• **Fight silo mindset** (teams) • Build culture of curiosity, listening and constructive debate • Need for integrated IT systems to support collaboration • S,LS: Use, train, reward around **agile manifesto** principles (it's the mindset)

- S: In the teams, decision making must happen as quickly as possible
- Resolve **interdependence** issues with non-agile parts
- Needs structure for retrospectives (learning from failure)

- LS,S: Real-time **measures**; strong KPIs
- S: Co-location, **office space** redesign
  - S: Co-location rule can be relaxed over time
  - S: During remote work, team rituals/ceremonies may need adjusting
- **Timing** S: Adapt the cycle when necessary
- Protect time for learning

- Needs incentives, rewarding collaboration to resolve **interdependence** issues

- **All-employees ownership:** Do not let **vocabulary** serve the gigs only
- Values: Shared values of collaboration are required to resolve **interdependence** issues
- **Leaders** need to build **trust:** Tolerating failure provided there is **learning**

Be Mindful of Configuration Issues

Chapter 5 described three distinct organizing approaches that established corporations chose when implementing agile methods. Each reflected a specific context and set of circumstances. Each produced its own types of benefits and also implementation challenges. You will next find some guidelines that are related to the three transformation journeys.

Enclaves

GE Digital was set up as a separate business, in part because the vision was to sell digital solutions to GE as well as non-GE customers. GE Digital's salespeople typically partnered with buyers from within customers' C-suites. As such, deep knowledge of the industrial products was not essential. By contrast, salespeople in the industrial verticals were selling to a strong installed base of customers and were trained to know the ins and outs of every product.

GE Digital was about agile at scale. It employed software developers who were accustomed to fast test-and-learn ways of working and shared the mindset from the very beginning. By 2016, 20,000 of them were developing the Predix platform. Meanwhile, in the industrial verticals, GE's FastWorks incorporated principles of design thinking and lean start-up methods. Its main objective was to accelerate the design of machinery and to involve customers in the process.

The persistent challenge was building strong links between GE Digital and the industrial verticals so that the two camps could learn to partner, co-create and envision things together. In order to deliver complete industrial and digital solutions, GE needed to create a shared culture. The industrial salesforce had to learn the language of digital and to sustain digital conversations with clients.

Historically, GE's strength was in strategizing and executing from the top down. But in this case, GE found the prospect of overhauling the entire conglomerate's operating structures and regulations overwhelming. In consequence, it opted for quick experiments, hoping that new paths forward would emerge naturally. Pushing digital and evangelizing about it versus actually absorbing it within GE, especially with GE Digital operating as a standalone entity, were two different ballgames. The GE culture of different divisions serving different industries was too entrenched to allow for new levels of collaboration across silos.

The decades-old mindset of one-model-fits-all created roadblocks, eg by forcing Digital staff to use FastWorks terminology in contexts related to FastWorks deployments – although for software engineers, FastWorks was just one of the many tools at their disposal. To deepen the divide further, scrum as the most commonly used agile process was not included in FastWorks, which GE saw as a pioneering instrument of lean start-up methodologies, enriched with elements of design thinking. The industrials people who used FastWorks demanded company-wide shared vocabulary but for the staff at Digital, FastWorks posed limitations in software development.

Importantly, the targets and incentives for the two salesforces remained unchanged. Salespeople in the industrials were rewarded for shifting machines and signing customers on to service contracts. What mattered in their minds was volume and contract size. Sales staff in Digital were thinking in terms of outcomes, selling subscriptions to the Predix platform on the promise of future earnings and savings. In some cases, GE spoke to customers with two voices, making its digital solutions appear as ancillary to the traditional industrial offerings.

Recruitment and compensation practices also varied widely between GE Digital and the rest of the organization, with software engineers in an increasingly competitive market demanding top dollar and stock options. While managers in the industrials division who received bonuses often remained with the company for 15–20 years, most of the techies at GE Digital expected to stay for 18 months before moving on to other opportunities.

On the leadership front, GE always thrived on a top-down culture where managers and experts took pride in the superiority of their expertise. Suddenly, to be faced with juniors who possessed more knowledge and sharper skills in the emerging tech areas was a rude awakening to managers. The idea of discarding behaviours and skillsets that were once a source of excellence and prestige was unimaginable. In consequence,

Figure 9.2   GE's challenge: Absorbing the satellite back into the fold

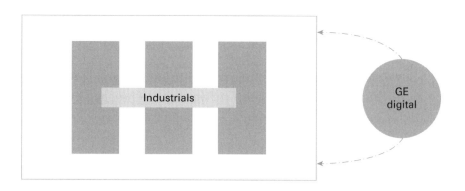

too many people at GE perceived GE Digital as 'not GE' – a complication they did their best to ignore or neutralize (Figure 9.2).

To think in terms of both industrial and digital – and in fact to leave this dichotomy behind and move into a space where industrial *is* digital – required constant connecting, translating and reconciling. Organizational and thought leadership was needed so that GE could place the customer front and centre, run through speedy experiments, test and measure their outcomes and kill off less-than-promising projects in order to prioritize the value-adding ones.[20]

In the end, GE recruited a chief learning officer for digital industrial. In 2016 and 2017, the company held eight bootcamps for a total of 400 senior leaders who, despite all the talk of digital, had yet to create their own impression of what it meant in their world. The aim was to build a personal connection to a digital future, one that came with a lot of experimental strategizing – a stark departure from the old GE approach of 'Here's the strategy; now go execute it.' This was coupled with a programme to explain the differences between the agile methods used in FastWorks vs Digital.

The message – revolutionary in GE's context – was that there is more than one way and that it's okay to use a multitude of tools to achieve the objectives of digital transformation. To make managers comfortable with digital and to learn in a safe environment, GE created gamified experiences, eg going through a virtual city (a microcosm of GE's own structures and workings) with an AI assignment. Predix Decoded was a mobile interface that allowed users to 'play' with Predix and create their own apps. These formats encouraged employees to become tactile with digital tools and to extrapolate the learning points into their current roles and business units. Finally, many were beginning to see for themselves the need and the value of digital for GE's future and its customers.

According to Janice Semper, GE Culture Transformation Leader, 'What we've learned is that you can't control this change, so you have to approach and lead it in a very agile way. Because you can't control it, the best you can do is be really clear on the outcome and then continue to measure where you are at, the impact and then test and try and learn through different efforts and then determine whether they're working or not. As long as you are making progress, you continue.'[21]

What can you take away from this transformation journey?

GE got many things right – including training, peer-to-peer learning and adopting agile from the bottom up. In 2017, the company reported revenue from the Predix portfolio products of $550 million, with sales growing rapidly.[22] But the concepts of simplicity, responsiveness and speed went against the grain of what the old GE stood for. Additionally, digital talent was brought in at a great cost but wasn't necessarily organized for success.[23]

The leadership style did not change enough, largely due to incentive problems. Top leaders weren't quite convincing as role models because they continued to be rewarded on traditional metrics and with traditional career paths. Traditional top-down and very bureaucratic ways survived, creating an obstacle to employee empowerment. One breakthrough GE did produce was in formalizing the role of 'translators' between business and digital, appointing chief digital officers (CDOs) for each business unit. These CDO-Bs reported to both the unit's CEO and the company's CDO to execute digital transformation.[24]

Where GE faltered was on the interface issue between digital and non-digital parts of the company. The biggest lesson is that if there is no strategic alignment around the purpose – ie why the transformation matters – usually associated with a new strategy, the interface issue will not be solved. GE also realized, albeit long into the process, that although not all parties need to work with agile (or the same version of agile in this case), they need to be bound by a single set of values that will nurture collaboration, trust and innovation. By the time GE started to define new values to encourage and measure those behaviours and to align incentives accordingly, it was too late to make the outcomes last. Table 9.4 lists practices that will help you pre-empt these issues and better coordinate your approach.

Building in-house digital capabilities and the gradual take-up of FastWorks represented big steps towards nimbleness. After all, GE traditionally lived and breathed stability, with industrial product development cycles stretching to several years. In the past, change programmes like Six Sigma were mandated from the top and rolled out with fierce discipline. By contrast, the uncharacteristically laissez-faire approach that GE took to FastWorks yielded only elusive simplicity. In fact, having two sets of agile methods (ie scrum in GE Digital vs lean start-up and design thinking, under the FastWorks umbrella, in industrials) fuelled new complexity in standards, vocabulary and collaboration.

Table 9.4   Next practices in implementing agile methods: Enclave configuration

Why	✓ Use when you need well-contained visibility on the agile method and its outcome
	✓ Use when you want to create a common way of working in one division
	✓ Create strategic alignment around the purpose of using agile and the sense of joint effort across the company
	✓ Communicate relentlessly about why agile matters across the company, even if only implemented in one part
Who	✓ Early on, define a set of cross-company values that are rooted in collaboration, trust and innovation
	✓ Measure relentlessly collaboration progress in and across teams
	✓ Extend support to middle managers
What	✓ Align incentives throughout the company to reward collaboration between agile and non-agile parts when it is necessary
	✓ Formalize a process to make interdependence issues explicit and use an agile approach to resolve them (eg scrum of scrums)
The journey	✓ If agile is the right thing, make it mandatory (top-down engine for scaling)
	✓ Provide platforms for peer-to-peer, cross-company communities (bottom-up engine for scaling)

Ad hoc

PharmaCo, a European multinational healthcare company, took a very different approach to implementing agile methods and processes within its organization. First, the methods were promoted in a grass-roots fashion, as opposed to decreed from the top. Second, the fulcrum of the change process was in managers' personal transformation. Where for GE the starting point was specific methods like scrum and lean start-up, for PharmaCo these were a finishing touch in a deeper process of change, one that aimed to understand and redesign how individuals at the firm worked together.

The main reason that PharmaCo in 2016 chose to explore 'How we do things' rather than 'What we should do' was that peering into the future of pharma, it saw mind-boggling uncertainties and possibilities. The What of the transformation simply defied description. Additionally, the Why was hardly a bone of contention as the company's purpose never steered away from patient-centricity. Hence the overarching objectives were to maximize the outcomes of innovation and to improve the company's ways of working.

An experience-based leadership programme was organized in order to shift executives' mindsets from reactive to a creative space of self-awareness, hyperawareness, authenticity and systems thinking. Encouraging executives to cooperate, the programme was also an instrument for mapping their collective leadership patterns. Operationally, PharmaCo pursued small, incremental changes and experiments (eg removing one layer of administration; shrinking teams to a size that could be 'fed by two pizzas', Amazon-style; self-selecting team members and relinquishing titles). These would set off avalanche effects.

The resulting momentum proved to be strong. The small, on-the-ground experimenting laid the foundation for meaty changes. For instance, the top layer of the firm's global governance was transformed into an enabling team of just a few people. The bonus structure, which was once the domain of individual divisions, was replaced by a single global sales target for the entire pharma commercial organization. PharmaCo did away with long-term annual budgeting, shortened the planning cycles in its pharma business and streamlined compliance processes. These were pragmatic steps that contributed to simplification.

As a next step, PharmaCo beefed up local initiatives with training in agile. As influence from programmes and leaders spread down-wards, employees started to take up agile methods. The results fur-ther steered the company towards nimbleness and simplicity by establishing a strong sense of direction and accelerating delivery of innovation outcomes to patients. Meanwhile, top management en-couraged the setting up of chapters, networks and communities that shared a vision, purpose and values.

Although the journey created significant areas of simplification, it also resulted in some new, unexpected complexity. Leaders who took part in transformation programmes were encouraged to bring the new mindset to their own businesses, creating momentum but also fragmentation. PharmaCo succeeded in engineering the tipping point as intended, but it had to take a step back and develop a set of or-ganizational interfaces across the company. It involved balancing in-dividual and team-based rewards in an intricate pharma setting where little can be achieved by an individual worker. Much of the agile

Figure 9.3   PharmaCo's challenge: Centralize; re-impose a single direction to rein in complexity

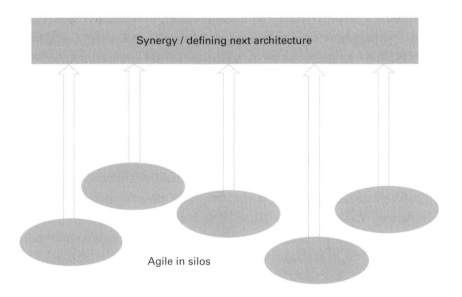

method adoption took place in silos, and was sometimes leading to duplication. Moreover, agile processes in IT worked quite differently from product development and bringing products to market; a lot of training was required as IT staff had the knowledge but not necessarily the skills to support their peers in other functions. Defining sets of shared data, systems, processes, career paths and vocabulary soon became a pressing issue for PharmaCo's leadership (Figure 9.3).

Consequently, an agility working group was created in 2017. Two years later, another initiative followed, aiming to bring together the transformation's successful but hitherto disparate elements and results. The initial 'touchy-feely' tone of personal transformation and leadership made way for far more granular initiatives that sought to define the company's 'next architecture'.

The next practices that will help you navigate the challenges of this journey are shown in Table 9.5.

Table 9.5 Next practices in implementing agile methods: Ad-hoc configuration

Why	✓ Co-create future ways of working based on a common understanding of the changing environment ('how we do things' rather than 'how we should do things')
	✓ Empower leaders, middle managers and employees to find the form of agile that suits their circumstances; that way, change will be more likely to take hold
Who	✓ Focus on leaders' personal transformation; let the change trickle down to their teams
	✓ All employees have a say and can experiment
What	✓ Nurture chapters and network communities that share values, purpose, vocabulary
	✓ Make experiments widely documented and available, including successes and failures
The journey	✓ This journey is particularly appropriate when the business is successful and there is time to adjust and learn progressively
	✓ Start from broader needs and strategic objectives to choose the most appropriate methods and agile ways of working
	✓ Let chaos reign, then rein in the chaos
	✓ Make 'how we work together' the foundation for finding further opportunities to reduce complexity
	✓ Metaphor of 'urban planning' – there is great diversity but underpinning it are common rules and shared infrastructures

PharmaCo's push towards nimbleness was successful; the bottom-up change started to gain strength. However, the company was not entirely effective in reducing complexity. At the time our study concluded, the company was actively working on reducing unwanted duplication and complexity.

Hub

Rabobank's Digital Hub approach to digital transformation was to 'infect' the rest of the company with the energy and excitement of its pilot agile team.[25] From the outset, the new heads of digital transformation, who joined the bank in late 2017, sensed that the hub must share the same roof with headquarters. It also foreshadowed the mammoth task, later on, of bringing all of its dynamics and accomplishments 'back' into the old organization. In a power-sharing quid pro quo, the managing board acceded to give the hub substantial autonomy (nimbleness) – in exchange for results, expressed in stringent KPIs (stability). With the company's annual IT spend of €1.5 billion, top management demanded more transparency on workloads and metrics.

Soon, the hub size grew from 30 employees to nearly 300, making a visible impact and inspiring some of the traditional divisions to come forward and declare, 'We want to be next.' What turbocharged the drive towards agile methods and processes was Rabobank's decision to use the hub as a launch pad for its Simplify@Scale programme. The programme was formulated as a driver of further simplification in client journeys, products and systems. The philosophy was to deliver results quickly – and also to let any hidden issues surface sooner rather than later. Thus between 2019 and 2020, 3,000 staff (representing 10 tribes and 300 squads) transferred to agile ways of working (Figure 9.4).

The single-minded push towards digital and a data-driven culture effected a great deal of simplicity for the bank: 95 per cent of customer interactions were now taking place in the app, as opposed to bricks-and-mortar bank branches. These trends also emboldened managers to seek radical rather than incremental change. As such, it was not uncommon to see a process redesigned from 19 steps to three (simplification).

Figure 9.4 Rabobank's challenge: Coming up against the limits of growth

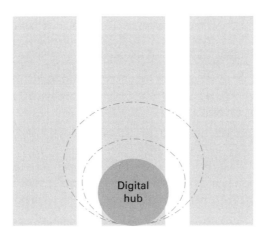

As with GE and PharmaCo, the scaling up produced its own interdependences to be managed, as well as some unforeseen consequences. The bank's operating units were happy to accommodate the hub while it was a small entity – but supporting it through fast growth was much more of a juggling act. Line managers became anxious about 'lending' ever more resources. They were still responsible for evaluating their direct reports but if these were in the hub, they lacked the visibility to do so. Given that 70–80 per cent of the new teams' headcount was coming from IT – and often from countries other than the Netherlands – there were new levels of diversity to take into account. Meanwhile, IT staff, who previously built a solid track record in DevOps, looked askance at the new kid on the block, wondering whether its goal was to rectify or supplant some of their own previous effort.

Because of the interdependence issues and because its digital offerings were growing fast, Rabobank decided the time had come to tackle these interdependences and to scale agile further. The digital hub itself fulfilled its purpose and was disbanded. Its founders agreed that applying two different management philosophies to the same organization should not be done indefinitely. Moving forward, agile methods found growing use in the bank's corporate functions as well as in its wholesale banking and international franchise businesses. Rabobank drew the line at operations including physical branches, salesforce and call centres.

Table 9.6   Next practices in implementing agile methods: Hub configuration

Why	✓ Use when you cannot dedicate talents full time to agile
	✓ Use when you want to pilot and showcase agile on a smaller scale (gradual and focused ramp-up of investments if you are facing resource constraints)
Who	✓ Staff at first with talents who know agile best
	✓ Provide training to all other employees so that they feel involved already
	✓ Make the middle management of the mainstream organization part of the process
What	✓ Address interdependences between agile teams and previous IT teams' efforts in agile areas like DevOps
	✓ Create win-win outcomes for the mainstream organization
The journey	✓ Take an early focus on the interdependences; make them surface fast to learn and correct
	✓ Recognize that the hub may be a useful temporary solution

In many ways, Rabobank was a first mover that didn't have all the knowledge at hand. Drawing on its experience will give you inspiration on how to plan better, as Table 9.6 illustrates.

Rabobank's hub initiative was contained and successfully piloted. In hindsight, it was a constructive format for testing and learning fast. Nevertheless, the hub quickly reached a limit – in staffing, incentives, eliciting support from other parts of the organization, and managing legacy issues with IT.

Conclusions

What are the lessons you can apply to your own organization?

1 **In the journey, remember that introducing agile methods is a piece of organizational design.** Companies and executives who implement agile methods tend to focus on the mechanics and procedures, overlooking the other dimensions of organizational design – purpose, people and rewards. Without sharing and communicating the purpose and values, and without recognizing the people aspects and implementation

struggles, jumping on the agile bandwagon may produce results but it may also lead to unhealthy disruption, confusion and resentment.

Agile methodologies are often popularized as a toolkit that comes out of a box – which means anybody can presumably learn how to handle it. In addition, companies are increasingly pressured into 'agile' by external partners. In those situations, it becomes all too easy to go through the motions, replicating the process without considering the other dimensions of what makes an agile process implementation meaningful.

2 **To build agility at scale, consider the challenges stemming from the three common configuration approaches.** As the three company stories in this chapter illustrated, each configuration will come with its own set of pros and cons. Inevitably, there will be tensions and clashing requirements to manage:

- The original impetus behind GE Digital was to set up a bold satellite – physically as well as in other ways separate from the rest of the conglomerate – which marched to its own rhythm. Later on, that approach set off issues that had to do with bringing this entity back into the fold.

- For PharmaCo, agile methods were meant to be the icing on the cake of its leadership and personal transformation journeys. Eventually, however, their introduction necessitated a global round of conventional reorganization.

- Rabobank's hope was to use its Digital Hub as a catalyst of change in the rest of the company. Yet the broader demands of digital on top of the agile process would eventually redefine nearly every aspect of the bank's identity.

Rather than acting as a great equalizer, introducing agile methods produced successes but also side effects of unforeseen complexity which the companies had to address. At the same time, accomplishments in cultivating nimbleness had to be counterbalanced with moves to ensure a healthy measure of stability.

3 When rolling out agility at scale, you need to manage the issue of interdependences. The three company stories will help you anticipate the common interdependence challenges your business is likely to face as it introduces and expands the take-up of agile methods:

○ From GE's experience, you learnt the importance of not bringing agile methods into silos. If you believe your company needs to master multiple methods, you will do well to anticipate the issues. What you unveil to employees should be a complete toolbox.

○ PharmaCo's trajectory showed you that prioritizing the personal aspect of transformation ('the ties that bind') can be powerful in embedding meaningful change. But at some point, more forceful top-down governance will be needed to reduce the unintended complexity.

○ Rabobank's track record in deploying agile served up some good lessons for dealing with a hub initiative that has outgrown its initial experimental phase.

Despite the challenges, these bold first-mover companies changed the landscape of 21st-century organizational design for good, and are bound to be widely imitated. In the meantime, specific next practices continue to emerge which will help you navigate the landscape and implementation of agile methods with growing aplomb.

Anticipating the above scenarios will be a powerful source of stability in your organization. On the other hand, crafting coherent responses to unintended consequences will be a test of your company's nimbleness. Whatever the situation, your business shouldn't descend into an unstructured, directionless free-for-all where everyone is in charge and therefore no one is in charge.[26]

Evolution vs reset

Solving issues of interdependence and building meaningful interfaces in adopting agile methods are at the core of management reset in the age of agility. As shown, companies who opt for large-scale adoption of agile methodologies often learn on the go. Conventional, evolutionary management provides limited lessons and resources to guide their journey – a gap this book aims to fill by sharing specific guidelines.

Tackling the fissures that inevitably appear during scaling up – no matter how successful the original agile experiment turned out to be – involves all of the Star Model dimensions.

- From the outset, top management needs to provide clarity of purpose (Why).
- Engaging with HR very early on will help address the people (Who), incentives and rewards parts of the equation.
- Timing can be just as essential: As a big portion of the workforce (and possibly of the executive suite) will remain in wait-and-see mode or even a disengaged state, companies will need to draw on all the strengths and resources they can mobilize. They will have to abstain from concurrent big strategic moves and other distractions.
- Where mass adoption of agile processes is a vehicle for digital transformation, there are bound to be unanticipated issues that the firm will have to resolve promptly.

Similarly, the agile methods-based transformation journey is a topic that classical literature on management is unlikely to discuss. It combines elements of planning with fast adaptation. It typically requires a manageable-size pilot that will be subsequently scaled up or replicated. Lastly, it is punctuated with brief episodes of equilibrium when firms need to reflect, learn and absorb before advancing to the next phase.

Endnotes

1 Liedtka, J (2018) Why design thinking works, *Harvard Business Review*, **96** (5), pp 72–79
2 Hart, R (2019) Design thinking can deliver an ROI of 85% or greater, Forrester, 8 June, https://go.forrester.com/blogs/design-thinking-can-deliver-an-roi-of-85-or-greater (archived at https://perma.cc/S8GX-9M36)
3 Campanelli, A S, Bassi, D and Parreiras, F S (2017) Agile transformation success factors: A practitioner's survey, *International Conference on Advanced Information Systems Engineering*, Springer, pp 364–79

4   State of Agile (2020) *14th Annual State of Agile Report*, https://
     stateofagile.com/#ufh-i-615706098-14th-annual-state-of-agile-
     report/7027494 (archived at https://perma.cc/Y3AY-AK9H)

5   Khinda, B (2017) *The State of Project Management Report 2017*,
     Wellingtone, https://wellingtone.co.uk/wp-content/uploads/2017/03/
     The-State-of-Project-Management-Survey-2017-1.pdf (archived at
     https://perma.cc/5AT4-5JDB)

6   Brosseau, D, Ebrahim, S, Handscomb, C and Thaker, S (2019) The
     journey to an agile organization, *McKinsey & Company*, 10 May,
     www.mckinsey.com/business-functions/organization/our-insights/
     the-journey-to-an-agile-organization (archived at https://perma.cc/
     VCC6-YRWK)

7   Leatherbee, M and Katila, R (2020) The lean startup method: Early-
     stage teams and hypothesis-based probing of business ideas, *Strategic
     Entrepreneurship Journal*, **14** (4), pp 570–93

8   Ersoy, L A (2018) Why design thinking is failing and what we should
     be doing differently, UX Collective, 19 June, https://uxdesign.cc/
     why-design-thinking-is-failing-and-what-we-should-be-doing-
     differently-c8842f843b44 (archived at https://perma.cc/G3J5-JFPF)

9   Kates, A and Galbraith, J R (2010) *Designing your Organization:
     Using the STAR model to solve 5 critical design challenges*, John Wiley
     & Sons

10   Layton, M C (2015) *Scrum for Dummies*, John Wiley & Sons

11   Rigby, D K, Sutherland, J and Takeuchi, H (2016) Embracing agile,
     Harvard Business Review, **94** (5), pp 40–50

12   Beckman, S L and Barry, M (2007) Innovation as a learning process:
     Embedding design thinking, *California Management Review*, **50** (1),
     pp 25–56

13   Dreyfus, S E (2004) The five-stage model of adult skill acquisition,
     Bulletin of Science, Technology and Society, **24** (3), pp 177–81

14   Jurisic, N, Lurie, M, Risch, P and Salo, O (2020) Doing vs being:
     Practical lessons on building an agile culture, *McKinsey & Company*,
     4 April, www.mckinsey.com/business-functions/organization/our-
     insights/doing-vs-being-practical-lessons-on-building-an-agile-culture
     (archived at https://perma.cc/DC5A-35J6)

15   Naslund, D and Kale, R (2020) Is agile the latest management fad? A
     review of success factors of agile transformations, *International
     Journal of Quality and Service Sciences*, **12** (4), pp 489–504

16 Conboy, K, Coyle, S, Wang, X and Pikkarainen, M (2011) People over process: Key people challenges in agile development, *IEEE Software*, **28** (4), pp 48–57

17 Waldman, D A and Bowen, D E (2016) Learning to be a paradox-savvy leader, *Academy of Management Perspectives*, **30** (3), pp 316–27

18 Handscomb, C, Mahadevan, D, Schor, L, Sieberer, M, Naidoo, E and Srinivasan, S (2020) An operating model for the next normal: Lessons from agile organizations in the crisis, *McKinsey & Company*, 25 June, www.mckinsey.com/business-functions/organization/our-insights/an-operating-model-for-the-next-normal-lessons-from-agile-organizations-in-the-crisis (archived at https://perma.cc/D8PM-UYXS)

19 Dunne, D (2018) *Design Thinking at Work: How innovative organizations are embracing design*, University of Toronto Press

20 Girod, S J G and Duke, L (2018) Digital transformation at GE: Shifting minds for agility, Case Study, IMD-7-2011, IMD International, Lausanne

21 Girod, S J G and Duke, L (2018) Digital transformation at GE: Shifting minds for agility, Case Study, IMD-7-2011, IMD International, Lausanne

22 Lohr, S (2018) GE makes a sharp 'pivot' on digital, *The New York Times*, 19 April, www.nytimes.com/2018/04/19/business/ge-digital-ambitions.html (archived at https://perma.cc/3LLY-PETA)

23 Govindarajan, V and Immelt, J R (2019) The only way manufacturers can survive, *MIT Sloan Management Review*, **60** (3), pp 24–33

24 Govindarajan, V and Immelt, J R (2019) The only way manufacturers can survive, *MIT Sloan Management Review*, **60** (3), pp 24–33

25 Wade, M and Duke, L (2019) Rabobank: Building digital agility at scale, Case Study, IMD-7-2070, IMD International, Lausanne

26 Dönmez, D and Grote, G (2018) Two sides of the same coin: How agile software development teams approach uncertainty as threats and opportunities, *Information and Software Technology*, **93**, pp 94–111

10

Managing the Trade-offs of Radically New Organizational Forms

FIVE LESSONS FROM THIS CHAPTER

1 Learn to anticipate the unforeseen consequences of implementing new organizational forms of agility. With its radically new organization, ING successfully addressed the tensions between stable and nimble; complex and simple. Yet the process of transforming for agility didn't end there: As old trade-offs disappeared or were minimized, new ones emerged in their place.

2 ING recognizes that within its agile structures, squads are the cardinal building blocks that generate value. As such, the company is committed to testing and improving the squads' size, composition and work dynamics.

3 In a new organization, HR has a crucial role to play in ensuring the agility transformation's success, particularly by defining new paths to career progression and new career transition opportunities.

4 Observe how agility supports digital transformation and how, reciprocally, digital nurtures an environment that is conducive to building agility.

5 Go slow to go fast. Approach the journey that is agility transformation in an agile way. Run small trials in quick succession, even if you don't have every detail pre-planned. Learn – improve – grow are the rules of the game. As your teams get a taste of agile ways of working and a sense of shared destination, their motivation and commitment will climb.

Even Radical Redesigns Occur in Stages

In Chapter 6, you learnt about the workings of ING's pioneering organization. The results included not only sizeable cost reductions and improved financial performance but also a leaner, data-driven organization that deservedly saw itself as a tech player with a banking licence. These successful outcomes explain why several banks are now following suit. How did ING do it? The next few pages will examine the company's transformation as a journey, paying particular attention to the trade-offs that ING's leadership managed to minimize as well as the new, unexpected trade-offs that often emerged in their place.

The accepted view of the organizational transformation that took place at the bank's Netherlands headquarters in 2015 is one of a Big Bang. Morphing large parts of a conventional bank into networks of tribes and squads certainly merits that metaphor. On closer inspection, however, even a Big Bang approach to building agility must be supported by strong reservoirs of organizational readiness – and those can only be mobilized in stages (Figure 10.1).

Laying the Groundwork

In the first stage (laying the groundwork), ING saw a grassroots adoption of agile as early as 2012, with several teams in IT and marketing taking up the agile methodology in order to prioritize and manage requests from other parts of the company. This was largely a spontaneous move – but nonetheless, a few years later it would stand the bank in good stead: At least among some ING staff, the technical concepts and principles behind agile methods were not totally new and unheard of. This was the modest early stage, where knowledge of agile within the company was at a level of barely 'better than nothing' and contained in small technical pockets, with no impact on business: A first step in a long journey.

Before a big structural overhaul could take place, ING turned its focus to articulating the vision and the underlying values that would support the imminent large-scale change. It continued laying the groundwork with the 2014 launch of its Think Forward initiative

Figure 10.1 Growth stages in ING's organizational readiness

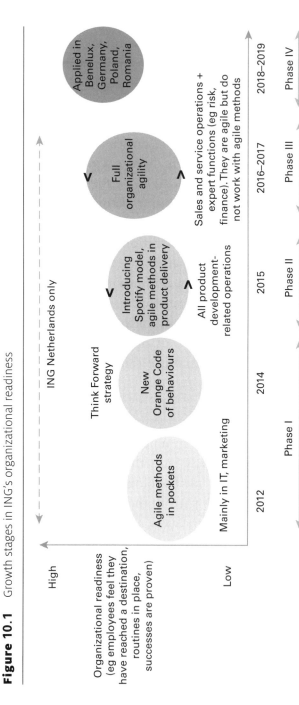

and the Orange Code. The latter turned out to be particularly important in creating the right mindsets and behaviours during the later phases. Transforming for agility couldn't start with a 'We like what Netflix are doing'; it needed an overwhelming Why – in other words:

1 The end result: A set of concrete objectives; and

2 The means to this end: A clear understanding of why agile would enable ING to meet these objectives.

Testing and Adapting

Transitioning to the testing-and-adapting phase, what was distinctive in ING's top management approach was the decisiveness. There was the need to launch fast even if not everything was carefully planned and ready, to learn and adapt rapidly. Creating the collective ambition and strong momentum were the main imperatives at this stage. Once the reorganization yielded results, these would have to be improved on over time.

The 2015 roll-out of agile processes, contained only in the product development-related operations at ING Netherlands, was the great leap; the most visible part of the change process. In hindsight and in terms of ING's growing organizational readiness, this phase was the de facto pilot. Inspired by tech and agile leaders such as Google, Netflix, Spotify and Zappos, ING created a specific form of organizational agility, covering product development and delivery. It copied leading companies' ideas but adapted them to its own strategy and context (Chapter 6).

Anchoring, Replicating

During the anchoring phase (Phase III) in 2016 and 2017, ING extended agility principles (although not outright agile methods) to its sales and service operations as well as expert functions such as HR, risk and finance. Outside the tech industry and digital-native businesses, executing this push into such a new organizational form was very nearly (apart from Haier) a globally unprecedented move.

Finally, with a well-defined transformation template in place, ING was in a strong position to replicate the revamped model in other countries (Phase IV) – including challenger markets such as Germany as well as growth markets in central and eastern Europe.

On several occasions this book has emphasized that agility transformations have little in common with conventional restructuring: it's not about an 'unfreeze–change–refreeze' approach to change, no matter how exceptional. At the same time, particularly from staff perspectives, building agility cannot be a process of wholly open-ended, incessant and unrelenting change. At some point in the transformation, visible contours of maturity must be achieved within the new organizational models.

Looking back, there were very few alternatives ING could pursue: Having gone through a drastic restructuring in the aftermath of the 2008 financial crisis where its total revenues shrank nearly by half, it wasn't tenable to repeat the process in 2015. The main objectives included becoming quicker to market, strengthening employee engagement and reducing impediments and handovers. In total, meeting these objectives was bound to improve client experience. Much of the transformation hinged on achieving cost savings amidst interest rates falling to zero. It was also a quest for relevance at a time of rupture where fintechs and digital giants encroached on different parts of the traditional banking business. ING Netherlands eliminated 6,000 jobs in the first two years of the transformation (30 per cent of the total workforce at headquarters). This was largely on the strength of its newly gained simplicity as manifested in staff collocation; teams taking on end-to-end product and returns responsibility; and the lesser need for coordination and bureaucracy. The physical network of retail branches was similarly rationalized. By the time COVID-19 struck in 2020, ING Netherlands was ready to face the crisis with great resilience, having stripped out €400 million in costs and established a ROE of 25 per cent.

ING's transformation process wasn't linear. It involved a number of discrete phases and was punctuated by milestones and spaces that were dedicated to continuous adaptation and improvement. Keeping people motivated enough to continue on the journey was one of the main challenges. On that count, the layoffs that accompanied the change process may have looked counterproductive and morale-sapping. At the same time, they created a watershed in the bank's history and sent a clear message that the status quo was no longer viable. Having thousands of staff reapply for positions in the 'new' ING further signalled renewal and rebirth. In the process, ING let go of those middle managers who did not possess the right empowering and collaborative mindsets to start with.

Try, Learn, Adapt: Be Prepared to See Old Trade-Offs Disappear and New Ones Emerge

Transforming for organizational agility is about minimizing the trade-offs of stable vs nimble and complex vs simple. However, in the course of the transformation process, new outcomes and consequences often emerge which the organization didn't anticipate. Some of the old trade-offs are replaced by new trade-offs. Becoming stable *and* nimble, complex *and* simple is a key objective of agility transformation but it is not the end of the journey. This is what ING discovered in Phases II and III of its transformation.

Moving ahead, these were the two central dilemmas (Figure 10.2) that manifested in a number of unintended consequences ING had to tackle over the next few years. Many features of the new setup turned out to be a work in progress and had to be continually fine-tuned and on occasion reversed (Figure 10.3).

Figure 10.2   ING met with new challenges on its way to agility

How do we balance our focus on meeting the company's objectives with our employees' need for autonomy as they grapple with fast-changing conditions?

How do we ensure sufficient diversity in our ways of working without sacrificing efficiency and constantly reinventing the wheel?

Figure 10.3   New, unintended trade-offs emerged at ING

- Incentives and rewards: should they target the individual or the teams?
- How to overcome the initial fear of empowerment?
- What is the best role for agile coaches?
- Expertise vs shared values: Too brutal a change?
- How to transition towards new leadership styles?

- What should be the shape of career management in a flat structure?
- How do we overcome resistance from national cultures (eg Belgium was highly resistant at first)?
- How to allocate sufficient time to chapter leads for craftsmanship development?

Individual or Team-Based Incentives and Rewards?

One of the biggest stumbling blocks to overcome was redefining incentives and rewards in the agile setup. On the surface at least, the new structures provided a better view of team output rather than individual contributions. However, retaining too much of the previous reward scheme, which revolved around individual bonuses, might create incentives for staff to slide back, consciously or unconsciously, into the ways of the past. If the reorganized workplace was to be a success, employees had to be rewarded for empowering others, aiding team-wide learning and energizing their squads as well as their chapters. ING eliminated individual bonuses and replaced them with team-based incentives alongside ING-wide performance criteria.

On the other hand, social comparison is an innate human instinct. As ING leadership found out, many employees considered the new incentive structure demotivating. Over time, the company had to reintroduce individual incentives on top of the other incentive types.

Empowerment: Boon or Bane?

There was also the initial fear of empowerment to be acknowledged and dispelled. In teams of nine, there was nowhere to hide. Peer pressure would be exerted even more than before. Whereas this suited entrepreneurial individuals, many staff felt intimidated.

ING had to build on the employees' sense of intrinsic motivation and make them observe quickly the additional impact they were creating through the revamped team dynamics. People would only commit to working in a different way if they could see why a change was needed, if leaders played their role in it, and if they could visualize for themselves a future where delivery would be smoother and more beneficial for all concerned.[1]

Re-examining this phase in ING's journey, it was clearly the make-or-break point in the entire transformation. In a conventional organizational structure, companies can hobble along, temporarily at least, even with a disengaged workforce. With agile, that is not the case: The majority of ING's workforce at this time had been with the bank through traumatic events like restructuring, the bailout and lay-offs. Now it was crunch time. Fortunately, the impact of agile on ING's performance and employee engagement was overwhelmingly positive, with NPS scores improving steadily and staff engagement rates in some tribes climbing over 90 per cent. The proposition behind implementing agile was now validated; ING executives could breathe easy and let go of the prolonged anxiety (in interviews, some used the word 'terror') that the change process could go off the rails. At this point, the bottom-up engine really switched on.

Crucially, a host of interdependence issues cropped up during this phase in the transformation. The C-suite had a tendency to focus on the loss of alignment. What it underestimated was that if employees were to be granted autonomy, that autonomy had to be deliberately designed. End-to-end empowerment cannot work if teams are overly dependent on others. Far from it – to make autonomy work, businesses have to organize meticulously for autonomy and anticipate the interdependence problems so that these can be addressed. For example, ING used the QBR as an opportunity for teams to report their interdependence issues, allowing the bank to add resources where necessary by shifting staff.

Coaching People or Coaching the Business?

Defining the remit of agile coaches was fraught with ambiguity. What backgrounds should the coaches have to provide a good fit with the challenges ahead? What should be the coaching outcomes? How long should coaches work within a particular squad? These questions had to be figured out on the go. Early on, the coaches were greatly outnumbered by squads. Through trial and error, ING learned that poor coaching could lead to poor individual as well as team performance, in addition to psychological fatigue and stress.

ING's instinct was to go beyond the 'people experts' mandate, which would limit the coaches' role to making staff comfortable with agile methodologies and their implications. ING experimented with making coaches report to the transformation office rather than HR. It also sought to make coaching drive actual KPIs, albeit without direct accountability for meeting them. Therefore, initially, a lot of coaching activity revolved around epics – series of request-based user stories. Coaches were expected to mould squad members' thinking along these lines:

- Were the epics' goals clear?
- Were the epics resolved on time?
- Were they processed within budget?
- Did they create the envisaged impact?
- Can we do better next time?
- Is the speed of delivery improving?

Thus, from the outset, coaching was about business performance, not just a feel-good factor. It created transparency and helped ING's CFO directly link the agile mechanisms with business performance. Consequently, coaches were expected to be as disciplined as scrum masters and equally focused on business priorities. By the same logic, they were discouraged from staying with a squad for too long and becoming perceived as a de facto leader or 'boss'. Coaches with engineering backgrounds turned out to be the best suited to the challenge, but HR management skills and prior hands-on experience in scrum were just as valuable.

Are Shared Values Too Vague a Concept? Will They Displace Expertise?

Similarly, the introduction of agile signalled a deeper change from a work environment that endorsed individual expertise to one that was propelled by communities of expertise, anchored in a set of shared values. As ING asked all its staff to apply for a job, many middle managers sought to become chapter leads. Some were great banking experts, but could not cope with the fact that they should refrain from prescribing what to do. Focusing on the How, and not on the What, turned out to be too much of a leap, and eventually they left the bank.

Armed with the confidence that the new model would prove to be attractive to plentiful fresh talent, ING made the deliberate bet to retain staff on the basis of their collaborative mindset and how well they would fit in, rather than expertise alone. The physical layout of the bank's headquarters was reconfigured along the same lines, setting up rooms and spaces for squads and domain discussions.

Leadership Agility: Where? By Whom? How?

ING's C-suite was quick to learn that agile leadership demanded much more engagement from them than traditional leadership. In the past, top executives ruled by decree: They could retreat into the corner office, look at data, ruminate, and issue a decision. The revamped C-suite didn't have rooms to begin with, just an open space that forced them to dialogue continually with other executives. In the same vein, in any QBR session, the entire C-suite was expected to speak with one voice and present a single portfolio of briefs and requests. Collectively, the executives were expected to spend as much time as possible in the trenches, with rank-and-file employees. This infused their positions with a great deal of vulnerability; suddenly, asking how others would approach a problem and coming up with questions rather than solutions was prized more highly than the old vantage point of intellectual and managerial superiority. Likewise, the CEO had to galvanize group support before instituting changes, not announce these unilaterally or abruptly like in the old days.

This sweeping change necessitated new leadership styles: Tightly linked to KPIs and the QBR, leadership was now about strict alignment across tribes. It was also about setting direction in experimenting with new technology while ensuring accountability in performance, delivery progress and customer experience. The emphasis on KPI-oriented coaching sent a message to managers that 'If you cannot lead people, there is no future for you at ING.'

Several central questions gradually reared their heads in this distributed model of leadership:

- When push comes to shove, where exactly does accountability reside in this new landscape? (Accountability in this context didn't necessarily mean reporting lines, but rather a sense of 'the buck stops here'; these are the pressure points in the system that can be relied on to provide leadership and create impact.)
- Should coaches be looked upon as the new organizational leaders?
- What are the best mechanisms to replace the old hierarchy? Without identifying these, will new, invisible hierarchies come to the fore and potentially paralyze progress?

Coaches played an important informal role in the early stages of the agile roll-out, often acting as the glue that held the new roles and processes together. However, to lead was never their mission. As it gained experience, ING slowly moved away from the coaches-as-leaders blueprint.

At a time when a lot of the responsibility for leading people devolved to chapter leads, the chapter lead role continued to be precarious for many employees to fulfil. Unlike tribe leads, whose responsibilities were outlined quite clearly and who reported to the bank's management board, a chapter lead's time and focus was perpetually divided between a squad and elsewhere in the organization. This created bottlenecks the company had to address.

A hidden trade-off that emerged in this leadership reconfiguration was between functional expertise on the one hand and cross-functionality as a way of improving speed and empowerment on the other hand. In the long term, could experts thrive in an environment where they were no longer surrounded by other experts and had to communicate their insights constantly and in more or less layman's terms? ING would have to observe and gauge this new quality of interactions closely.

Meanwhile, the cognition aspect of leadership included leading from a position of craftsmanship, eg guaranteeing superior quality in software coding. After all, the entire vision of organizational renewal rested on the idea of ING as a tech company with a banking licence. Why not instil in the workforce a sense of pride in engineering and creating code – not just coordinating others to write code?[2]

HR's Role: Blending in the Background or Setting the Agenda?

In Phase II, HR was excluded from the transformation. As staff switched to a self-organizing mode, HR perpetuated its old role of a bureaucratic gatekeeper who granted employees permissions to take annual leave or participate in learning-and-development modules. Finally, expanding the agile model to the entire organization meant that HR's own way of working had to reflect the fundamental principles of agility. The chief expectation of HR was now to respond more quickly to business needs, as well as to improve the employee experience and drive the people agenda throughout the business. As a result, HR's focus shifted to sustaining high-performing teams; upholding the value of craftsmanship; setting big-picture priorities; and organizing for simplicity.

In the spirit of agile, HR set out to advance and automate continuous conversations among employees as a way of boosting a culture of performance and improvement. These conversations took place in a range of formats, from very short and informal to longer and formal. HR also discovered that switching from descriptive to impactful in the way it labelled work roles was a hidden source of energy and in fact a self-fulfilling prophecy: The effects of referring to workers as customer loyalty team members rather than call centre agents, for example, or customer journey experts instead of marketing managers went far beyond an exercise in semantics. The greater sense of purpose and impact was as palpable in the staff as it was visible in the titles.

Although HR was late in adopting agile in its own operations, as a consequence of the organizational transformation it came to enjoy a prominent seat at the table. HR collaborates tightly with IT on achieving business KPIs. It also actively designs career management solutions that allow employees to grow in a flat hierarchy. Given ING's ongoing shift from a generalist model to one of networked experts, HR in concert with chapter leads is tasked with promoting training that mirrors ING's future needs (push) but also employees' personal aspirations (pull). Mirroring the agile way of working, HR had to become comfortable with co-creation and the idea of actively learning from the rest of ING.

Career Progression: How to Climb the Ladder in a Flat, Agile Organization

Diversifying the ways of working released great creativity and resilience among ING's employees. The next overarching task was to sustain this diversity without sacrificing efficiency and without constantly having to reinvent the wheel. As such, one of the questions on everyone's mind was what the shape of career progressions in the revitalized but considerably flatter organization. With the metaphors of climbing the corporate ladder and eyeing the corner office relegated to the past, what were the new career peaks and perks employees could aspire to?

Reflecting the nature of agile work, conventional career management at ING gradually ceded ground to a fluid, ecosystem-based career landscape. For instance, with fewer steps separating different levels of the company, some employees accept international postings as a halfway step. There are other such diagonal and even lateral career paths that workers are willing to explore. These steps are coupled with developing deep specialization through craftsmanship. Fundamentally, working at ING was reframed as a lifelong journey of learning, developing, anticipating change, exploring and networking. Looking to identify clearer, evidence-based patterns in employees' career prospects, in 2018 and 2019 ING's HR launched studies of agile work's impact on careers, both from a customer journey specialist's and a tribe lead's point of view.

ING recognizes that many of its employees are eager to gain exposure and boost their employability. As headcounts may continue to shrink in the future, the bank set up a digitally powered Talent Fluidity matching platform that lists opportunities at ING as well as its ecosystem partners – NGOs, public sector agencies, academic institutions and other entities. The platform helps ING workers visualize and plan their next career move to a role inside or outside ING that provides the best match for their current set of competences and skills.

During the 2020 lockdowns, staff from retail branches who found themselves in a work vacuum were encouraged to step forward and volunteer to work with their peers in the Know Your Customer teams whose capacity remained stretched. The 150 volunteers who agreed to participate received brief onboarding and IT training. From there on, the exercise served as a great catalyst for networking, deep learning and cross-fertilization of customer-related observations and ideas. At the same time, ING solicited for volunteers to take part in discussions on social and business reform in collaboration with its ecosystem partners among non-profits and academia.

The Model Was a Success. Could it be Replicated in Other Countries, Copy-and-Paste Style?

A big test of gearing for simplicity without setting off too much additional complexity came in the form of bringing the organizational agility blueprint to other markets and having to integrate it with their national cultures. ING had to translate its 'one way of working' within the organization into a 'one ING' operating model that spanned national boundaries. The objectives were to leverage scale, achieve a high level of standardization across countries, amortize investments over a larger pool of customers, share operating costs, and improve efficiency and time-to-volume indicators.

Belgium was the logical next-door frontier for integrating the bank's platforms with the Netherlands. Unlike the Netherlands' more experimental model of implementing agile, in Belgium the agile processes were rolled out in a top-down fashion, thus setting up a cross-border network of tribes, squads and coaches within six months. Squads with a total of 6,000 staff started working across the two countries. Yet the Belgian culture of team effort turned out to be more formal and hierarchical than ING's planners in the Netherlands expected. In many instances, the situation was one of 'two countries separated by the same language', and it took time and attention to iron out the differences. Another unanticipated consequence of the operational merger was that following this latest round of extensive layoffs, the headcount started creeping up again in response to local regulatory requirements. Some squads initially straddled two countries, with members putting in long train commutes every day. Eventually, this practice proved exhausting and the collocation requirement had to be dropped.

Further internationalization of the agile way of working, this time to incorporate ING operations in Poland and Romania, as well as a contact centre in the Philippines, led to further discussion on where to locate specific competences. IT, for its part, went ahead and set up global tribes, the only ones within ING's international footprint. It is of note that while executing this complex transformation, ING delivered strong financial and commercial results in areas such as primary customer growth and core lending growth. Its integrated banking platform was successful in attracting third-party offerings in banking and beyond (eg ING Shop, ING+ deals, apps for all housing needs throughout a customer's lifetime, Funding Options including crowdfunding, factoring and other services).

Drawing On Agility Principles to Help Your Digital Execution

ING's transformation story cannot be told without considering in depth the role of digital in making the implementation of agile a success. It also raises broader questions about the links between the two types of transformation. For example, you may be wondering:

- Looking at evidence from large legacy businesses, what are the links between building agility and adopting digital?
- Can transforming for agility and embracing digital run in parallel, or will one eventually 'hijack' the other?
- How reciprocal and mutually reinforcing is the relationship? Eg is one the soil in which the other will grow? Or are other paradigms emerging in this agile/digital combination?

This book has shown that digital disruption is one of the drivers of agility in that it infuses strategy-making with a large measure of uncertainty (Chapter 1). In addition, scrum as an agile method was born in the software industry as a way of accommodating the ambiguity and speed required by software development: It is about driving speed and simplicity by using iterative cycles and user-centric priorities (Chapter 5). You also saw that digital was often the missing link in achieving strategic agility (Chapter 8).

Reciprocally, ING's experience suggests that agility can help companies embed digital transformation by drawing on:

- *both* the experimental mindset (nimbleness) *and* the discipline required to implement digital strategies (stability); and

- *both* inner and outer collaboration across silos (simplicity) *and* the ability to orchestrate networks for learning (complexity).

ING realized early on that any company that wishes to take the lead in omnichannel must be able to bring improvements to new products and services to the market very quickly. Therefore, in the new architecture of work, squads became the cornerstone of this change, representing a distributed model of producing code. 'Agile' is often presented as a methodology that any company can adopt. Realistically, though, up to 70 or 80 per cent of seats in a squad are necessarily staffed by IT programmers, user-experience (UX) designers and data analysts. The key issue is getting software to production. Thanks to the squad composition and dynamics, software is designed with discrete business and systems integration requirements in mind, rather than in a vacuum. Developers and operations staff are equally responsible for the delivery and stability of code.[3] The aspiration is to go live with new software releases on a much more frequent basis – every two weeks rather than having five to six 'big launches' a year.

Because squads are where the action is in terms of creating value, maximum decentralization of coding is taking place. Squads are accountable for the quality they produce. On top of that, they build new capabilities through the constant customer feedback loop of lean start-up (MVP, test and learn). If each squad were working in its own silo, ING would disintegrate in chaos. How does ING maintain consistency, quality, common infrastructure and continuous evolution of technological solutions? It applies a minimum degree of centralization and alignment at the top, which cuts through two hierarchical lines:

- Competences such as digital craftsmanship are the responsibility of chapters. Chapter leads report into area leads who then report to ING's CIO.

- On the business side of the equation, customer journey experts report to tribe leads. For example, the omnichannel tribe is at the core of ING's strategy to deliver a seamless omnichannel experience to its customers.

There are other, additional structural arrangements in place that serve to create a common architecture with discipline and accountability (Figure 10.4). For instance, on the infrastructure aspect, ING set up a tribe in charge of determining the bank's infrastructure needs and their evolution. This tribe is linked to ING's global technology function. It scouts new technologies, enables the tribes' continuous delivery pipeline, pushes the latest solutions and educates the teams about them. It must also produce quality guidelines about how to use the technology.

Figure 10.4   ING's organization for digital espouses agility principles

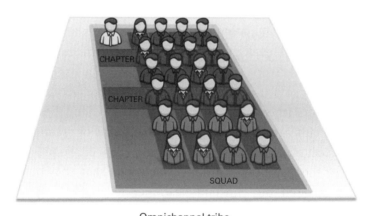

Omnichannel tribe
Infrastructure tribe
Data management tribe
One Analytics tribe

One Analytics is the tribe that analyses customer data and builds predictive models. It owns the data analytics and builds the engine for it, ie the capability for personalization. Composed of data analysts and scientists, One Analytics is in charge of providing the right data for all the tribes. It also aims to bind customers to ING by making communications more personal and relevant.

The Data Management tribe owns the data lake and the environment in which the data resides. It is also tasked with regulatory and financial reporting with regard to data integrity and other aspects of managing data within the bank. Ultimately, all of the skillsets that are organized into tribes must also be infused with the capability to field questions from the organization, handle time pressure, and tackle issues that will generate real value-adds for the customer and therefore for the bank.

With the bulk of customer interactions taking place in the digital app, ING discovered it also had to live up to its duty of care and the many social repercussions and responsibilities that are related to inclusiveness. Customers who adopted the app include those who are not digitally proficient. Some are visually impaired and need assistance to adjust the app to their preferences.

Underlying the role of digital in ING's operations is what top executives describe as an 'obsession' with data as driver of better transparency, decision making, context sharing and performance. From digitizing routines to improving hypothesis testing, ultimately data is the fuel that powers both continued cost reduction and superior customer experience. This is where digital enhances agility and the relationship between the two transformation efforts becomes reciprocal. Meanwhile, in the leadership dimension, data enables leaders to steer on output rather than input, as output becomes more easily measurable. This is helpful in making leadership agility take root in the organization.

Conclusions

With these lessons in mind – and with the entire practice of management going through a reset as you read this book – how will you respond? Here are a few guiding recommendations:

1 **No room for half measures. Organizational innovation is a powerful source of competitive advantage – so be brave!** By inventing radically new organizational forms in their time, IBM and Procter & Gamble (P&G) leapt forward and created competitive advantage that sustained them for many years to come.[4] In banking, firms like Rabobank, Danske Bank, ABN Amro and Sberbank have all started to play catch-up with ING. Redefining competitive advantage is not just about fancy AI. Organizational innovation can play a big role as well.

2 **Think in stages.** At times the tale of ING's transformation is presented as a Big Bang – not dissimilar to what happened at IBM in 1995 and P&G with Organization 2005. In those instances, a lot of time was dedicated to designing and planning the new organizations. ING's approach was in reality a staged one and included a pilot phase and much improvisation. ING did not want to wait until a perfect design was in place. It figured out 80 per cent of it; the rest it was prepared to learn and correct on the fly.

   The staged approach was also important psychologically: It is well-nigh impossible for a transformation process of this magnitude to take off unless the top-down engine and bottom-up initiatives meet in the middle and work together in sync. Humans are not designed to spend long years trekking in a dark tunnel with no light at the end. Customers will not be served better by a workforce that goes through a fun-free grind and constant disarray, day after day. Without long-term rituals and habits in the workplace to fall back on, employees are bound to lose their sense of work as an anchoring experience in their lives. ING's skilful phasing of the transformation provided sufficient early successes and tangible outcomes to prevent this nightmare scenario.

3 **Define a destination; do not let the journey meander endlessly.** You might often hear: 'Agility is a journey, not a destination.' This is not completely true. At ING, as more and more employees in the organization were becoming comfortable with agile work (corporate functions, bricks-and-mortar retail branches, call centres), there was indeed a moment where the leadership could declare victory. You cannot sell endless change to employees under the pretext of agility. Agility is a state that enables ongoing flexibility (as opposed to occasional change).

Evolution vs Reset

ING's journey illustrates that a transformation should be necessarily agile. To get it right, even on a less ambitious scale than ING's, takes a great deal of ammunition. You will be running experiments and iterations; learning and absorbing lessons; sharing the learning points with other parts of your organization and with operations in other countries.

Along this journey, there are traditional, pre-agility practices you can continue to rely on safely. Changing an organization still requires top-down championing; lots of patience and dedication over time; giving the ongoing change some space to mature and take shape every once in a while; showing sensitivity to national cultures, which can otherwise become a minefield. Unity and alignment in the top team are even more important in the agility approach, and so is functional expertise – all cornerstones of traditional change management.

Sustaining a sense of social contract with your workforce similarly remains a top priority. ING's modern take on the social contract reflects a world where organizational, industry and ecosystem boundaries are blurring and sometimes disappearing. ING therefore encourages workers' exposure to partner organizations along with creating generous training and development opportunities. This equips employees with the learning and networking tools they need for the next step in their career development and transition, within or outside ING.

Reset: Next Practices and Why Change is Changing

This type of transformation signals a paradigm shift. New trade-offs will continue to appear as the agility journey unfolds. Yet the new mindset is one of grappling with them and minimizing them rather than settling for either/or choices.

As this book keeps reminding you, the way you go about changing your business is also changing. Unfreeze–change–refreeze cycles are a thing of the past, even if you have a definite organizational template in hand. Instead, you have reached a stage where adaptation is continuous, on-demand. Changing for agility is a non-linear process that requires multiple feedback loops. Bringing people on this journey with you demands that despite all the improvising and adjusting, the process yields tangible achievements: Employees can see, feel and touch the change in their own work and in the impact it has on customers. There cannot be a transformation without both top-down and bottom-up engines firing on all cylinders.

ING's phased approach offers you a wealth of inspiration. Granted, it cannot be copied without thinking. But sticking to these guidelines may help you:

1 In the early phases of preparation, locate your own organization's pockets of agile (they may have been flying below the radar all this time); put in place an agile-conducive culture.

2 In terms of testing, don't try to script everything in advance. Go in – the agile, minimum viable way of piloting, testing, learning, adjusting. There's no need to wait until you have every detail figured out; that's not what agility is about. 'Go slow to go fast' is your mantra now: Exert a lot of pressure to drive the experiment fast; afterwards allow time for the new ways to take hold and for employees to see the initial outcome; then learn from it and make it better. Repeat in another part of the company (to achieve simplicity) – but also adapt and differentiate (boosting healthy complexity).

3 Make sure that change is occurring both in a top-down and a bottom-up direction.

4 Once you get going with strong, inspired experimenting and planning, traditional functions will eventually emerge as profit maximizers as opposed to the old cost centres, as ING's HR story bears out.

5 Autonomy sounds great at first, but in reality it isn't easy to install. To make it happen, you need to organize deliberately for end-to-end autonomy (nimbleness), not just for alignment (stability).

6 In carrying out these changes, don't follow blindly what other companies have done. Start with clear objectives of what you want to achieve – and why agility is precisely the capability that will bring you to those objectives.

7 Manage functional expertise extra carefully. Your experts will now be dispersed in cross-functional teams; they may feel isolated and underappreciated. To compensate, give them the time and space to meet with other experts and to develop new skills. Similarly, talents in your company may soon be faced with a pancake-flat organizational structure. That means you will have to search actively for avenues that will provide them with the experience and the perks of career progression.

8 Use agility and digital to support one another.

Throughout, a new quality of leadership – decisive yet vulnerable – must be in place. The CEOs of truly agile businesses have earned the right to champion change, instead of imposing it on their collaborators. They understand that in order to lead, change must start from within themselves.

There is no such thing as a perfect organization. As a result of your best effort, you will see old trade-offs vanish and new ones sometimes take their place. With time, you will learn to anticipate and shape these new trade-offs. The above guidelines are not a panacea. However, the model they outline provides your business with a better fit for organizing in the age of uncertainty than any traditional model could.[5]

Endnotes

1 Agile Business Consortium (2019) Case study: ING Bank's Digital Platform tribe goes agile, www.agilebusiness.org/page/Resource_casestudy_INGBANK (archived at https://perma.cc/V3HZ-NX96)

2 Jacobs, P, Schlatmann, B and Mahadevan, D (2017) ING's agile transformation, *McKinsey & Company*, 10 January, www.mckinsey.com/industries/financial-services/our-insights/ings-agile-transformation (archived at https://perma.cc/6SM3-AQBR)

3 Bossert, O, Ip, C and Starikova, I (2015) Beyond agile: Reorganizing IT for faster software delivery, *McKinsey & Company*, 1 September, www.mckinsey.com/business-functions/mckinsey-digital/our-insights/beyond-agile-reorganizing-it-for-faster-software-delivery (archived at https://perma.cc/D9FP-SJ8J)

4 Galbraith, J R (2011) *Designing the Customer-Centric Organization: A guide to strategy, structure, and process*, John Wiley & Sons

5 The authors would like to thank in particular Maarten van Beek, CHRO of ING Benelux, Vincent van den Boogert, former CEO of ING Netherlands and Tanja Tierie, Tribe Lead Omnichannel of ING for their contributions to this chapter.

Final Words

If you are a mid-level or senior executive, or aspire to become one, in the next decade you are going to be incentivized to create a much more adaptive, flexible and entrepreneurial business. Boards will increasingly scrutinize how executives create the conditions of business agility, defined broadly as the ability to achieve the right level of adaptability and to 'play to win', not just survive, in fast-changing and uncertain environments.

Too many large, non-digital-native firms are rigid. They favour today at the expense of tomorrow, especially if they are successful. The way they strategize and lead is simplistic, a case of command and control. Organizationally, they are overly bureaucratic, hierarchical and complex. For these companies, uncertainty is something to fear, or at best to react to.

In the management reset currently underway, businesses that thrive will embrace uncertainty. They will reset how they create competitive advantage at the strategic, organizational and leadership levels. They will use digital tools to embed agility and, vice versa, agility principles to accelerate their digital transformation. Although not everything will change in the practice of management up ahead, this reset is of the same magnitude as the one that gave birth to the modern corporation a hundred years ago. Resetting management with business agility is what it takes to be a manager in the 2020s.

To embody this reset manager authentically, here is what will be expected from you:

Understand What Business Agility Is and How It Works

Given that your mandate will be to form better conditions of flexibility and growth, you ought to be clear about what business agility is and how it works. This is not an academic exercise. Misconceptions abound. Unless you see through them, they will lull you into procrastination (hiding behind the 'buzzword' excuse), or send you down the wrong path during implementation.

Learn to Unleash Agility By Minimizing Trade-Offs

To gain flexibility, you will need to minimize dangerous 'either/or' trade-offs and create instead the conditions for 'both/and' solutions. This is tough because, inevitably, tensions come creeping into the picture. But think of it this way: If you can juggle several tasks, it gives you extra options to change tack when uncertainty strikes.

1 If your company is a legacy, non-digital-native business, you will have to be nimble, ie experiment and improvise faster. However, nimbleness with no stability brings dilution and chaos. The secret to resolving this tension is to discover which sources of stability are healthy (eg clear and well-communicated direction; cautious sense-making; analysis and synthesis for good strategizing) and which ones you should stay clear of (eg risk avoidance).

2 Large businesses must simplify. That way their business portfolio is focused and allows for good resource allocation. Bureaucracy gets trimmed down. Yet legacy businesses cannot afford to be simplistic, either. Complexity is not all bad. Especially when it resides in networks of organizational learning; the ability to reduce risk through diversified portfolios; and a differentiation of structural choices by business line, country or function.

3 When executives say we want to be agile, they mean nimbler. What they overlook are the other three dimensions of business agility: Simplicity alongside a healthy degree of stability and complexity.

Embrace the Entrepreneurial Energy

Business agility cannot be understood solely as a reactive quality, or even as resilience. To be resilient is merely to bounce back in conditions of hardship. Business agility surpasses resilience through the power of entrepreneurship and innovation. It is about playing to win – and that's what this book is about. It shows you how to be proactive and create a competitive advantage, reshaping the future of industries and of your own business thanks to the entrepreneurial energy that strategic, organizational and leadership agility create.

Strategic Agility

Protect and renew competitive advantage with flexibility

Strategic agility is about minimizing five trade-offs, ie reconciling five pairs of seemingly contradictory strategic options to find new growth opportunities in an adaptive way. Some of these deal with the What of strategy (where to play, how to win) and some with the How (how to strategize). It's important you start by identifying which trade-offs may be impeding your business growth and flexibility.

Make better choices to factor in uncertainty

Minimizing trade-offs doesn't mean there are no strategic choices to be made. In the traditional paradigm, companies would launch costly initiatives outright without testing them with future users first. Often the results were innovation failure, loss of strategic focus and waste. The management reset involves small-scale, bottom-up experiments coupled with eliciting feedback from users early and regularly to reduce the entrepreneurial uncertainty and make better choices.

Calibrate the effort to reflect your circumstances

Strategic agility is not a balancing act because that would imply finding an ideal 50–50 position. Rather, you should choose where to place the cursor along the stable–nimble/complex–simple continuum based on your company's circumstances. What is important is to include the opposite end of each continuum. It is also important that you look at the trade-offs exhaustively, as they are mutually reinforcing. For instance, simplifying your business portfolio may mean that you will create partnerships to pursue certain strategic initiatives, which in turn creates its own degree of complexity.

Use digital to resolve the tensions

Once you are clear on which strategic trade-offs matter to you, you can then start thinking about how you will achieve your 'both/and' objectives and minimize the resulting tensions.

As the chapters in this book showed, when it comes to dialling down the tensions, digital is often the missing link.

Organizational Agility

A key message of this book is that organizational innovation is a source of competitive advantage in its own right. And yet it is often overlooked. By inventing new designs for agility, you can leap ahead of your competition. Specifically, what you can do is:

Reverse your organizational design priorities

In essence, organizational agility is about reversing the priorities of organizational design. It's about empowering small cross-functional teams to improvise around the customer (nimble). At the same time, you need to fix concrete, inspiring and easy-to-remember directions on top of setting clear accountability (stable). It is empowerment within a framework. Moreover, you need to streamline and/or standardize your bureaucracy and hierarchy to achieve efficiencies (simplicity). In tandem, you will want to step up the organization's ability to learn and adapt continuously (complexity). If most companies are rigid it is because their priorities run the other way round.

Find the degree and shape of agility that suits your business

This book is not about selling a formulaic and fashionable approach to agile. Instead, it focuses on eight principles of organizational agility and encourages you to adapt them to a business's circumstances by using the building blocks of organizational design. This is why different companies cluster around different choices in the nascent agility landscape.

There is no 'one way'. Agile methods or working in squads and tribes should not be your default choice. Agile and agility are not equal. Neither is moving towards radically new organizational forms necessarily about scaling agile. What it should be about always is securing a competitive advantage.

The book's chapters review the challenges you may encounter on the different paths to agility. They provide you with the key to overcome these challenges by learning from the pioneers. They make it clear that neither agile nor agility aim for a state of 'anything goes'. On the contrary – for all the improvisation, a great deal of discipline needs to be in place.

Connecting organizational and strategic agility

Agile methods are not meant just for continuous improvement. They can be successfully deployed in radically new strategic initiatives. For example, GE Healthcare established a billion-dollar new business in portable medical equipment by empowering local cross-functional teams in China and India and linking them with core business talents and scientific experts; and by systematically implementing testing and learning from the customer in conditions of uncertainty as to what the final solution should look like.

Leadership Agility

In building leadership agility, the C-suite is a study in paradox. Technically, the changes that took place as part of building organizational agility (such as flattening the organizational structure) should free the top management from mechanical tasks. It should redirect the C-suite's attention to listening, motivating and connecting different parts of the company. In reality, the shift from ego leadership to a distributed model of leadership can be traumatic as it entails the fear of losing power. There is a risk that leaders not only become the transformation's weakest link but also unconsciously steer the company towards the old, hierarchical ways of doing things. To prevent this common scenario, you will do well to:

Become proficient in multiple leadership styles

Leadership agility has to do with the mastery of four leadership competences (4Cs). To strike the right level of nimbleness, leaders must prove their ability to coach teams by asking tough questions and helping them remove bottlenecks. The necessary measure of stability comes from cohesion – the ability to set purpose and ensure direction, alignment and performance. By providing connections, leaders help break down silos and strengthen collaboration. To bring about the right level of complexity, leaders need to rely on the cognition parameters of their leadership style.

Be an inclusive yet decisive leader

Just as strategic agility thrives on diversity, leaders in the distributed leadership space must similarly draw on diversity yet continue to take responsibility for strategic direction. In consequence, this has blurred the lines between leaders as thinkers and leaders as doers. In an agility transformation, leaders are expected to 'signpost' the journey. They must demonstrate to employees that change is the new constant. But far from being unrelenting and morale-depleting, that change creates successes, milestones and more exciting ways of working all around.

Present a united top team

Correspondingly, building strategic agility requires leadership unity. The C-suite needs to speak with one voice and increasingly address the board with a single portfolio of results and demands. The leaner, agile organization leaves substantially less room for egotism and turf wars within the top team.

Secure the success of (remaining) middle managers

Dismantling the old bureaucracy means fewer organizational layers and less need for middle-management functions like oversight and handovers. Middle managers will be faced with vulnerability and will need support and coaching as they take on new roles.

Change the Way You Change

Now that your task is to set up the conditions that will be conducive to flexibility and growth, you also need clarity in terms of how to change for agility, how to approach the transformation, and how to deal with the unanticipated issues that will crop up as part of building agility. Keep in mind that:

Change is cultural, not exceptional

Business agility is a state of continuous adaptation where change, led by self-organizing teams in a framework defined by the top, takes place as and when necessary. This is a significant departure from the conventional cycle of unfreeze–change–refreeze.

Think of agility transformation as a journey and a destination

It would be a mistake to see agility as just a journey. When your workforce and its leadership are alert, stay curious and hyperaware and recognize that there are other possible routes, you know you have reached your destination. Employees who can be inspired to connect their personal purpose with the company's purpose are more likely to be resilient to change and deal with the stress and fatigue that comes with it.

Managing change comes with its own paradoxes

In the world of developing agility, there are no perfect organizations, just organizations that have become better suited to different circumstances. What this means is that preparation is useful but you will have to improvise as well. You will act decisively, but also run pilots and prototypes to correct course. You will apply agile methods not just as a process but also as an exercise in organizational redesign. You will learn to 'go slow to go fast', to combine top-down with bottom-up transformation, and to anticipate new trade-offs that will replace old trade-offs.

Risk of reduced creativity

Agility and digital transformations are mutually reinforcing – but also produce risks and ethical dilemmas. Involving customers in every step of product development can extinguish radical innovation. The same is true of placing highly talented specialists and creatives in cross-functional teams.

Risk of teams drowning out the individual

Unless the interests of individual workers are carefully considered in terms of career trajectories and personal rewards and incentives, business agility may turn out even more impersonal and mechanistic than the model it was supposed to replace. If everything is about 'communities' and creative outliers are excluded because they are deemed not collaborative enough, it will be a great loss to large organizations. In the absence of deviations from the 'one' corporate mindset, rigidity will set in. And that is the antithesis of agility.

Digital lends itself to collaboration and crowdsourcing – but also surveillance and replacement of humans by machines

There is much about agility that emulates the workings of the human mind: Iterative, intuitive, empathetic, creative. Nonetheless, at the core of agility transformations are objectives such as productivity, efficiency and speed. As automation and AI continue to advance, more jobs will be eliminated, and team sizes reduced. Data is in a strong position to determine if not hijack the entire decision-making process.

It will be your moral responsibility to explore and weigh these ethical issues and make sure that the humanistic potential of business agility is not crushed. They should not be an excuse to sit on the fence, however. Digital transformation is forcing momentous changes in strategizing, working and leading. The 2020s might be even bumpier and more volatile than what we have witnessed recently on all fronts: Geopolitically, technologically, ecologically and socially. Only the businesses that are fit to their context and can adapt in the short term yet stay focused on the long term will thrive.

What's Next?

There hasn't been a huge number of radically new organizational forms in evidence among large corporations. The Haiers and the INGs of this world largely maintain their pioneering status. Leaders remain fearful, not least of what the change means for them.

Circumstances and younger population cohorts may bring about bolder change in this opening decade. In the meantime, the agility landscape is dotted with many hybrid forms, a trend that the COVID crisis has accelerated.

Talent is the currency of 21st-century economy. Talent is also what can make or break many agility transformations. Young people are resentful of the gap they see between promises of empowerment and realities on the ground. In many ways, this further accentuates the need to shift to business agility. At the same time, talent clouds are emerging; they give workers located anywhere in the world the flexibility to pursue multiple, including complementary and non-competing, careers. This is a trend that businesses and their HR departments will have to come to grips with.

As the middle management layer continues to dwindle, there will be many more start-ups coming onstream, including start-ups that are orbiting corporate ecosystems and open collaboration networks. Corporations will likewise shrink in size, allowing for greater flexibility in learning and relearning but jeopardizing job creation or pushing it onto their ecosystems.

This book equips you with the right skills, tools and capabilities to understand what business agility is and to implement it well, including by helping you reflect on what level of agility is right for your business. Depending on their performance, ambition, industry conditions and level of foreseeable disruption, not all companies will need the same level and shape of business agility. But what's certain is that most businesses will need some degree of it.

Agile methods may one day become so mainstream (like Six Sigma has become) that no one will talk about them anymore. But agility that manifests as minimization of tensions and trade-offs will remain a hot topic in 21st-century business, not least because it is a difficult but exciting exercise. In the journey ahead, you will have to reconsider how you lead and inspire others. Equally important will be your ability to combine the power of bottom-up entrepreneurship and innovation with top-down decisiveness and sense of purpose. Tomorrow's reset managers will pull away from the rest on the strength of their ability to adjust both capabilities and mindset... to whatever is coming. Will you be one of them?

INDEX

NB: page numbers in *italic* indicate figures or tables